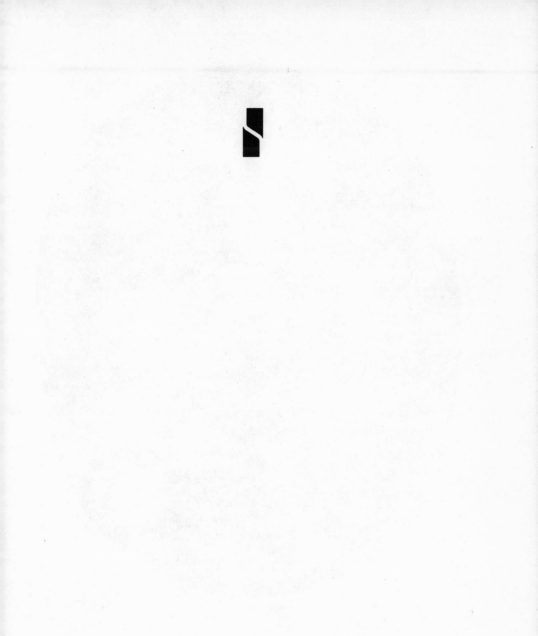

Mr. Thomas Betterton

Totus Mundus Agit Histrionem

THOMAS BETTERTON

AND THE

MANAGEMENT

OF

LINCOLN'S INN FIELDS 1695–1708

Judith Milhous

SOUTHERN ILLINOIS UNIVERSITY PRESS

CARBONDALE AND EDWARDSVILLE

FEFFER & SIMONS, INC.

LONDON AND AMSTERDAM

Library of Congress Cataloging in Publication Data

Milhous, Judith, 1946–
   Thomas Betterton and the management of Lincoln's Inn Fields, 1695–1708.

   Includes index.
   1. Betterton, Thomas, 1635?–1710. 2. Theater—London—History. 3. London. The Duke's Playhouse. 4. English drama—Restoration, 1660–1700—History and criticism. 5. English drama—18th century—History and criticism. I. Title.
PN2598.B6M54   792'.094212   78-21017
ISBN 0-8093-0906-8

To Rob and Kit Hume

CONTENTS

PREFACE

THE ultimate object of this book is to show the importance of theatre management policy and company history to English drama in the pivotal years 1695–1708. Competition between the King's Company and the Duke's Company in what Hume calls the Carolean period (the reign of Charles II) had an immense influence on the amount and types of new drama produced. In the Carolean heyday of the 1670s twenty or more new plays were mounted each year. Following the union of 1682 the United Company operated conservatively, putting on only three or four new plays per year, and those by established authors who were following proven formulas. When competition resumed after the actors' rebellion of 1695, a flood of new plays (again more than twenty each year) was an immediate result. The bulk of this study will be devoted to a detailed survey of the circumstances in which the Lincoln's Inn Fields and patent companies competed, and a chronological analysis of their shifts, devices, and fortunes over a dozen years of rivalry.

Betterton is the key figure in this theatrical warfare. His prestige made the Lincoln's Inn Fields breakaway possible; he was the leader of the rebel company and later officially its manager. By 1695 he was an old man, and he was trying to operate in a very difficult period. The Court-centered audience of the first three decades was breaking up, and new classes of playgoers had to be sought. The moral criticisms of the stage reached their peak at the turn of the century, and that uproar proved very damaging to theatrical prosperity. In such troubled circumstances neither company flourished.

Betterton's management is seldom much discussed. Most sketches of his career depend heavily on Cibber, who idolized the actor but gave the manager short shrift. Lowe's "biography" (1891), though a landmark in its day, inevitably suffers from lack of a performance calendar; and he did not know of the Lord Chamberlain's warrants and the lawsuit testimony gradually unearthed in the Public Record Office during the twentieth century. Lowe's picture is further skewed by his determined avoidance of anything which reflects negatively on Betterton's business morals—evidence involving management, not acting. In recent years scholars have tended to assume that Lincoln's Inn Fields's problems were Betterton's fault. Shirley Strum Kenny, in a pioneering investigation of this competition, mentions Betterton's managerial career only to dismiss him as "incompetent" ("Theatrical Warfare 1695–1710," *Theatre Notebook* 27 [1973]: 130–45). That Lincoln's Inn Fields was in deep trouble around 1700 is clearly true. However, the cliché—that it never really improved its situation until the union of 1708—is demonstrably false, and Betterton should be credited with rescuing Lincoln's Inn Fields, not ruining it. The supposition that he was a "bad" manager is peculiar and inaccurate. He had, after all, served as manager of the Duke's and United companies for some twenty years—with great financial and artistic success. Betterton's problems at Lincoln's Inn Fields seem to me largely the result of difficult external circumstances and Betterton's failure to adapt sufficiently to changing times and new audiences. And we may note that overall the Drury Lane managers did no better.

To understand the rebellion of 1695 and subsequent events, one must know something about the way theatre companies had been organized and run since the Restoration. Consequently chapter 1 is devoted to a brief explanation of Charles II's patent grants in 1660; description of the rights of owners, actors, and managers; and an account of the original Davenant-Killigrew competition back in the 1660s. Chapter 2 concerns Betterton's long experience in management, first with the Duke's Company 1668–82 and then with the United Company 1682–94. As Sir William Davenant's apprentice, assistant, and successor Betterton was from the start exposed to a definite philosophy of management. His lifelong fascination with opera and scenic spectaculars came straight from Davenant. His sense of competitive tactics was undoubtedly derived from Davenant's success with a company of young unknowns playing innovative new dramas against a more conservative veteran company of leading actors with a near monopoly in the classic repertory and less interest in spectacle. Betterton's success with Davenant's policies in the seventies and eighties left him less than ideally prepared to run a company of aging star performers, putting on standard repertory shows in a cramped and inadequate theatre. Some of the apparent anomalies of the Lincoln's Inn

Fields management policy are clearly traceable to Betterton's earlier experience in different circumstances.

Chapter 3 explains the theatrical situation in 1695, offering a fresh analysis of the reasons for the rebellion and the nature of the competition which resulted: aging prima donnas bickering among themselves versus young hopefuls suffering under Rich's tyranny but enjoying the immeasurable advantage of holding rights to the only two good theatre buildings in London. Chapters 4 through 7 trace the course of their competition through four phases—the initial success of the rebels; a standoff; the confusing years 1702–5; and finally the period when spoken drama was offered at the Haymarket. The survey reaches a natural conclusion in 1708 with the new union decreed by the Lord Chamberlain. At that time the company which Betterton had led away from Rich in 1695 ceased to exist and the competitive circumstances studied here came to an end. At a number of points I challenge long-accepted views of the two companies. In the third phase of competition, in particular, I argue for drastic reevaluation of the usual interpretation—that Lincoln's Inn Fields was in desperate straits. On the contrary, there seems to me good evidence that the rival managers arrived at a *modus vivendi* around 1702, and that insiders, at least, enjoyed a modest prosperity after that. Reinterpretation also helps explain the otherwise astonishing events of 1706, when Rich allowed his best actors to join the company at the Haymarket, taking with them a large number of stock productions.

Throughout this chronological survey I will be paying particular attention to several factors: a) the rival companies' organization and personnel; b) repertory policy, especially in new plays; c) competitive devices—including entr'actes, double bills, variety shows, singers, dancers, jugglers, and animal acts. Again and again we will find Betterton and his fellows driven to respond to Rich's challenges, while scrambling to find effective innovations of their own. In repertory, as in management generally, we will constantly see the importance of competition between the two houses. Changes in the drama of the pivotal time ca. 1700 are commonly ascribed to political and social circumstances—and to a significant degree, rightly so. But as we will see, trends in the drama 1695–1710 were also influenced by theatrical circumstances, and in these years patterns were established which exerted a profound influence on drama and theatre in the first third of the eighteenth century.

The plays produced in the period I am covering have been expertly surveyed in Robert D. Hume's *The Development of English Drama in the Late Seventeenth Century*. My account of this competition would not be possible without the performance calendar in *The London Stage, 1660– 1800*, a work to which I am indebted beyond acknowledgment. I have depended on Leslie Hotson's historical investigations in *The Commonwealth and Restoration Stage*—a study which unfortunately becomes quite sketchy after 1682. A great deal of my information about company organization and policy, however, has been derived from unpublished and partially published documents in the Public Record Office, The British Library, and the Harvard Theatre Collection.

In conclusion, I want to make two points about the kind of study this is. It is, I believe, the first strictly theatrical history to make extensive use of *The London Stage* to help re-create a sense of the circumstances in which theatre companies operated and plays were mounted. *The London Stage* has a multiplicity of uses beyond the verification of dates and the calculation of plays' popularity. The performance calendar is a book in which the initiate may read the hopes and fortunes of living institutions. Second, my focus on management policy is unusual and, I believe, advantageous. Looking at a string of plays, successful or not, and reading the high-flown pronouncements of playwrights, one may come away with little sense of the practical factors which influence the history of drama. Close study of the circumstances in which plays were actually brought to the stage reminds us that the gritty and intractable day-by-day problems of running a theatre often outweigh the grand aspirations of playwrights.

For advice, assistance, and encouragement I am much indebted to Arthur H. Scouten, Robert D. Hume, and Edward A. Langhans. The University of Iowa has provided me with a congenial working atmosphere, a cooperative library, a much-needed grant to visit British libraries, and the encouragement of Samuel L. Becker and J. Dudley Andrew. For various kinds of help, and for permission to quote from manuscripts, I am grateful to the staffs of the Public Record Office, the British Library, the Westminster Public Library, the University of Nottingham Library, the Bodleian, the Guildhall, the Newberry Library, the Folger Shakespeare Library, the New York Public Library, and the Harvard University Library. I am particularly indebted to Edwin E. Williams of Harvard, and to Jeanne T. Newlin and Martha R. Mahard of the Harvard Theatre Collection.

Documents in the appendixes are transcripts of Crown-copyright records in the Public Record Office, and they appear by permission of the controller of H. M. Stationery Office.

JUDITH MILHOUS

University of Iowa
October 1978

A NOTE ON TEXTS
AND DATES

QUOTATIONS from prologues, epilogues, dedications, and the like are from the first London edition unless otherwise specified. All dates are Old Style, though the new year is treated as beginning 1 January. Play dates are normally from *The London Stage*. Where they differ, the reason for the change will be explained in the new editions of parts 1 and 2 on which I am now at work in collaboration with Arthur H. Scouten and Robert D. Hume. References to Lord Chamberlain's documents (LC) and lawsuits in the Public Record Office (P.R.O.) are based on my own photocopies and notes except where I have specifically indicated otherwise. In quoting seventeenth and eighteenth-century manuscript sources and literal transcriptions published by modern scholars I have retained the original spelling and punctuation but have followed a policy of silently lowering raised letters and expanding all abbreviations except ampersand and certain conventional abbreviations such as "Esq" and "Bart." Ordinal numbers (e.g., "2d") have been spelled out. Terminal periods have been added where necessary for clarity. *U* and *V* and *I* and *J* have likewise been silently regularized. Italics have usually been silently reversed in quotations from printed prologues, epilogues, and prefaces.

WORKS FREQUENTLY CITED

A Comparison between the Two Stages	Anonymous, *A Comparison between the Two Stages* (1702), ed. Staring B. Wells (Princeton: Princeton University Press, 1942).
Biographical Dictionary	Philip H. Highfill, Jr., Kalman A. Burnim, and Edward A. Langhans, *A Biographical Dictionary of Actors, Actresses, Musicians, Dancers, Managers, and Other Stage Personnel in London, 1660–1800*, 16 vols. in progress (Carbondale and Edwardsville: Southern Illinois University Press, 1973–). The authors very kindly allowed me to use their files on people in the latter half of the alphabet.
Cibber, *Apology*	*An Apology for the Life of Mr. Colley Cibber, Written by Himself*, ed. Robert W. Lowe, 2 vols. (1889; reprint ed., New York: AMS, 1966).
Hotson	Leslie Hotson, *The Commonwealth and Restoration Stage* (1928; reprint ed., New York: Russell and Russell, 1962).
Hume	Robert D. Hume, *The Development of English Drama in the Late Seventeenth Century* (Oxford: Clarendon Press, 1976).
The London Stage	*The London Stage, 1660–1800*, 5 parts in 11 vols. (Carbondale: Southern Illinois University Press, 1960–68). Part 1, ed. William Van Lennep, Emmett L. Avery, and Arthur H. Scouten (1965). Part 2, ed. Emmett L. Avery (2 vols., 1960).

Nicoll   Allardyce Nicoll, *A History of English Drama 1660–1900*, 6 vols., rev.ed. (Cambridge: At the University Press, 1952–59).

Roscius Anglicanus   John Downes, *Roscius Anglicanus, or an Historical Review of the Stage* (London: H. Playford, 1708). I have used both the Augustan Reprint Society facsimile (1969), with an Introduction by John Loftis and a useful index by David Stuart Rodes, and the pseudo facsimile published in 1928 by Montague Summers (reprint ed., New York: Blom, 1968) for its notes. The pagination is identical.

Part I
BACKGROUND

Chapter 1

The Organization and Management
of the
Patent Companies, 1660–1668

W HEN Thomas Betterton undertook to run a rebel theatre company at Lincoln's Inn Fields in 1695 he had a lifetime of experience on which to draw. From the outset of his career in 1660 he was Davenant's principal assistant as well as a leading actor. After Davenant's death in 1668, he and Henry Harris shared the management of the Duke's Company. Harris retired in 1677 and William Smith, a lawyer and sometime actor, joined Betterton as comanager. They ran the United Company successfully from 1682 to 1687. From 1695 to 1705 Betterton was to head a company made up of aging stars, performing in a small and poorly equipped theatre, with severely limited financial resources. The circumstances he faced at Lincoln's Inn Fields were very different from those he was accustomed to. He had helped Davenant parlay a motley assortment of inexperienced actors into an enterprising and innovative company which set theatrical trends in the 1660s. He led the Duke's Company in the days of its greatest glory and the United Company in its most successful years. He was accustomed to strong, centralized management, and a well-equipped theatre that allowed him to indulge in the lavish staging he promoted. All of Betterton's experience, his predispositions, and his managerial habit of mind conditioned his thinking in ways that proved to be handicaps at Lincoln's Inn Fields. A survey of company organization and competition prior to 1695 will show why he tried to operate there as he did.

I
The Patent Grants

The theatrical situation was extremely unsettled when Charles II returned to the throne in May 1660.[1] Three groups of players were active,
headed respectively by Mohun, Beeston, and Rhodes. The details of the
power politics by which Davenant and Killigrew seized control of these
groups and established a monopoly are beyond my purpose here. But
since the whole structure of theatrical competition in this period was
determined by the establishment of a patent monopoly, a brief account
of it is required.

Theatre companies had traditionally been "licensed" by the Master of
the Revels. Consequently they operated at the pleasure of the monarch,
and the only limitations on the number of companies were the monarch's
whim and their ability to support themselves. Working in collusion,
Davenant and Killigrew persuaded Charles II to grant them a hereditary
monopoly with a guarantee that all competition would be suppressed.

By no means did this happen overnight. The infighting was protracted
and probably only gradually did the details get worked out. A temporary
"Privilege" was granted to Davenant and Killigrew on 21 August 1660,[2]
but Killigrew's patent did not pass the Privy Seal until 25 April 1662,
and Davenant received his on 15 January 1663.[3] Matters were complicated by the violent objections of Sir Henry Herbert to the infringement
of his traditional rights as licenser of theatres and censor of plays. In the
midst of the various parties' maneuverings Killigrew seems to have colluded with Herbert against his erstwhile ally Davenant, but the upshot
was a compromise in which the two courtiers got their monopoly while
Herbert kept his profitable right to censor and license plays. Killigrew's
motives seem to have been largely mercenary throughout: he saw the
theatre as a way to make money. Davenant was no doubt equally anxious
to make money, but he was a professional man of the theatre with previous managerial experience, and he had long dreamed of running a
fancy public theatre with changeable scenery.[4] The patent grants show
clearly the influence of Davenant's vision and his determination to avoid
the legal pitfalls which had blocked his enterprise twenty years earlier.

The terms of the two patents are substantively identical, but for convenience I shall summarize and discuss their provisions as they apply to
Davenant. The crucial provisions are these:

(1) Davenant can build a theatre anywhere he pleases "within our Cities of London and Westminster or the Suburbs thereof." Davenant's enemies had used a restricted location in his grant of 1639 to stall that project out of existence, and he wanted no such problems this time.

(2) "Davenant his heires or Assignes" have the right to present "Tragedies Comedies Playes Opera's musick Scenes and all other entertainments of the stage whatsoever." This clause takes specific note of Davenant's multimedia plans. The unrestricted variety of entertainments allowed under the patent became an issue ca. 1706, when Vanbrugh and others began to campaign for a separation of plays and operas.

(3) Davenant and his heirs have the right "to Acte Playes and entertaynments of the Stage of all sorts peaceablie and quietly without the impeachment or impediment of any person or persons whatsoever for the honest Recreation of such as shall desire to see the same." Puritan objections to the theatre continued after the Restoration. Charles is implicitly guaranteeing freedom from harassment, while making the point that only those people who want to see plays need do so.

(4) Davenant can charge patrons "such sume or sumes . . . as either have accustomably beene given . . . or as shalbee thought reasonable by him . . . in regard of the great expences of Scenes musicke and such new decorations as have not been formerly used."

(5) "The said Company shalbee under the sole Government and authoritie of the said Sir William Davenant his heires and Assignes And all scandalous and mutinous persons shall from tyme to tyme be ejected and disabled from playing in the said Theatre." In view of the monopoly and the restriction of movement imposed under No. 7 below, this gave Davenant great disciplinary power if he chose to exercise it.

(6) Charles declares his "dislike" of unlicensed companies, and declares that "onely the said Company erected and set up . . . by the said Sir William Davenant . . . and one other Company erected . . . by Thomas Killigrew Esq . . . shall from henceforth Acte or represent . . . entertainments of the Stage." "All other . . . Companyes" are hereby "silenced and suppressed." This is the monopoly clause on which Christopher Rich based his furious objections to the licensing of the Lincoln's Inn Fields company in 1695.

(7) The two companies are forbidden to steal each other's personnel. "And to preserve Amity . . . betwixt the said Companies and that the one may not encroach upon the other by any indirect meanes we will and Command that no Acter or other person . . . ejected by the said Sir William Davenant and Thomas Killigrew or either of them or deserting his Company shalbe received by the Governor or any of the said other Company . . . without the consent and obligation of the Governor of the Company whereof the said person so

ejected or deserting was a member signified under his hand and seale." This provision may well reflect squabbles over personnel during the initial phase of organization, and in particular (as Freehafer speculates) over the young Thomas Betterton.

(8) Offensive material is to be suppressed by the Patentees. "And forasmuch as many Playes formerly acted do conteyn several profane obscene and scurrilous passages . . . for the preventing of these abuses . . . we do hereby strictly Command and enjoyne that from henceforth noe new Playes shalbee acted . . . conteyning any passages offensive to pietye and good manners nor any old or revived play conteyning any such offensive passages . . . until the same shalbee Corrected and purged by the said masters or Governors of the said respective Companies." This provision has often been attacked as hypocritical, but such a view probably rests too heavily on hindsight. The early Carolean plays are not at all smutty, and we may suppose that Charles II wanted no more protest from Puritans than was inevitable. What is surprising about this provision is its silence on the subject of Sir Henry Herbert's rights as censor. In June 1662, two months after receiving his patent, Killigrew made a separate peace with Herbert, signing an agreement to pay him damages, back fees, legal costs, and £2 per new play, £1 per revived play as licensing fees.[5] Davenant fought on,[6] but must have reached a similar agreement by sometime early in 1663.

(9) Actresses are permitted. Because in the past "the womens partes . . . have been Acted by men in the habits of women att which some have taken Offence," the king gives permission that "all the womens partes to bee Acted in either of the said two Companies for the time to come may be performed by women."

(10) Finally the patent states that it shall "be in all Things Good and Effectual in the Law, according to the true Intent and Meaning of the same," regardless of precedents or of errors introduced by mistake. This clause, with the monopoly provision in No. 6 above, would allow Christopher Rich to argue in 1695 that issuing licenses to other companies was prohibited. Legal opinion did not agree with his interpretation.[7]

In most respects the patents simply confirm a status quo already arrived at. They validate and formalize the monopoly coveted by Davenant and Killigrew, and give them the power to keep their actors in line. Direct interference with the other company is forbidden in No. 7: the companies were to coexist, not to subvert each other. On two critical points the patents are silent: the rights of the two companies to old plays and their relation to Sir Henry Herbert. Obviously these hereditary grants infringed on his traditional powers. Previous licenses had been granted "during the King's pleasure," and the "Privilege" of August

1660 gave no hereditary rights. Attorney General Palmer objected even to the terms Davenant requested be embodied in that initial grant, arguing that "the matter was more proper for A tolleration; then A Grant under the greate Seale of England."[8] At what point Davenant and Killigrew wangled the concession of unprecedented hereditary rights there is no evidence to tell us—but the fact was to have great significance for future companies, particularly after the Licensing Act of 1737.

Little is known about Herbert's practices as censor.[9] He interfered extensively with John Wilson's *The Cheats*, mounted by the King's Company in 1663,[10] and examples of minor excisions may be seen in the manuscript of Elizabeth Polwhele's *The Faithfull Virgins* (1670?)[11] Definite proof that Herbert did censor and license Duke's Company plays (suspected by White, but something for which he could find no "actual evidence") is the license for Polwhele's play, and that for Cartwright's *The Lady Errant* in 1672, the latter signed by Herbert himself.[12] But the very lack of evidence about censorship by the Master of the Revels suggests that though the companies were forced to pay the fees, the control exerted was insignificant.

Reflecting on the terms of the patent grants, one sees that Charles II was giving the theatre a strong bulwark against opposition of all sorts. By creating a monopoly and giving it hereditary status Charles went far beyond the power granted in a license, and largely freed the theatres from legal harassment. By granting his managers (and their heirs) almost unlimited power to hire, fire, set prices, operate where they pleased, and suppress competition, Charles created for both companies a situation in which a strong, centralized management ought to have been able to run a theatre in an efficient and profitable way. Davenant and Betterton succeeded in doing just that. But the potential for tyranny is also there, and thirty years later Christopher Rich was to exploit it.

II
COMPANY ORGANIZATION
AND FINANCES

When Davenant and Killigrew set about organizing their troupes in the fall of 1660 one of their first problems must have been allocation of personnel. How this was done we have no evidence to show, but the

process was more complicated than it might have been. Killigrew was
able to select eight senior actors from Mohun's troupe (a descendant of
the Caroline King's Men): Mohun himself, Burt, Hart, Robert and Edward Shatterell, Wintershall, Clun, and Cartwright. To them he added
Lacy, Baxter, and Loveday (probably all from Beeston's troupe), plus Betterton and Kynaston from Rhodes's.[13] Beeston's Company remained largely
intact, and on 24 December 1660 its leader, George Jolly, received a
separate license to act, "notwithstanding any former grant [i.e., the
"Privilege" of August 1660] made by us to . . . Thomas Killegrew Esqr
and Sir William Davenant."[14] (How the patentees combined to cheat Jolly
out of his license is beyond my subject here.) Consequently what Davenant got was basically Rhodes's young company. Freehafer comments
that "Although it is usually said that Davenant had second choice of the
London actors, it is more likely that he had third choice." This may well
be correct: certainly both Killigrew's and Jolly's companies were far more
experienced and professional than Davenant's as of November 1660.
Whether Davenant was unhappy about this, however, is open to question. Killigrew's veteran actors proved both troublesome and expensive.
Desiring absolute control of his company, Davenant may have been
happy to let Killigrew take the stars while he set about building a company from more malleable materials. Davenant's one dire lack was a
leading male, and he seems to have solved the problem by hiring Henry
Harris and "seducing" Betterton away from Killigrew, back to the troupe
for which he had been leading man the previous year. Betterton was
definitely a member of the King's Company in October 1660; by the
fifth of November he was a signatory to the Duke's Company's sharers'
agreement; on 12 December the Lord Chamberlain forbade transfer of
actors from one company to another.[15] Killigrew probably objected more
to the principle of the theft than to the loss of Betterton. With the King's
Company he would have been a hireling, not better than fourth in line
for lead parts. With the Duke's Company he instantly became a sharer
and one of two leading men. Why Betterton was willing to make the
switch is clear.

    A Restoration theatre company involved five persons or groups: 1) the
patentee, who had the authority to operate a company or to delegate its
operation to a manager of his choosing; 2) the senior actors—males
only—who were "sharers," i.e., stockholders in the acting company, and
hence entitled to their due proportion of the profits in lieu of salary; 3)

the "hirelings"—junior actors (and women), paid a set wage; 4) other personnel, usually called "servants"— carpenters, dressers, et al.—paid set salaries out of general income before the distribution of profits; 5) the person or persons who financed and owned the theatre in which the company performed, and were owed some profit on their investment.

The Articles of Agreement signed 5 November 1660 between Davenant and his ten sharing actors give a very clear idea of the way the company was structured and run. Omitting details having to do with the organizational period, the provisions are as follows:[16]

1) "Davenant shall provide a newe Theatre with Scenes."

2) "The generall receiptes of the said Theatre (the generall expence first beinge deducted) shalbee devided into fifteene shares." Of these two are to be used by Davenant "towardes the house-rent, buildinge, scaffoldinge, and makeing of fframes for Scenes." A third share is to be given to Davenant to pay "for provision of Habittes, Properties, and scenes." Of the remaining twelve shares, seven go to Davenant, who will pay all the actresses out of this income; the remaining five shares are to be divided among the ten sharing actors, though not necessarily in equal proportions.

3) Admission to the theatre will be by ticket. Davenant will hire three people to handle ticket sales; they will be paid out of the general fund, before division of profits for shares is calculated. The sharing actors are to "appoint two or three of themselves, or the men hirelinges deputed by them" to oversee and check on the ticketsellers.

4) Davenant will appoint support personnel (e.g., barber, wardrobe keeper) as he thinks fit and set their salaries, which will "bee defrayed at the publique Chardge."

5) When any sharing actor dies, Davenant has the right to appoint his successor.

6) Davenant has the right to set the wages of the hirelings.

7) Davenant is not obliged to pay for sharers' hats, feathers, gloves, ribbons, sword belts, bands, stockings, or shoes, "Unless it be to Properties."

8) Killigrew is given free use of a box large enough for six people. (We may guess that Davenant had a like privilege at the King's theatre.)

9) All sharers bind themselves in a £5000 bond for performance of the agreement.

10) Finally, "it is mutually agreed by and betweene all the parties to these presentes, That the said Sir William Davenant alone shalbee Master

and Superior, and shall from time to time have the sole government of the said Thomas Batterton [et al.]."

Two features of this agreement are peculiar. Nothing is said about the financing of the theatre building or the nature of payment for use of it. Evidently Davenant financed the conversion of Lisle's Tennis Court and paid himself "house-rent" out of the two shares reserved for that purpose. The income derived thereby was probably quite inadequate. House rent in the 1670s was usually at least £3 per acting day, and nothing like that sum could have been generated by the two shares allotted. In this respect Davenant seems to have shortchanged himself. Why he chose to pay the actresses himself, rather than treat them like the male hirelings, is also unclear. He had them live in his own house in a usefully paternalistic way—the King's Company had endless trouble with pregnancies and unexpected departures from the stage. And Davenant may have seen financial advantage in paying the actresses out of his share money. This arrangement was dropped after his death.

What the sharers' agreement really makes plain, however, is just how totally dominant Davenant was in the company. He had the sole right to hire and fire personnel and to set salaries. He chose replacement sharers. He alone was "master and superior," with "sole government" of all sharers and hirelings. In a word, Davenant was the Boss. He would run the theatre, choose the shows, and superintend rehearsals. Decision-making was his province. The company would be as successful as Davenant's skill and judgment could make it.

On matters of overall authority the agreement could scarcely be clearer. On some other points it is silent or vague. The system of recruitment and training is left unspecified—perhaps because Davenant was just gathering his troupe, and felt no need to look ahead to the inevitable problem of replacements. By July 1663 a plan for a joint King's-Duke's Nursery was in train, and by 1667 such a theatre was in operation. It lasted a number of years, but little is known about it.[17] The sharers' agreement, we may notice, assumes that there will be a profit: at this date people believed that the patent monopoly was essentially a license to rake in large sums of money. No provision is made for company operations after Davenant's death. His heirs were presumably free to carry out any kind of reorganization they chose. Nor does the agreement say anything about the actors' retirement or disablement. Of course this was a very young company and no doubt retirement was not uppermost in anyone's mind. Nothing is said about the sale of shares. Actors are implicitly forbidden to sell their shares, even to other actors. But could Davenant sell his shares to outsiders? In fact, he promptly did so. Over a period of years he actually sold (or, technically, leased for one thousand years) 7.7 shares. The first of these sales came in March and June of 1661 while he was trying to make the Lincoln's Inn Fields theatre operational and needed cash.[18] The price realized per share seems to have been £600–£800. By selling more than half his interest in the company Davenant received about £5000.

This maneuver seems to have made no immediate difference to the operation of the company, and I am aware of no protest. The practice does, however, pose interesting questions. What rights over theatre operations did investors in shares have? If a creditor obtained control of Davenant's shares, did that confer the rights of the patent? Could Davenant, his heirs, or assigns operate the theatre in such a way that all proceeds were swallowed up and there were no profits to declare? In the halcyon days of 1660 no one anticipated the broils in which Rich's companies found themselves entangled between 1693 and 1709. Back in the Caroline period, however, squabbles between actors and outside investors had generated major controversy in the King's Company.[19] As long as good dividends were paid, there was no problem. Let the dividends fall, and there was a fatal conflict of interest. But without selling shares, how could a group of actors raise a substantial amount of capital? This problem was to haunt the Lincoln's Inn Fields Company in 1695.

The arrangements of Killigrew's King's Company make an interesting contrast. We possess no document comparable to the Duke's Company's agreement of 5 November 1660, but the basis of the competing operation is evident from a variety of sources. An agreement of 10 January 1662 tells us that the acting company had 12¾ shares.[20] Of these 2 belonged to Killigrew; Mohun, Hart, and Lacy had 1¼ each; Wintershall, Cartwright, Burt, Clun, and Bird had 1 each. Two shares were unassigned at this date: later in the decade Dryden was given 1¼ in a special agreement. The difference is striking: Killigrew held less than a one-sixth interest in the profits of the acting company. What Davenant actually realized from his two-thirds of the Duke's Company after paying for a theatre building, scenery, and actresses we have no way to tell—but obviously Davenant had much greater control over the daily operation of his theatre.

Killigrew made no attempt to manage his company on a day-by-day basis. At the outset of the decade he gave "Letters of Attorney to Moone Hart, and Lacy, to be superintendants over the rest."[21] For this they split three-fourths of a share among them while paying the two actors (unspecified) who were displaced from that share out of the general fund, to the great discontent of the other sharers. Killigrew, the arbitrators report, "hath made very little use" of the powers granted in his patent, leaving the operation of the company up to his deputies. Sometime after the death of Bird in March 1663 Killigrew withdrew his Letter of Attorney, restored the three-quarters of a share to the company—and attempted to keep Bird's vacated share for himself. The company objected violently, but the arbitrators held that Killigrew was within his rights. Killigrew may have tried to run the company himself in the middle of the decade, but by 1667 the Lord Chamberlain's orders to the theatre name Hart as manager. Apparently the King's Company had no strong, centralized management, and no routine procedures for reassigning vacated shares. Who made decisions about hiring and salaries is vague—and was probably somewhat unsettled. Of course Killigrew would have had trouble getting Mohun's troupe to accept the kind of absolute control Davenant was able to impose upon his fledglings. But squabbles over management and shares were to characterize the King's Company throughout its stormy career, and ultimately they led to its downfall.

Unlike the Duke's Company, however, the King's Company did from the outset have a clear agreement spelling out the use of its theatre. On 20 December 1661 a group of investors made an agreement to build a modern theatre with changeable scenery. Davenant's success with his Lincoln's Inn Fields theatre forced the King's Company to follow suit. Thirty-six shares in the building were apportioned to investors, who were responsible for the ground rent: nine to Killigrew; nine to Sir Robert Howard; four to Lacy; two each to Hart, Mohun, Burt, Robert Shatterell, Clun, Cartwright, and Wintershall. The theatre was to cost at least £1500; it actually did cost about £2500.[22] The acting company—including Killigrew and the eight actors with building shares, plus five others—then signed an agreement to occupy the planned theatre, and to pay £3 10s. rent for every acting day. This arrangement, by which the actors rented their theatre from a holding company partly owned by some of their own members, was to become standard.

If the acting company operated regularly and was able to pay its rent, the building shares would be a very good investment. Each investor wound up paying approximately £70 per share. At a nightly rent of £3 10s., only about 714 acting nights would be required to repay the entire investment—well under four years at only 200 acting nights per year. Hotson reports that in November 1663 Clun was able to sell his two shares for £430—a rather tidy profit on a £140 investment made in installments over the previous two years.[23] Of course the plague could interrupt acting, and wooden theatres could burn down—as this one did in 1672. And long before a company went out of business it could fail to pay its rent—as the King's Company did in the later 1670s.

The financing of the Bridges Street theatre shows another side of a constant dilemma. The actors were well advised to avoid raising capital by selling shares to outside investors, even in buildings: if they did so they would pour money out of the theatre operation, and would do so indefinitely. This is why, in 1674 when the King's Company built the Drury Lane theatre, the actors kept the contract for the adjoining scene-house entirely separate.[24] The £2040 required to finance the scene-house, new scenery, and costumes they raised by levying contributions on acting company shareholders, who were then to be repaid at the rate of £10 per week for each full share. This excessively rapid repayment—the whole would have been repaid in only sixteen weeks—proved disastrous, since the profits would not cover the total and a mutiny resulted. But the principle of raising money from within was sound.

Our complete lack of box office receipts or general financial records for the 1660s makes any account of company finances hypothetical, but the general outlines are clear enough.[25] The basic cost of operating a theatre for one performance in the 1660s was about £25. These "house charges," as they were called, included salaries, theatre rent, and all miscellaneous disbursements. They did not, of course, cover remuneration for sharers. Thomas Cross, Duke's Company treasurer from 1660 to 1674–75, reports that he received 25s. per week for duties which included

the sole trouble of paying the whole charge of the House weekly, that is to say, the Salaries of all hireling Players both men and Women, Music Masters, Dancing Masters, Scene-men, Barbers, Wardrobekeepers, Doorkeepers, and Soldiers, besides Bills of all kinds, as for Scenes, Habits, Properties, Candles, Oil, and other things, and in making and paying (if called for) all the Dividends of the Sharers, dividing each man his particular share according to his proportion, and . . . the paying the sharers of the Ten Shares (being the Assignees of the said Sir William Davenant) who came or sent for their moneys when they pleased.[26]

If we make the assumption of a two-hundred-performance acting year (using the round number for convenience),[27] the fixed expenses would come to 200 × £25, or £5000. We must also allow a minimum of something like another £1000 (£5 per day) to cover the costs of new productions, money lost to authors' third days, and so forth. If the theatre actually took in an average of £35 a day, then there would be a £1000 profit, which would amount to £66 for each of the fifteen shares. This may not sound like much of an annual income for the holder of a full share, let alone for part-share holders—but we must remember that even after 1700 the annual salary for a senior actor amounted to something between £80 and £150. Salaries in this range would have been generated for holders of half shares in the 1660s if the theatre averaged more than about £40 per performance. In a 1670 lawsuit the painter Isaac Fuller estimates that the King's Company could expect "usually to receive above 40 or 50*li* per diem," and states that £100 represented a very large house.[28] According to John Downes, the largest receipts for a single performance at ordinary prices for the Drury Lane theatre were £130.[29] More than half that was probably exceptional.

   The price structure was as follows: boxes, 4*s.* per occupant; pit, 2/6; first gallery, 1/6; second gallery 1*s.* (The first Restoration theatres probably had no second gallery, but we will ignore this technicality.) How many spectators would be required for a house to break even? Hypothetically, 30 patrons in the boxes, 130 in the pit, 60 in the first gallery, and 30 in the second would yield a return of about £28—which would have meant thin pickings for the sharers. The seating capacity of the first Lincoln's Inn Fields theatre is not known, but we may say with some assurance that a theatre needed something like 200 spectators to come close to breaking even, and more if the sharing actors were to be paid. The relatively small budget projected here makes an interesting comparison to the cost of the scene for *Tyrannick Love* over which Isaac Fuller sued the King's Company and was awarded £335. Restoration companies did invest heavily in scenic spectacle, but this is an imposing bill for a single scene. We may suppose it was altogether exceptional for the King's Company at that time. They conceded they should have paid Fuller £100, and he contended in reply that he had spent nearly that much in "providing materialls and paying Servants for and about the Same." Even at that rate, the potential expense of scenery tells us something about the financial priorities of a Restoration theatre.

III
THEATRICAL COMPETITION,
1660–1668

In November 1660 an impartial observer might have felt that Davenant was in dire straits. True, he had concluded an agreement with his sharing actors, hired Harris, and enticed Betterton away from Killigrew. But the King's Company was already acting daily in what was said to be "the finest play-house . . . that ever was in England." And the glamour of the veteran actors was undeniable. Pepys remarks with awe that he has seen Mohun, "who is said to be the best actor in the world."[30] Worse yet, Davenant's company had almost no plays to perform once it did get organized. The company did not manage to open in temporary quarters until late January 1661, and from the start it had an acute repertory problem. Quite undismayed, Davenant set about coping with his situation, and he did so with such success that by the end of a year the King's Company found itself getting much the worst of the competition. A survey of the interaction between the two companies during the remainder of Davenant's lifetime shows a very simple pattern. Davenant led and Killigrew followed. The circumstances demanded exactly what Davenant's inclinations led him to anyway—innovation. Pulling together a young and well-disciplined company, he established a theatre with changeable scenery, added music and dance, and made the most of new play types. He never achieved the scale of production he dreamed of, but he set his company on the path toward it, and Killigrew tagged along behind. Killigrew sometimes boasted of grandiose plans, but nothing ever came of his vague schemes for Italian operas.[31] Basically Killigrew was inclined to rely on his extensive repertory of pre-Commonwealth dramas. He mounted plenty of new plays, but only because he was forced to do so.

The rights of the Carolean theatre companies in earlier drama are a confusing subject. Cibber asserted that "they had a private Rule or Agreement, which both Houses were happily ty'd down to, which was, that no Play acted at one House should ever be attempted at the other. All the capital Plays therefore of *Shakespear, Fletcher*, and *Ben. Johnson* were divided between them by the Approbation of the Court and their own alternate Choice."[32] This was very far from the truth. At the time he organized his company, Davenant apparently had rights to only two plays known to have been in the repertory of Rhodes's troupe (*The Changeling* and *The Bondman*), and even they may have been the subject of dispute.[33] To give his company a minimal basis for a repertory Davenant evidently petitioned the King, for on 12 December 1660 the Lord Chamberlain issued an edict. In response to Davenant's "proposition of reformeinge some of the most ancient Playes that were playd at Blackfriers and of makeinge them fitt," Davenant is granted exclusive performing rights to eleven plays, including nine of Shakespeare's. He is further allowed "liberty . . . to represent by the Actors under his Comand all the playes written by himselfe formerly."[34] This was by no means a minor or *pro forma* concession. It doubled the number of plays to which the company had rights, and Killigrew's company had staged Davenant's *The Unfortunate Lovers* as recently as 19 November. The Lord Chamberlain went on to say a) that transfer of actors between the two companies without the joint agreement of Killigrew and Davenant is forbidden, and b) that Davenant is granted liberty "dureinge the space of two Months after the date hereof" eof" for his actors to perform six plays (*The Mad Lover, The Maid in the Mill, The Spanish Curate, The Loyal Subject, Rule a Wife*, and *Pericles*) which had been in Rhodes's repertory.

The implication of the order is clear. The "two month" plays could be performed on an interim basis, but after this transitional period Davenant's repertory would be some twenty-three plays specifically allotted to him, new plays, and whatever other old plays he could negotiate rights for. (In fact Davenant seems somehow to have kept four of the two-month plays in his permanent repertory.) In the Caroline period play manuscripts seem almost to have been treated as physical theatre properties. They belonged to a company of actors. To publish a play was to lose exclusive control of it. This is why Brome's contract with the Salisbury Court Company in 1635 forbids him to publish a play without the express consent of the actors, and why so many of the "Fletcher" plays were never published until 1647—at a time the actors had despaired of ever reopening their theatre.[35] Attempts at usurpation and infringement were by no means unknown. Thus in 1639 we find the Lord Chamberlain forbidding "all other Companyes of Actors . . . to intermedle with or Act" any of the plays in a list claimed by William Beeston's troupe.[36]

In 1660 the rights of the new companies to the old drama seem to have been a subject of doubt and confusion.[37] Killigrew's veteran actors had performed in various Caroline troupes, and they laid claim to most of the preexisting repertory on that ground. But because plays had been bought and sold as physical entities, and because many plays had been published during the Commonwealth period, the situation was by no means simple. A letter of 30 August 1660 from the publisher Humphrey Mosely to Herbert denies negotiating with Rhodes: "I never so much as treated with him . . . neither did I ever consent directly or indirectly, that hee or any others should act any playes that doe belong to mee."[38] Mosely owned a large collection of play manuscripts: arguably, at least, he had some control over the performance rights. One of the mysteries of the Restoration theatre is the lack of explicit testimony about the division of the older English drama and the nature of the companies' rights in plays. At least initially, actors may have felt that even new plays belonged to them. Thus in a will made in March 1663 Theophilus Bird of the King's Company left to his sons "right and title in all the playes and play bookes that are mine by payment and survivour shipp"—something he considered entirely distinct from his share in the acting company.[39]

However Davenant and Killigrew settled the matter, they did so without formal litigation and without much open conflict. Very early in the 1660s we have records of some direct collisions. In March 1661 both companies mounted Heywood's *Love's Mistress*, and after Davenant scored a success with *The Bondman* that spring Killigrew promptly mounted the same show. But such head-to-head competition could only damage both companies, and the managers seem to have been able to agree not to do something so stupid. The long silence about play rights which followed is more surprising. The next we hear of the matter is a list of "Playes allowed to be acted by his Royall Highnesse ye Duke of Yorkes Comoedians" in an order issued by the Lord Chamberlain on 20 August 1668— four months after Davenant's death.[40] The order specifies that "This is the list of the playes allowed to His Royall Highnesse Actors and none other has right to them." None of the twenty-three old plays specified was much of a catch. The Duke's Company can scarcely have been anxious to

receive rights to these plays. We may guess that Davenant's successors
set out to see what old plays they could pry loose from the sweeping
claims of the King's Company, and the answer was—not much worth
having. Alternatively, we might hypothesize that in the confusion following Davenant's death the King's Company made a grab for whatever it
could get. On 14 October 1668 the Duke's Company gave a special
performance at Court for the Duke of York's birthday. The play chosen
was Habington's *The Queen of Arragon*, one of the plays to which they had
just received rights. Samuel Butler wrote a special prologue for the occasion, in which he says:

> We bring you only, what your great Commands
> Did rescue for us from ingrossing Hands,
> That would have taken out *Administration*
> Of all departed *Poets* Goods i' th' Nation;
> Or, like to *Lords of Manors*, seiz'd all Plays,
> That come within their Reach, as *Wefts* and *Strays*;
> And claim'd a Forfeiture of all past Wit,
> But that your Justice put a stop to it.[41]

The plays the Duke's Company got were, however, sufficiently unattrac-
tive that we have records of only two of them performed without alteration. Probably as a result of this imbroglio the King's Company got the
Lord Chamberlain to issue "A Catalogue of part of His Majesties Servants
Playes as they were formerly acted at the Blackfryers and now allowed of
to his Majesties Servants at ye New Theatre" (ca. January "1668/9").
More than one hundred plays are named—among them practically all
the popular old plays in the English dramatic heritage. And this seems
to be merely that "part" of their holdings to which the King's Company
wanted to lay specific claim.

The acuteness of Davenant's repertory problem in the early sixties is
made even plainer if we consider what was required. In the first year his
company did not perform every day, and novelty brought people flocking
to the theatres. But after that a normal acting year would be some 200
days or more. If the company mounted four "new" plays which averaged
10 days each (which would be pretty fair success), they would still need
to fill 160 days. To run twenty different plays an average of 8 days each
during the year would do the trick. But Davenant had rights to barely

more than twenty plays; new plays were scarce until 1663; and without variety in his repertory audiences would soon dwindle.

I have explained this problem of rights to plays at such length because it is so crucial a factor in 1695. The Lincoln's Inn Fields and patent companies made no attempt to divide existing repertory, and they deliberately engaged in vicious head-on collisions, mounting the same plays. As far as we know, the healthy competition in the sixties rarely included such stunts. And Betterton, we must note, had an opportunity to watch firsthand in a situation where star actors, with exclusive rights to almost the entire classic repertory, failed to compete successfully against a company of beginners who mounted new plays. Little wonder then, with exclusivity lost, that Betterton and his fellows scrambled to produce new plays in 1695.

Over the years, Davenant could not hope to compete without new plays at his disposal—and that would take time. But even in the first fragment of a season he was remarkably successful. As early as March 1661 Pepys found the Duke's Company's production of *Love's Mistress* preferable in some respects to their rivals', which is quite surprising. And during that first spring Davenant was readying his special lure. On 28 June 1661 he opened his new Lincoln's Inn Fields theatre with a revamping of his own *The Siege of Rhodes* (1656) which featured changeable scenery—its first use in the English public theatre. This sensational innovation made *Rhodes* such an event that it brought Charles II to a public theatre for the first time. It also emptied Killigrew's theatre. On 4 July Pepys wrote: "I went to the Theatre and there I saw *Claracilla* (the first time I ever saw it), well acted. But strange to see this house, that use to be so thronged, now empty since the opera begun—and so will continue for a while I believe." Later in the summer Davenant produced *The Witts* and *Hamlet*, both "with scenes" (as Pepys admiringly notes), and both with great success. *Love and Honour* received a fancy production in October, and *Cutter of Coleman Street* was a hit in December. A year earlier the King's Company's new Vere Street theatre had seemed splendid; now it was manifestly inadequate. To stay in business against Davenant's upstarts, Killigrew would have to erect a theatre equipped with changeable scenery. The building-sharers' agreement is dated 28 January "1661/2": just seven months after the opening of Lincoln's Inn Fields Killigrew and his men had bowed to the inevitable. When their new Bridges Street theatre finally opened, 7 May 1663, it was the best in the land, and it immediately made the King's Company fully competitive. On the twenty-eighth of the month Pepys and his wife went "to the Royall Theatre but that was so full they told us we could have no room"—so they had to go to the Duke's house to watch Betterton as Hamlet.

One can scarcely overestimate the importance of scenery and costume in the Restoration theatre. Davenant had dreamed of changeable scenery for more than twenty years. A hint of this interest appears in the 5 November 1660 sharers' agreement, in which Henry Harris, who was to become an actor of note, is specifically mentioned as a "painter." A year later Davenant stole a march on Killigrew when he persuaded the King, the Duke of York, and Lord Oxford to give his company their coronation robes for the production of *Love and Honour*. The success of Davenant's fancily clothed and staged *Henry VIII* in December 1663 pressured the King's Company to reply in kind with *The Indian Queen* a month later, a play for which they persuaded the King to give them a special grant of "forty pounds in silkes" for the Royal musicians.[42] They succeeded: Pepys reports gossip that the new play "exceeds" even *Henry VIII* "for show," and the grumpy John Evelyn says admiringly that *The Indian Queen* was "beautified with rich Scenes as the like had never ben seene here as happly (except rarely any where else) on a mercenarie Theater."[43] Escalation was the order of the day; both companies made expensive plunges into spectacle. On 11 December 1667 Pepys reports a rumor from Henry Harris (of the Duke's Company) that the King had promised the King's Company £500 for "sixteen scarlett robes" in a projected production of *Catiline*. Rumor may have magnified the sum, and given the state of Charles's finances we may doubt that such a promise was ever fulfilled—but already both companies felt compelled to put a lot of money into scenes and fancy clothing. The payment to Isaac Fuller was not an isolated expenditure, except that prompt reimbursement might have saved the King's Company the expense of going to law over *Tyrranick Love*.

Audiences could be very fussy about costumes. The Duke's Company put on *Pompey the Great*, by Waller et al. in January 1664, "acted in English habits, & that so aprope that Caesar was sent in with his feather and Muff, till he was hiss'd off ye Stage."[44] In March, mounting *Heraclius*, they were careful to provide "authentic" Roman garb, on which Pepys commented approvingly (8 March 1664). Again in August 1667 he was fascinated by the King's Company's display of "the true garbe of the queens in those days" in *Queen Elizabeth's Troubles*, a play he otherwise disliked. The phrase Downes uses so regularly in describing successful new Duke's Company plays—"all new Cloth'd"—is no empty formula, but a very expensive and important competitive device.

How smoothly were the two companies operating? On the principle that no news is good news we may infer that the Duke's Company went along very efficiently. No disputes over authority or shares are known in this period. The most serious upheaval came in the summer of 1663 when Henry Harris tried to desert to the King's Company.[45] According to a rumor reported by Pepys, Harris was receiving "a stipend from the other House privately." Although no one seems to have suggested the possibility, I wonder if the motive was Harris's capacities as "painter"? The King's Company had just opened a theatre in which the services of a scene painter were needed. In any event, the King forbade the transfer. In contrast, the King's Company had a stormy time. The appointment of Hart, Mohun, and Lacy as managers did not work out; Killigrew threw the company into an uproar requiring government mediation when he seized Bird's vacated share in 1663; in December 1667 the company ceased acting for some days when Hart and Mohun quarreled (Pepys, 7 December). Such broils were to be all too typical of the King's Company in the 1670s. Lack of discipline had a bad effect on their performances. Pepys often grumbles that their actors are "out," something he rarely charges Davenant's players with. (Neither house was sure to be very accurate at premieres.) By 1663 Pepys is regularly commenting on his preference for the Duke's Company. The dizzying succession of brand-new actresses could not have helped Killigrew's performances, either. Davenant had these troubles too but seems to have coped more smoothly with them. He lost the popular Hester Davenport to the Earl of Oxford's private service in January 1662, only half a year after her triumph as Roxolana in *The Siege of Rhodes*. Pepys feared that her loss "would spoil the house," but by 18 February he found himself delighted with Moll Davis, her replacement. Moll Davis departed to the service of the King himself in due course, but on the whole Davenant's personnel remained stable and he recruited skillfully.

Competition in the 1660s was reasonably friendly but definitely hot. A success by either company could leave the other with a dangerously empty house. Thus on 7 March 1664 Pepys found Lincoln's Inn Fields "very empty, by reason of a new play" at the King's theatre. More often, especially late in the decade, he remarked on scant audiences at Bridges

Street. "The house mighty empty—more than ever I saw it" (1 August 1667, at *The Custom of the Country*). The following 5 October he watched Nell Gwyn dress, and commented: "But to see how Nell cursed for having so few people in the pit was pretty, the other House carrying away all the people at the new play, and is said nowadays to have generally most company, as being better players."

Successes and innovations could not go unanswered. Killigrew seems to have "replied" to Davenant's use of the coronation robes in October 1661 by sending an actress out in men's clothes after Glapthorne's *Argalus and Parthenia* to show off her legs (Pepys, 28 October—he loved them). If we match their new plays by type and then chronologically, we find that almost every time Davenant led and Killigrew followed. In January 1663 the triumph of Tuke's *Adventures of Five Hours* at Lincoln's Inn Fields crushed Dryden's *Wild Gallant* at Vere Street. A year later Killigrew mounted Dryden's imitation of Tuke, *The Rival Ladies*. In the fall of 1663 Davenant's triumph with *Henry VIII* was matched by the King's Company's production of *The Indian Queen*, but in March 1664 the smashing success of Etherege's first play, *The Comical Revenge*, at Lincoln's Inn Fields was to swamp *The Rival Ladies*. Davenant's house pioneered the popular Spanish romance mode, and Killigrew's followed, not too successfully.

Killigrew's foot-dragging was especially flagrant in that notorious genre, the rhymed heroic play. Orrery had given the script of *The Generall* to Charles II in 1661, and the King passed it on with an enthusiastic recommendation to Killigrew, who did nothing with it for more than two years. Yet when Davenant mounted Orrery's second play, *Henry the Fifth*, in August 1664 (reusing the coronation robes and adding other fancy costumes), Killigrew scrambled to get *The Generall* on stage in September. Despite its even "finer Clothes" Pepys found the production disappointing.[46] Davenant followed this with his own successful revamping of Shakespeare in *The Rivals*; Killigrew replied with his own *Parson's Wedding* (October 1664), "acted by nothing but women," as Pepys informs us. Evidently such titillation was considered necessary to make the play viable. The following spring the two companies clashed again with fancy new productions of heroic plays—*The Indian Emperour* (King's) and *Mustapha* (Duke's). Downes says of the latter: "All the Parts being new Cloath'd with new Scenes, Sir *William's* great Care of having it perfect and exactly perform'd, it produc'd to himself and Company vast Profit."[47]

The Indian Emperour evidently did well enough, but the company econo-
mized and reused scenery and costumes from *The Indian Queen*, as the
prologue notes apologetically—"The Scenes are old, the Habits are the
same / We wore last year."

Competition after the reopening of the theatres in December 1666
follows the pattern established before the plague. We see the Duke's
Company mounting interesting new shows and the King's Company unhappily trying to compete by relying on its classic repertory. Davenant
and Dryden's reworking of *The Tempest* in November 1667 made the
King's Company's production of Fletcher and Massinger's *The Sea Voyage*
seem "but a mean play" in comparison.[48] By the following fall Killigrew
had mounted a counterextravaganza, a revamping of *The Island Princess*
complete with "a good scene of a town on fire."[49] In the spring of 1669
Pepys exclaimed over the "infinite full" house for the Lincoln's Inn Fields
production of Shadwell's *The Royall Shepherdess*; the next day he went to
Bridges Street, where the King's Company was countering with Fletcher's
old *The Faithful Shepherdess*, and he says: "but Lord, what an empty
house, there not being, as I could tell the people, so many as to make up
above 10*l* in the whole house" (26 February).

The one great advantage possessed by the King's Company was John
Dryden. Had Davenant not died suddenly in April 1668, even that prop
might have been lost. Dryden's promise was evident to Davenant from
the success of *Sir Martin Mar-all* (on which Dryden had assisted New-
castle) in August 1667. Davenant invited him to collaborate on *The
Tempest*. Until 1667–68 Dryden had given his own work to the King's
Company, in whose theatre his brother-in-law Sir Robert Howard was a
major shareholder; but the collaborations suggest that Dryden (then
quarreling with Howard) might have shifted his allegiance, had not the
King's Company retained his services by the unprecedented expedient of
giving him a full share and a quarter in the acting company.[50] Little is
known about the financial arrangements between companies and authors
in this period. Many plays by amateurs or free-lancers were produced.
Professional writers usually stuck with one company, and some of them
were evidently given a salary in addition to the customary third night
profits. The extraordinary lengths to which the King's Company was
willing to go to reserve Dryden's services are testimony both to his value
and to their need.

If Betterton had learned nothing else from working with Davenant, he would certainly have seen the advantage of setting the trend. In view of Betterton's lifelong association with "dialogue opera," we should note a similar passion on Davenant's part. The concept behind Davenant's 1639 patent was that of the multimedia show, demanding music, dance, and scenery. Davenant had mounted "opera" under Cromwell. His concept was not, however, based on Italian opera but rather derived from the Stuart masque. He may have been influenced by seeing Italian opera during his exile, but his basic intentions did not change. He found *stilo recitativo* intriguing and used it in some of his poetry and for occasional passages in his plays. He may have seen *pièces à machines* at the Théâtre du Marais, and would have enjoyed the mechanics of those productions. But Edward J. Dent suggests that Corneille's *Andromède*, if Davenant saw it, would have provided an influence more congenial to his ideas. *Andromède* "is interesting as the experiment of an accomplished dramatist in the combination of speech, song and machinery, and though its influence on French opera was only slight, it ought probably to be regarded as the model for D'Avenant's version of *The Tempest* and the later English operas."[51] Davenant is called the "Father of English Opera" because he included elaborate spectacle and a fair amount of music in his productions; but as his patents show he never meant to devote his theatre to musical drama alone. However much scenery and incidental music a production might include, his main characters had speaking parts and were rarely involved in the songs. In this respect Betterton always followed him closely. Had Davenant lived, he would almost certainly have directed the building of Dorset Garden. Really fancy productions (utilizing the resources of that theatre) are a development of the seventies and eighties, most of them done under Betterton's direction. In mounting such spectaculars Betterton was elaborating a concept to which his mentor was deeply committed.

When in his old age Betterton faced the task of advising and leading his cohorts at Lincoln's Inn Fields, his memory of the original competition could not but have influenced his thinking. Davenant had shown that a young company with a passable theatre could put a veteran company with a fancier theatre (after 1663) at a disadvantage, just by continuing to stage new plays. Conversely, Killigrew had found that having a company of stars, even with exclusive rights to most of the classic repertory, carried no guarantee of success. The stream of new plays mounted by the rebel company after 1695 testifies to a resolve not to stagnate but instead to take the offensive, as Davenant had. The desirability of a strong central management was also plain from the original King's-Duke's competition, but that was a point over which Betterton did not have control in 1695. Of course he knew the advantages of a good theatre: Lincoln's Inn Fields had given Davenant a lead in 1661 that the King's Company never really recovered from, even after the opening of Bridges Street in 1663. Davenant loved and exploited the multimedia approach to play production, and this influence on Betterton in his formative years affected his whole outlook on theatre. Davenant might be said to have passed on to Betterton the motto "Think BIG." All the adjuncts to a bare script—scenery, dance, music—had put the Duke's Company ahead and forced Killigrew to scramble to keep up. During the next twenty years Betterton was instrumental in enlarging the scale of theatres and productions. When he had to return to a hastily refurbished Lincoln's Inn Fields in 1695, the outmoded building severely cramped his style.

Chapter 2

Betterton's Management Experience, 1668–1694

D AVENANT'S sudden death in April 1668 changed Betterton's status and considerably enlarged his responsibilities. The reorganization which made him comanager of the Duke's Company opens a new phase in his career: for nearly twenty-five years he was to share responsibility for operating a stable, profitable, and well-disciplined theatre. In the seventies he watched the opposition falter and fail, and following the King's Company's protracted death agonies, Betterton continued as manager of the new United Company. In 1687, according to a theory propounded by Hotson, the Betterton-Smith management was "deposed": in fact, the situation was a good deal more complex than that. I shall leave the messy details of the later days of the United Company for the next chapter. Here, my purpose is to review briefly company management and competition prior to the stalemate which led to the rebellion of 1695. Those who wish to belittle or denigrate Betterton as a manager after 1695 must reckon with an important fact: at the time of the Lincoln's Inn Fields breakaway, Betterton was the most experienced and successful manager in England. He had, indeed, enjoyed quite a distinguished career as a manager.

I
THE DUKE'S COMPANY, 1668–1682

Davenant died intestate a fortnight after the opening of his last play. His widow found herself with numerous children and stepchildren to care for out of an entangled inheritance which included a theatre as well as a boardinghouse. The complexities of the Davenant family's internecine squabblings need not detain us here.[1] Pepys reports Davenant's death and adds that who "will succeed him in the mastership of that House is not yet known."[2] Charles Davenant was still a minor; consequently Lady Davenant took control of the estate (such as it was) and had a voice in the operation of the theatre for some years. But though she was a canny businesswoman, she was no theatre manager. According to a Chancery deposition made by Henry Harris in 1691, he and Betterton "were chose by all Parties interested in the said Theatre to manage the same." The job of management had "always before" belonged "to the Patentee without any salary or consideration for the same beside the share or shares he had therein." For their work in running the company Harris and Betterton were allowed "twenty shillings a week . . . to each of them"—quite a considerable salary.[3] The two men ran the company smoothly for about ten years. Harris was replaced as comanager by William Smith about 1678 and had left the company to pursue other interests by the time of the Union of 1682.

One of the first steps taken by Betterton and Harris was to overhaul the financial structure of the company.[4] Davenant's original plan used some of his ten shares to supply operating funds out of which to pay actresses and theatre rent and to mount new plays. Such a system was no longer workable, especially since outsiders now held some of those shares. The new system was simpler and much more rational. The company reduced the shares to ten by decreeing that *all* expenses would be paid before profits were divided into shares. Thus out of general receipts they would pay rent, salary of all actresses and hirelings, and the cost of new productions, and the like, and then they would split up the balance. For convenience in dealing with half shares they also divided the ten shares into twenty, half of which belonged to sharing actors and half to "Proprietors." This increased the sharing actors' take by one-sixth (from one-third to one-half), but also entirely disencumbered the other sharers of the obligation to pay operating expenses assumed by Davenant in 1660. The proprietors thus waived their rights to one-sixth of the profits, but thereby considerably reduced their responsibility and liability. From now on the sharing actors would assume their full share of risk. If productions were extravagant or unsuccessful, their profits would immediately suffer—something which had been much less true in the Davenant regime.

Previously they had been carefully sheltered children; now they were adults whose competence and cooperation would determine the success or failure of their business.

We have little evidence about the day-to-day operation of the Duke's Company in the seventies. To keep the theatre functioning, somebody had to decide which plays (old and new) to rehearse and perform; assign roles in new plays and fill vacancies in stock productions; hire and fire support personnel; coach beginning actors; supervise the design and construction of Dorset Garden theatre and maintain it thereafter; approve payment of bills; assess fines for misbehavior; award prize money when appropriate; consider pensions and charity for widows and disabled persons; and do the socializing which made important friends for the theatre at Court.

To identify individual responsibility for any single phase of Duke's Company management after 1668 is very difficult. Betterton and Harris both continued to perform old and new roles—a time-consuming commitment Davenant never faced. We have no evidence that Harris ever wrote or adapted plays, nor does he seem to have had much interest in the mechanics of operatic productions—matters which fell to Betterton. Both men did some training of actors. Downes tells us that Joseph Williams served his apprenticeship under Harris, and tradition holds that the Bettertons adopted Anne Bracegirdle and raised her to be an actress.[5] From the Reply of the Patentees in 1694 we know that Betterton was then receiving 50 guineas per annum for duties which included "ye Care he tooke as principall Actor in ye nature of a Monitor in a Schole to looke after rehearsalls" (article 8). In 1703 the author of the plan for a United Theatre Company penciled Betterton in at an annual salary of £150—plus £50 "more to teach."[6] Little is known about the processes of recruiting and training, and information on the succession of "Nurseries" is scanty in the extreme. Trained or not, recruits had to be walked through stock productions and coached in new shows.

One of Davenant's major functions had been providing plays. He wrote no new pieces after 1660, but instead turned his hand to a stream of adaptations and translations, most of them extremely successful. The evidence is strong that when Betterton and Harris took over, Betterton (who had apparently never done any writing) immediately set out to take up the slack. In May 1669 *The Unjust Judge, or Appius and Virginia* (a production alteration of Webster's *The Roman Virgin*) was mounted by the

Duke's Company, and we have Downes's word that Betterton did the alterations, whatever they may have been. During the next year Betterton rigged out *The Woman Made a Justice* (lost—probably based on Mont-fleury's *La Femme Juge et Partie*) and *The Amorous Widow* (from Molière and T. Corneille), both extremely successful.[7] In the summer of 1670 agreements were made for the building of Dorset Garden, and Betterton busied himself with that. In the seventies the Company found that it had plenty of writers, and Betterton apparently felt no desire to do more such work.

The principal event in this phase of the history of the Duke's Company is the building of Dorset Garden. This "most magnificent of the Restoration playhouses" will be discussed briefly in section IV.[8] It fulfilled all of Davenant's dreams, and gave the company the ability to mount the lavish scenic spectaculars Betterton favored. According to the authors of the *Biographical Dictionary*, Betterton made at least one trip to France to do research on machinery for the theatre, which opened in November 1671. Both managers lived in apartments over the theatre—Harris until about 1678, Betterton until about 1694. In 1691 Betterton testified that "by his own Care & Management of the playhouse and by his nearness and diligence he hath several times preserved the Playhouse from being burnt."[9] In the days before fire insurance, this was an especially important service.

Finances were evidently kept as open and aboveboard as possible. I have already quoted Thomas Cross, one of the "Receivers," on the treasurer's duties. The books were subject to inspection and even confiscation at any time. Cross tells us that the members of the company

might and did almost dayly view and examine this Defendant['s] Accompts which one or other of them did or might have done when they pleased. . . . [Holders of the ten Davenant shares] came or sent for their moneys when they pleased having free accesse by themselves servants or Agents to the Books of Accompts of all the Receipts and disbursements of the foregoing week with the severall Dividends, this Defendant being ever ready when required to Sattisfy them in every particular and to deliver them their shares at every weeks end.[10]

Cross, we may note, was caught embezzling from the Dorset Garden building fund and fired in November 1674. He was replaced by Dame

Mary's son, Alexander Davenant, a piece of nepotism which boded the company no good.

Harris's successor, William Smith, gives us a picture of the system of petty fines and rewards used by the company.

The Actors and Musitians forfeitures according to the Method of the Dukes Company which were made by reason of their not attending to performe the Rehearsall of their parts and other Offices of the Stage were never looked upon as this Defendant Conceives as any part of the cleere profitts ariseing by acting in any of the said Theatres. . . . Some of them [the fines] have been remitted to engage further diligence in those that made them Or else spent in Treats amongst the Actors or given as Extraordinary Rewards to such whose meritts deserved it & often disposed of in Charityes according to usuall Custome.[11]

The fines for missed rehearsals or other misbehavior went into a special "kitty" which could be used by the managers as a party fund or a source of special rewards—the money "belonged" to the acting company as a whole, it did not constitute profits to which the "Adventurers" were entitled. Christopher Rich, in sharp contradistinction, was convinced that he could levy fines and pocket the money.

Both managers did some useful socializing, particularly Harris, who as Yeoman of the Revels had good political connections in society and government. When the Royal Family decided to mount Crowne's *Calisto* at Court for its own amusement, the Bettertons were invited to coach Princesses Mary and Anne, both future queens of England.[12] In a letter of May 1678 Nell Gwyn mentioned that Lord Buckhurst was spending a lot of time at Dorset Garden, drinking ale with Harris and the playwright Thomas Shadwell. In 1695 that same peer, by then Earl of Dorset, was serving as Lord Chamberlain and was a key figure in authorizing the Lincoln's Inn Fields breakaway.[13] When Rich moved to suppress the rebellion he found "People of Quality" almost unanimous in the actors' favor. Betterton and his fellows used their social connections to the utmost.[14]

The overall picture shows us a business efficiently run by people who knew their jobs and understood the necessity of working together comfortably. Doubtless some were lax; certainly some of the actors got in trouble, mostly for nonpayment of debts,[15] though such problems were far more typical of the members of the King's Company. Lack of lawsuits from tradesmen suggests that, unlike the King's Company, the Duke's

Company could and did pay its bills. The very limited financial records extant for this period (approximately from 1675 to 1677) suggest an annual income of £50 or £60 per share on a basis of twenty. Times got much harder during the Popish Plot and the following Exclusion Crisis: prologues and epilogues complain of thin houses. But we have every reason to believe that the company remained stable and profitable, and in these respects the contrast with the King's Company is striking.

II
THE DISMAL HISTORY OF THE
KING'S COMPANY, 1668–1682

The later history of the King's Company is ludicrous. To lesser members of the company, events must have seemed a nightmare tangle of disaster, deceit, theft, and dissension. To the rival Duke's Company this tale of woe must have seemed a comedy of errors. Some of the problems were no one's fault—wooden theatres do burn down. But overall, the history of the King's Company in the seventies is an object lesson in how not to operate a theatre company. The Duke's Company ran successfully, but one has to admit that Betterton and his comanagers were given little competition.

For detailed discussion of the King's Company the reader should turn to Hotson, and particularly to John Harold Wilson.[16] Here I will merely note the key points of the company's decline and collapse.

January 1672. The destruction of the Bridges Street theatre by fire left the company homeless and bereft of a decade's accumulation of scenery and costumes. Coming just two months after the Duke's Company opened their splendid new theatre, the blow was doubly crushing. The only silver lining—not much of one—was the availability of Lincoln's Inn Fields, in which the King's Company reopened on 26 February. A series of revivals "acted all by Women" was the best competitive expedient they could think of that spring. The Duke's Company had done well with *Charles the Eighth of France* that winter, and scored a blockbuster success with Ravenscroft's farcical *The Citizen Turn'd Gentleman* sometime in the spring or early summer. So woebegone was the King's Company that rumors of a union were bandied about. Shipman's epilogue for *Henry the Third* (May or June 1672) complains that the audience has deserted them, and hopes that people will "sometimes range / Fro'th' *other House*."[17] Dryden's epilogue for a revival of *Secret-Love*, delivered by Mrs Reeves "*in mans Cloathes*," observes

> Here we presume, our Legs are no ill sight,
> And they will give you no ill Dreams at night:
> In Dreames both Sexes, may their passions ease,
> You make us then as civill as you please.
> This would prevent the houses joyning too,
> At which we are as much displeas'd as you.[18]

The company avoided collapse, however, and survived two lean years at Lincoln's Inn Fields—during which time their rivals were busy exploiting the potentialities of Dorset Garden.

June 1673. By this time Thomas Killigrew had "pawned, not merely his building shares, but his patent and interest in the acting profits as well, in return for ready money."[19] This meant that Killigrew's interest in managing the theatre was greatly reduced. If it made no money his creditors would not be paid, but he was never much of one for paying creditors anyway.

March 1674. The opening of the new Drury Lane theatre ought to have restored the company to a fully competitive position. Though they felt obliged to apologize for a "Plain Built House,"[20] Drury Lane was in fact a fine theatre. It had cost only about £4000, as opposed to a reported £9000 for Dorset Garden. Nonetheless it proved in time the more satisfactory building for staging ordinary plays, and after the union, the United Company used Drury Lane except for productions which required special machinery.

January 1675. Thomas Killigrew complained to the Lord Chamberlain that he was being cheated by the actors. Noting that they have been charged with having "violently taken and shared Money against an Agreement betweene you and his [the Lord Chamberlain's] positive order to the Contrary," that official summoned the actors to a hearing and ordered them (in the meantime) to "continue Acting without any disturbance."[21] Evidently a walkout had been threatened. The resulting agreement (given in LC 5/141, p. 114) basically calls for all parties to abide by company rules; it afforded only a temporary peace.

December 1675. A new set of rules and regulations was agreed upon between Killigrew and the actors. The provisions summarized here suggest the shambles the company was now in. Actors are forbidden to "dispose of theire parts"; must perform what parts are assigned to them; and must attend rehearsals. Costumes and properties must not be taken out of the theatre for private use. No hireling may leave the company without three months' written notice. "To prevent the Disorders of the shareing Table by an Inundation of People," Henry Hayles is appointed to stand at the door and to admit people one by one.[22] This picture of company members mobbing their treasurer vividly suggests the level of misbehavior and disorganization to which the company had sunk.

February 1676. Attempts at enforcing discipline proved ineffectual, and in this month the company "left off actinge upon private differences and disagreements betweene themselves." Charles II, "very much displeased thereat," promptly ordered "the said Company forthwith to act and play as formerly."[23] The company ignored this order, and the Lord Chamberlain had to have the chief actors arrested and hauled before him to patch up yet another operating agreement.[24] The actors simply did not want to work for Thomas Killigrew.

April–May 1676. Recognizing their intractability, Killigrew offered to give his son Charles his entire right in the patent and the company (mortgaged though they were), if Charles could persuade the actors to cooperate and perform. Charles succeeded—basically by bribing Hart and Kynaston £100 and £60 respectively—and the actors signed a sharers' agreement on 1 May.[25] Thomas Killigrew promptly reneged on his promises to Charles, and great confusion ensued.

September 1676. Attempting to put the company in better order, the Lord Chamberlain silenced the house on 3 August, and then ordered that management be assumed by a committee consisting of Mohun, Kynaston, Hart, and Cartwright (9 September). This arrangement failed to work, and so the Lord Chamberlain tried appointing Hart sole manager at an unknown date during the fall.[26]

January–February 1677. Charles Killigrew took his father to court, and won. Of course what he won was (theoretical) authority over the company: any profits paid on his father's shares would go to his father's creditors. And whether the actors would accept his rule remained to be seen.

July 1677. Disliking Charles Killigrew's management, the actors petitioned for self-government and were granted it on the conditions that they continue to act and that they pay any monies due on the "Killigrew" shares.[27]

September 1677. Charles Killigrew attempted to regain control of the situation by rallying a majority of the "building sharers" and signing an agreement with the younger actors. This was, in essence, an attempt to freeze out the "sharing actors," and replace them with a company consisting of former hirelings.[28] Little is known about the offerings of the King's Company this fall, but evidently the reshuffle did not work, for senior actors played all the leading roles in the premiere of *All for Love* in December.

March 1678. Disgusted with the chaotic and unprofitable condition of the King's Company, Dryden defected to the Duke's Company, which mounted his *Mr. Limberham* this month. To make matters worse, he encouraged his young friend Nathaniel Lee to come with him, "to the great prejudice, and almost undoing of the Company, They being the onely Poets remaining to us,"[29] as the King's Company protested. Why the authorities allowed Dryden to defect, but not Lee (who managed to leave in 1679), remains a mystery.

April 1678. The Lord Chamberlain was compelled to forbid the actors to remove costumes and properties from the theatre, implying that they had been pawning or selling company property again. At about the same time some of the sharing actors charged Charles Killigrew with secretly mortgaging the stock, and sued to keep the "Stock of Clothes and Scenes belonging to the Royal Theatre" together until the interested parties could decide what to do with them.[30]

March 1679. Toward the end of a very lean season the King's Company ceased acting, and three of the younger actors went off to work for Thomas St. Serfe in Edinburgh. No definite King's Company performance is known for a year thereafter, though presumably the company did act intermittently.

July 1680. Charles Killigrew persuaded the wanderers to return in February 1680 and then reneged on his promise to pay their travel expenses, occasioning a lawsuit he finally lost four years later. In July we find yet another new sharers' agreement.[31]

February–May 1681. In February the company found itself unable to pay the £5 14s. daily rent due on the Drury Lane theatre. The hirelings and building sharers agreed to accept half of what was due them, but the company soon found it could not manage even that. During this spring receipts sank as low as £3 a performance—and on other occasions the company returned what little money was collected and refused to act. In short, the situation had become desperate.

March 1682. The company struggled to continue operating during the 1681–82 season, but torn by dissension, heavily in debt, and entirely lacking direction and discipline, it finally lurched to a halt. On 21 March, "there happened a difference between the Senior and Young men belonging to the King's play house which grew to such a height that they all drew their swords which occasioned the wounding of severall. But in the end the Seniors shut up the dores."[32]

In the company's last years bills went unpaid and authority for making managerial decisions became entirely unclear. When Robert Baden, a copperlace man, sued for £73/2/10 worth of trimmings sold to Cardell Goodman and others in October 1681, Charles Killigrew replied that he had not ordered the goods, and had given tradesmen notice that they were not to "Deliver out or Trust them [the actors]" with any goods but those Killigrew himself called for. Though the company was heavily in debt, the actors allegedly took what money they found in the till and "spent the same for dinners att Tavernes & otherwise."[33]

This catalogue of chaos, theft, and mismanagement only seems worse when we recall that in these years the King's Company actually mounted some splendid new plays—for example, *Aureng-Zebe, The Country-Wife, The Plain-Dealer, All for Love,* and *The Rival Queens.* As late as 1680 they staged Settle's successful *The Female Prelate,* and even in their last season they mounted some respectable new plays—Durfey's *Sir Barnaby Whigg,* Tate's *The Ingratitude of a Commonwealth,* and Southerne's *The Loyal Brother.* The problem was eternal disarray and incompetent management. In the course of just six seasons, I count *nine* major reorganizations.

The King's Company was never again genuinely competitive after the burning of the Bridges Street theatre in January 1672. Despite the successful design of Drury Lane, the company remained so short of operating funds that its productions could not match its rivals'. The Duke's Company was drawing audiences to expensive operas. When the King's Company tried to "answer" by mounting an opera, Pierre Perrin's *Ariane* (30 March 1674), they felt too straitened to give it the sort of lavish production it needed. Indeed, they borrowed the necessary scenery from the Court theatre—a loan authorized for only fourteen days.[34] This was scarcely the way to compete with a rival company able to mount the 1674 "operatic" *Tempest* a month later.

Another of the King's Company's problems late in the seventies was simply age. By 1679 Hart and Mohun were old and sick—and acting irregularly. Wintershall died that summer, and Nicholas Burt stopped acting entirely. Back in the mid-seventies the Duke's Company had replenished itself. Downes reports that "About this time the Company was very much Recruited," and names such stalwarts as Anthony Leigh, Gillow, Jevon, Percival, Williams, Bowman, Mrs Barry, Mrs Currer, and others.[35] The King's Company, in contrast, found itself crippled by the defection of three or four actors to Edinburgh. Indeed lawsuit testimony alleges (perhaps with some exaggeration) that "no plays . . . could well be shown or Represented . . . for want of the said Players."[36] Some hirelings were elevated in the company's last years, but the likes of Griffin, Goodman, and Martin Powell were unsatisfactory replacements for the senior men in the company. An even more startling decline is apparent in the women, but the culprit was not age. Contemplating the decayed state of the company in 1677, John Harold Wilson notes that "of the troupe which had played so admirably before the Theatre Royal fire in January, 1672, only three women were left"—Knepp, Boutell, and Corey.[37] Replacements were recruited, but most of them proved, as Wilson says, inept.

Before the fire, the King's Company was a potent organization. The production of Dryden's *The Conquest of Granada* in two parts in December 1670 and January 1671, with what Evelyn terms "very glorious scenes & perspectives" (painted by Robert Streeter), was the sort of thing on which their rivals were to make so much money. But as we have seen, even when the King's Company got into Drury Lane they lacked the machines and the money to mount competitive spectaculars. A long series of sour comments about "Scenes, Machines, and empty *Opera's*" (in Dryden's phrase) suggests how acutely the company felt itself at a disadvantage in this respect. The best it could do was try to capitalize parasitically on its rivals' successes by burlesquing them. Duffett's *The Empress of Morocco* (a travesty of Settle's popular play and the new Dorset Garden production of Davenant's *Macbeth*), *The Mock-Tempest*, and *Psyche Debauch'd*, are delightful and increasingly sophisticated spoofs. No doubt we would have had a *Circe Transform'd* in 1677 had Duffett not been in prison on a forgery charge. But entertaining though such hijinks can be, they are not the foundation on which to build a healthy repertory.

Given the political turmoil of the years 1678–82, the failure of one theatre company is not surprising. That the company very nearly folded after the fire in 1672 is likewise logical. That it should be in such a state of disarray in 1675 and on the verge of a complete halt in February 1676 is much harder to understand. The company had a good theatre in Drury Lane, some fine actors, and solid plays. The problem, obviously, was organizational and managerial. Conflict among proprietors and between proprietors and sharing actors proved utterly ruinous. The Duke's Company flourished because it left management in the hands of competent actors, an arrangement ultimately disrupted by Christopher Rich's secret acquisition of shares in the United Company. Under Rich the actors were to learn once again the lessons of the King's Company, and in this hard experience we see the basis for the actor-manager tradition which was to flourish in the eighteenth century.

III
The Organization and Operation of The United Company, 1682–1687

The Union of 1682 created a seemingly strong and stable theatre. Even to the Duke's Company, union seemed like a fine idea. Uniting the patents would eliminate all competition. From the King's Company's side the alternative to union was dissolution. Reconstructing Charles Killigrew's viewpoint, Betterton noted the company's debts, the refusal of some actors to perform, Killigrew's inability to "compose the said Differences," or to act without the dissidents, and concluded:

the said Complaynant [Killigrew] as this Defendant Beleives being in greate despondency of makeing any advantage Suitable to the charge of their future acting in the same Theatre and observing as this Defendant Beleives That by the Management and method of matters at the said Theatre called the Duke's Theatre the profitts ariseing out of and by the same had in a Reasonable measure answered the Expectations of the persons concerned therein Hee the said Complaynant applied himself not only to the said Charles Davenant but

likewise to William Smith Gent. . . . and to this Defendant . . . That both
the said Patents and the Powers and authorityes thereby granted might be
united.[38]

Killigrew was only trying to make the best of the inevitable. In the fall
of 1681 at the same time that Cardell Goodman was buying costume
trim in Killigrew's name, and Philip Griffin was eating out on company
money, Charles Hart and Edward Kynaston signed a secret bargain with
Betterton, Smith, and Charles Davenant, promising to subvert the King's
Company.[39] By this agreement of 14 October 1681 they promised 1) not
to act for or assist the King's Company; 2) "to make over" to Betterton,
Smith, and Davenant "all the Right, Title, and Claim" they have "to any
Plays, Books, Cloaths, and Scenes in the King's Play-house"; 3) to assign
their income from the King's Company (if any) to Betterton, Smith, and
Davenant; 4) to promote a union; 5) to sue Killigrew at their own expense in pursuance of this agreement, should that prove necessary. In
return, each man was to receive a salary of 5s. per acting day. Hart
evidently had no further plans to perform, but Kynaston, twenty years
younger, was promised a 10s. daily salary if he could get permission to
act with the Duke's Company. Obviously the rival managers were willing
to add to King's Company troubles if they could.

On 4 May 1682 Charles Killigrew signed the Articles of Union, and
the King's Company ceased to exist. His action was of dubious legality
(and Killigrew had to meet several court challenges in the next few
years), since he had not obtained the agreement of either the sharing
actors or the Drury Lane building sharers—but agreeing to a union was
probably the only way left to Killigrew to get any value out of his patent.
When his actors could not even agree to act, how could they be expected
to agree to sell out? By asserting his power as heir to the patent, Killigrew circumvented all kinds of difficulties, and managed to make quite
a good bargain for himself and even for the Drury Lane building sharers.

The Articles of Union are apparently lost, but their terms are known
in some detail from documents copied after 1700 in connection with a
lawsuit about Charles Killigrew's rights to shares, and from a Chancery
deposition in another case.[40] Both parties stood to gain. Charles Killigrew,
by scuttling the King's Company, cut himself in for a healthy 15 percent
of the United Company's profits. He became nominal cohead of the company, sharing the position with Charles Davenant—the wording of the

original patents essentially dictated such an arrangement. Day-to-day management continued in the capable hands of Betterton and Smith, who retained their 20s. per week management salaries. The exact share arrangement became a matter of legal dispute. The company started by treating the "three shares" allotted to Charles Killigrew as an addition to the twenty shares previously held (making twenty-three in all), and paid him 3/23 of the profits accordingly. He went to court and successfully maintained his right to 3/20.[41] One and a half of his shares represented compensation for his assuming the debts of the King's Company (said to be £500) when he dissolved the company. This was generous compensation, since a United Company share was worth about £600 in the mid-1680s. The other share and a half was said to be compensation for his patent rights, now indissolubly joined to the Duke's Company patent. In the terms recorded in Add. MS 20,726, the two "should be joyned and united" and "should be as one and soe for ever continued." Whether they could indeed be split apart again to legitimize two separate companies was an issue which was to exercise lawyers for more than a century.

At all events, Charles Killigrew had assured himself of a better income than the King's Company had produced in at least a decade. Provision was made for books of accounts to be kept wherein all receipts would be entered and all "chardges and expenses" would be noted. The possibility of disagreement between the two patentees was foreseen and provided for in a special clause.

All matters and things then after to be acted and done persuant to the Letters pattent should be acted and done by the joynt consent of the said Charles Killigrew and Charles Davenant . . . (except onely as in such cases as are therein excepted). . . . And that in case they the said Mr Killigrew and Mr Davenant should differr in any matter or thing to be done born or suffered concerning the premisses that then the same should be determined by 3 persons players that then should have the greatest share in the profitt of acting and should have binn longest Actors or the Major part of them. (Add. MS 20,726)

The provision for joint decisions was to be the basis for a special interpretation which will concern us in chapter 6.

Two clauses with some bearing on future management problems may be noted at this juncture. Both reflect concerns originating with the Duke's Company. First, the legal position of Betterton and Smith is somewhat ambiguous. Neither could be construed as a hereditary patentee, and yet they were the people who actually operated the theatre. Charles Davenant made them party to the Articles of Union as persons having "had some power or right to the same [the letters patent] from or under the said Sir William Davenant then lately deceased or by the said Charles Davenant." Their importance as managers could hardly have received stronger endorsement. Second, the rent agreed upon for Drury Lane—£3 per acting day—was contingent upon uninterrupted enjoyment of the monopoly by the United Company. If "the said Agreement should be interrupted by any person or persons in the quiett or enjoyeing of the same then the said rent of 3*l* per diem should be suspended untill any such interruption should be removed." This gave Charles Killigrew strong motivation to suppress any attempt to act by the disaffected remnant of the King's Company. One peep from them, and he would be out of pocket.

The Drury Lane building sharers are not specifically mentioned in the Articles of Union, but in June 1683 a majority of them signed an agreement which gave Charles Davenant a nineteen-year lease for a house rent of only £3 per acting day retroactive to November 1682—the sum negotiated by Charles Killigrew. Davenant agreed that the company would pay the ground rent.[42] We must note that Killigrew protected himself, and the interests of his fellow investors, by insisting that the Drury Lane rent (though reduced from £5 14*s*.) be paid every acting day, even if the performance occurred at Dorset Garden. This meant that the company's theatre rent was £10 every day they acted, a stiff overhead. Nonetheless, the company managers were thereby given a useful choice of theatres. And they also prevented any discontented building shareholder at Drury Lane from agitating for a second company by paying rent whether they used the theatre or not. Ironically, this arrangement was to give Christopher Rich a stranglehold on London theatre buildings which the Lincoln's Inn Fields Company was unable to break, even after the Drury Lane lease ran out in 1701.

By the union the Duke's Company gained the use of Drury Lane and freedom from competition. It also acquired the rights to King's Company plays. The Articles of Union apparently included an attached list of old plays reserved for the King's Company, plus plays written for them since 1660, all now available to the United Company. Since the play list was not in dispute, it was not copied in our sources of information about the articles. Downes tells us that soon after the union, "The mixt Company then Reviv'd the several old and Modern Plays, that were the Propriety of Mr. *Killigrew* as, *Rule a Wife*, . . . *The Scornful Lady. The Plain Dealer. The Mock Astrologer The Jovial Crew. The Beggars Bush. Bartholomew-Fair. The Moor of* Venice. *Rollo. The Humorous Lieutenant. The Double Marriage.* With divers others."[43] All but one of these are old plays, and performance records are very scanty in the eighties, but we do know that over the next five years the company revived such King's Company originals as *The Destruction of Jerusalem, The Rival Queens, The Committee, The Chances, An Evening's Love, Secret-Love,* and *The Rehearsal.* Thus the United Company also benefited from the post-1660 repertory which had belonged to the King's Company.

An obvious problem created by the union was the surplus of actors it gave the United Company. A few, like Coysh and Disney, left London, and some women were squeezed out, but accommodation was made for as many performers as possible, perhaps as a means of ensuring acquiescence. House servants were probably less lucky. What became of the King's Company's prompter, Charles Booth, for example? We have no idea. Only one new recruit, James Carlisle, seems to have joined the company for the 1682–83 season, so full was the roster. The company run by Betterton and Harris jumped from twenty-seven known performers to forty-two in this season, twenty-four from the Duke's Company and eighteen from the King's. Attrition was rapid, however. At the end of five years the company was back to approximately fifteen men and eight women. The older players died or retired; some of the younger ones went off to Ireland. Hart received a generous pension of £2 per week, but died in August 1683. One sign of the inevitable friction in the integration of the companies is Mohun's petition to the King in the fall of 1682. Mohun protests that his share in scenes, clothes, and plays has been rented to Charles Davenant by Charles Killigrew for his own benefit, and Mohun has been told that he can sue Killigrew for some share in the rent. Worse, he is offered 20*s.* per day "when they have occasion to use him," which Mohun fears will be seldom, "they haveing not studyed Our Playes."[44] The King ordered that Mohun be given "the same Conditions as Mr Hart."

Such problems of readjustment aside, the United Company found itself in a very comfortable position. House charges after the union seem to have risen to about £30,[45] but from the "Legard report" we know that between 1682 and 1692 the company averaged about £50 per day and declared an actual profit (overall) of £9 6s. daily.[46] Thus on the basis of two hundred acting days (a slightly low approximation), a single share (of twenty) would have been worth about £90 per annum. Even though the shares were diluted a little by the assignment of 3/20 to Charles Killigrew, this is a very respectable return. We must also remember that these figures include heavy losses sustained on *Albion and Albanius* at the time of Monmouth's invasion in 1685; a bad year in 1688–89 during the Revolution; and what all parties agree were unprofitable operations in 1691 and 1692. With the exception of 1684–85 (already a bad year because of the suspension of acting after King Charles's death), the United Company must have been a highly profitable operation in the five years Betterton and Smith managed it.

The lack of competition brought about by the union was naturally seen as an advantage by managers and proprietors. Safe enjoyment of a monopoly was what they sought and got. An immediate result, however, was stasis in English drama. In the mid-seventies the Duke's Company had often mounted a dozen new plays each season, and together with the King's Company usually put on a total of eighteen to twenty-four new shows. In the five years after 1682 the United Company never mounted more than three or four new plays in any season. Why risk time and money? For variety the managers had a huge stock of proven King's Company plays. Looking back on the eighties, George Powell commented: "The time was, upon the uniting of the two *Theatres*, that the reviveing of the old stock of Plays, so ingrost the study of the House, that the Poets lay dorment; and a new Play cou'd hardly get admittance, amongst the more precious pieces of Antiquity, that then waited to walk the Stage."[47] After the Glorious Revolution, a few more new plays were tried, but too few writers were developed. The old stalwarts— Dryden, Shadwell, Behn, Lee, Otway—died or fell silent, and they were not re-placed. The best plays of the nineties are by nonprofessionals like South-erne and Congreve. The United Company managers had no reason to worry about developing new writers—but the direct consequence of their conservative repertory policy was a dearth of young professional dramatists when suddenly in 1695 there was an urgent need for new plays.

In the spring of 1687 the company must have felt secure indeed. It was expertly run and highly profitable. Attrition had disposed of the surplus personnel acquired with the union. Squabbles over share division had been settled without disruption. When on 30 August Betterton witnessed a deed of sale by which Alexander Davenant bought out his brother Charles, he could scarcely have imagined that the sale would matter. Members of the Davenant family had been juggling their shares for nearly thirty years. What no one knew, however, was that Alexander Davenant had secretly borrowed five-sixths of the purchase price from outsiders, and that when he defaulted on his obligations, those outsiders would assume control of the company.

IV
BETTERTON AND THE DORSET GARDEN SPECTACULAR

Throughout all the years he was officially manager, and indeed beyond that period, Betterton was the particular champion of "English opera." As we have seen, he inherited this predilection from his master Davenant, but under his direction the English theatre went on to unprecedented heights of costly spectacle. Indeed, so closely was Betterton associated with the staging of operatic spectacles that the penurious Christopher Rich was willing to pay him a special bonus of £50 to "gett up" the 1695 operatic version of *The Indian Queen*—a subject discussed in chapter 3. To understand Betterton's outlook, we need to comprehend the special appeal that Dorset Garden held for him.

We know very little about the building of Dorset Garden theatre. By 1669, if not earlier, the Duke's Company began to think of larger and better-equipped quarters. Who had the idea, who pushed it along, and the details of financing are mostly lost to us.[48] Betterton is said to have gone to France to study the latest developments in stage machines, but we do not even know who designed the new building for the company.[49] At all events, the resulting theatre, despite a 200 percent cost overrun, did the company proud. When Dorset Garden opened on 9 November 1671, even without new productions, Charles II was sufficiently pleased that he contributed £1000 toward the £9000 cost.[50] The theatre had some teething problems. A rumor apparently went out during the first month that the building was unsound,[51] and a temporary return to Lincoln's Inn Fields in the summer of 1673 suggests that the machinery was not fully rigged until then. As of March 1674, however, the Duke's Company had the facilities to produce "operatic" spectacle on a scale far beyond anything the English public had ever seen.

Most of the titles of the once-celebrated machine plays they mounted mean nothing to the twentieth-century reader, and the only illustrated edition of any of them, Settle's lurid *The Empress of Morocco* (1673), conveys little sense of the theatrical experience. What then was all the excitement about? What kinds of plays benefited from the new theatre, and what kind of writing did it generate? As I have noted, Drury Lane ultimately proved the better house for ordinary plays. Most comedies made little use of the theatre's technical capacity—the principal exceptions came in the machine farces of the 1680s, culminating in Mountfort's *Faustus* travesty.[52] Serious drama, whether of the "heroic," "horror," or "high tragedy" type,[53] often included a scene or two which showed off the perspective stage or used some of the simpler machines. The brief appearance of the Trojan Horse in *The Destruction of Troy* (1678) or the scene in *The Destruction of Jerusalem* (1677) of "the Temple burning, filled with Jews lamenting" are obvious visual high points of those plays. The omen scene in *The Rival Queens* (1677) is striking but of limited duration and relatively straightforward to stage: "The Scene draws, and discovers a Battel of Crows, or Ravens, in the Air; an Eagle and a Dragon meet and fight; the Eagle drops down with all the rest of the Birds, and the Dragon flies away. Souldiers walk off, shaking their Heads" (act 2, scene 1). In fact the two latter examples are Drury Lane productions: nothing made Dorset Garden a markedly preferable house in which to stage spectacle on this limited scale.

The "English opera" and its precursors are the plays for which Dorset Garden was built. The principal productions are as follows:[54]

1672–73   *Macbeth* (The Davenant version, with new costumes, scenery, machines, and flyings, plus songs by Matthew Locke, and fancy dancing arranged by Channell and Priest.)
             The Empress of Morocco (Settle).
1673–74   *The Tempest* (Dryden-Davenant version, "made into an Opera by Mr. *Shadwell*.")
1674–75   *Psyche* (Shadwell).
1676–77   *Circe* (Charles Davenant).
[1678–84:   no new operas during the period of political upheaval.]
1684–85   *Albion and Albanius* (Dryden).

1689–90   *The Prophetess* (Betterton adaptation).
1690–91   *King Arthur* (Dryden).
1691–92   *The Fairy-Queen* (Settle).

Staging these shows was different from mounting ordinary serious drama, though the distinction is more one of degree than kind. The difference lies in the amount of stage time devoted to special effects, and in the scale of the production. The Dorset Garden spectacular is really defined by the number of sets required and their elaborateness; the number of people called for, both performers and support personnel; the amount of money invested; and the length of time needed to prepare such a show.

A lot of stage time in the "operatic" works is spent on religious cere-monies, folk festivals, initiations, processions, and entertainments for royalty—often involving a masque within the play. Comparison of the original scripts with the musical adaptations makes this move into pure display very plain. Thus where Betterton cut the "Fletcher" *Prophetess*, he added scenic effects which are—given Dorset Garden to play with—logical extensions of the descriptive passages they replace. While an elaborate tragedy might feature one or two such effects, these plays are stuffed with them, and music becomes pervasive instead of incidental, even though speaking and singing parts are basically kept separate.

The difference in scale of production is hard to convey, though for people with any practical experience in theatre, a valid comparison would be the complexities of mounting a musical as opposed to a "straight" play. To put on *My Fair Lady* or *Man of la Mancha* is an immensely more complex business than to do *Arms and the Man* or *The Mousetrap*. Lacking any set designs except those for *The Empress of Morocco*, we can only say that most of the descriptions for later shows imply new effects, not reuse of stock pieces, as was routine for straight drama. When a script wanders off into fantasy or allegory, as most of these do, the settings bear little relation to the standard palaces and battlefields of the serious drama, a difference which was part of their appeal. Most opera sets were strictly opera sets, not usable on an everyday basis. Only in a dream—or in an opera—would Vulcan's smiths, dressed in satin, forge silver vases in a palace courtyard bordered by Corinthian columns festooned with gar-lands and topped by cupids (*Psyche*, act 3).

Very briefly, I want to indicate some of the kinds of effects used in Dorset Garden spectaculars. Transformations fascinated audiences throughout the period. The appeal of Davenant's *The Siege of Rhodes* at Lincoln's Inn Fields in 1661 lay in a very rudimentary demonstration of this technique. Writers enjoyed exploiting the contrast between (for example) Cupid's early baroque Garden and Palace and the Desert into which it is suddenly transformed when Psyche asks the forbidden question (*Psyche*, act 4). Transformations are also effective on a smaller scale. The witches, gods, and magicians who inhabit these plays frequently bring statues to life: the Prophetess changes statues into dancing butterflies; in *The Fairy-Queen* swans glide into view, then turn into fairy dancers. Altogether more difficult effects were achieved with elaborate trap and flying systems. The sacrifice offered in act 3 of *Psyche* is rejected by Mars and Venus from separate, airborne chariots, and the altar is immediately attacked and destroyed by Furies which "descend and strike [it]; . . . and every one flies away with a fire-brand in's hand." At a conservative estimate, we can suggest that Dorset Garden was equipped to fly at least four people simultaneously, and some of their machines could be guided to meet in midair. Earlier in that same play, "Two Zephiri descend and take *Psyche* by each arm, and fly into the Clouds with her." Perhaps this was done in the perspective stage with a double replacing Psyche, or even with children; but the stage direction implies great confidence in the rigging of the theatre. The more elaborate machines could move both down and forward, in one play carrying twelve people (*The Emperor of the Moon* zodiac). By the time of *The Fairy-Queen* attempts were being made to manipulate the dimension over which seventeenth-century designers had least control—lighting. "A Sonata plays while the Sun rises, it appears red through the Mist, as it ascends it dissipates the Vapours, and is seen in its full Lustre; then the Scene is perfectly discovered, the Fountains enrich'd with gilding, and adorn'd with Statues" (act 4). The final sequence of the opera begins the same way. In comparison to what was being done with lighting on the Continent, this is scarcely revolutionary—but in terms of English practice it represents a step forward.

Quoting four stage directions from *Albion and Albanius* may serve to suggest just how complex and exciting a visual display Dorset Garden spectaculars aimed at producing.

The Clouds divide, and *Juno* appears in a Machine drawn by Peacocks; while a Symphony is playing, it moves gently forward, and as it descends, it opens and discovers the Tail of the Peacock, which is so Large, that it almost fills the opening of the Stage between Scene and Scene. (Act 1)

Iris appears on a very large Machine. This was really seen the *18th* of *March 1684.* by Capt. *Christopher Gunman*, on Board his R. H. Yacht, then in *Calais Pierre*: He drew it as it then appear'd, and gave a draught of it to us. We have only added the Cloud where the Person of *Iris* sits. (Act 1)[55]

The Cave of *Proteus* rises out of the Sea, it consists of several Arches of Rock work, adorn'd with mother of Pearl, Coral, and abundance of Shells of various kinds: Thro' the Arches is seen the Sea, and parts of *Dover Peer*: In the middle of the Cave is *Proteus* asleep on a Rock adorn'd with Shells, &c. like the Cave. *Albion* and *Acacia* seize on him, and while a Symphony is playing, he sinks as they are bringing him forward, and changes himself into a Lyon, a Crocodile, a Dragon, and then to his own shape again. (Act 3)

Whilst a Simphony is playing; a very large, and a very glorious Machine descends: The figure of it Oval, all the Clouds shining with Gold, abundance of Angels and Cherubins flying about 'em, and playing in 'em; in the midst of it sits *Apollo* on a Throne of Gold: he comes from the Machine to *Albion*. (Act 3)

And these are only four of the fourteen such highlights in this one opera.

These productions stretched the company's resources to the utmost. If we look at relative cast size, act 2 of *The Tempest* calls for twelve winds; act 4 of *Psyche* specifies ten dancers for one of the many interludes; *The Prophetess* has at least sixteen small parts which cannot be further reduced by doubling. Twenty-four dancers appear in the finale of *The Fairy-Queen.* We have some idea how expensive scenery could be from the King's Company's problems with theirs for *Tyrannick Love.* According to Downes, the scenery alone for *Psyche* cost more than £800,[56] though the show nonetheless "prov'd very Beneficial to the Company." The old prompter remembered these operas largely in terms of whether or not they had made money. Discussing the 1674 *Tempest*, he observes that "not any succeeding Opera got more Money"—a comment which is painfully to the point. *Circe* "answer'd the Expectation of the Company," but *Albion and Albanius*, delayed by the death of Charles II and finally produced just when Monmouth invaded the country, "was perform'd but Six times, which not Answering half THE Charge they were at, Involv'd the Company very much in Debt" (p. 40). Speaking of a rehearsal, 1 January 1685, Edward Bedingfield reported that immensely raised prices were in prospect: "they have set the boxes at a guyny a place, and the Pitt at halfe. They advance 4,000*l.* on the opera, and therefore must tax high to reimburse themselves."[57] This was almost quadruple prices. Since the company's annual gross receipts were only about £10,000, this sum represents an absolutely staggering investment in a single production. The next fancy Dorset Garden show, *The Emperor of the Moon*, reused extant machines for the most part and did not impress itself on Downes's memory, though it seems to have been profitable.[58] The last three operas all broke even, but *The Fairy-Queen* seems barely to have managed to do so—"the Expences in setting it out being so great, the Company got very little by it," says Downes (p. 43). Narcissus Luttrell reported that its "clothes, scenes, and musick cost 3000*l*."[59]

Preparation time for these productions is hard to determine. *Psyche* seems to have been in the works for as long as sixteen months. From the original schedule for *Albion and Albanius*, we may guess that at least four to six months of planning, contracting, building, and rehearsing probably went into most of these pieces. In comparison, a new play got between four and six *weeks* of planning and rehearsal time (sometimes less), and simply reused stock scenery and costumes unless management decided to dress up a promising show, or oblige a friend.

We tend to think of the Restoration theatre in terms of the demands of *The Country-Wife* or *The Man of Mode*. Even *The Conquest of Granada* (theatrically a pretty simple play) is known more for its verbal grandeur than as a kind of wide-screen technicolor spectacular. But to the Restoration theatregoer, the big scene and machine shows were the height of theatrical splendor. Visiting ambassadors came and gaped—for more than thirty years newsletters faithfully report such theatre attendance. The company would not have put such disproportionate sums into opera productions if it did not feel that the publicity and interest warranted the investment. Betterton obviously adored shows like these. He had reached his highest flights in *The Fairy-Queen*: how paralyzing, then, for him to have to return to Lincoln's Inn Fields at a time when his theatrical imagination was still so active. And he had become accustomed to a budget of the sort enjoyed by Cecil B. DeMille. When he moved back to Lincoln's Inn Fields, Betterton lost the ability to operate as Davenant had taught him to. As an actor, Betterton needed no fancy theatre; as a manager-producer, he must have felt lost without one.

Part 2

THE
LINCOLN'S INN FIELDS
EXPERIMENT

Chapter 3

The Actors' Rebellion
of 1694–1695

THERE is no mystery about the cause of the actors' rebellion which led to the re-establishment of a second company. Christopher Rich's tyrannical ways and pinchpenny management have been made notorious by Cibber. But the details of the clash are worth investigating: the reasons for the actors' revolt, the power struggle which followed, and the intense ill will thus generated—all affected the nature of the resulting companies and their subsequent operation. Two documents provide most of our information about the rebellion: the Petition of the Players and the Reply of the Patentees. Since neither has been printed in full before, they are included as Appendixes A and B for easy reference. A discussion of the charges and countercharges in these two documents provides a vivid picture of the split that occurred in the winter of 1694–95—a split which produced competing companies with very different advantages and disadvantages in terms of their initial personnel, theatre buildings, equipment, and financial resources. Both groups, however, were faced with a basic and knotty problem: determining the tastes of an audience whose composition was rapidly changing. Consequently I have ended this preparatory survey with a brief discussion of the struggle to identify and please a "new" audience.

I

THE HISTORY
OF THE REBELLION

After the collapse of the King's Company in 1682 the United Company enjoyed several years of good profits, despite the unsettled times and the *Albion and Albanius* fiasco. To understand the breakaway of 1695 we must look behind the apparent success: the rebellion has its roots in company mismanagement. Indeed, the nature of the actors' grievances was to determine the way they were to organize and structure their own cooperative company. The problems began in 1687 when Alexander Davenant bought out his brother Charles with money which turned out not to be his own. Alexander reorganized the managerial structure of what had been a stable company, and his maneuvers brought them to the verge of major trouble at least twice before he decamped to the Canary Islands in 1693. The active intervention of Alexander's main creditors following his departure led to the confrontation which is the main subject of this chapter.

For convenient reference, I have included a tabular "time line" summarizing the events discussed below. This chronicle is drawn from materials in *The London Stage*, Langhans's "New Restoration Theatre Accounts," Hotson, Nicoll, and certain unpublished portions of LC 7/1 and 7/3.

Events Leading to the Rebellion of 1695

1687

30 August	Alexander Davenant buys his brother Charles's shares in the United Company with money borrowed from Skipwith.
12 September	Alexander contracts to "farm" shares for Skipwith.
ca. 24 October	The United Company resumes acting for the season.
29–30 October	Alexander "deposes" the Betterton-Smith management and installs his brother Thomas as manager. Betterton is given a quarter and one-half a quarter share on "private consideration."

1688

12 January	Smith's name is written but canceled in the Lord Chamberlain's Register of Players.
17 November	Smith makes his will, preparing to go to war for King James.

1689

January–February	Henry Killigrew et al. try to set up a rival company.
13 February	William and Mary ascend the throne. Betterton is working on salary.
11 March	Lord Chamberlain Dorset grants Mrs Corey's petition to be received back into the company "like the rest of the rebels."

1690

18 March	Alexander sells the one share he still owns to Rich.

1691

September	Betterton works for one share instead of a salary.
7 December	By court order Sir Robert Legard begins to investigate the finances of the company as a result of Charles Killigrew's suit for a three-twentieths share.

1692

February	The United Company has an £800 debt and is continuing to operate unprofitably.
17 March	Charles Killigrew attempts to have Alexander Davenant enjoined from taking the aftermoney.
13 May	The court hears the aftermoney case and decides for Davenant, ordering that profits be held in a separate account to defray company debts; both sides appeal this decision.
[n.d.]	Betterton loses his lifesavings, invested with Sir Francis Watson.
3 August	The accounts covered by the Legard report end on this day.
26 September	Betterton, Mountfort, Leigh, and others draw up a statement of the rights of sharing actors, a document apparently not extant.
December	The company is weakened by the deaths of Mountfort and Leigh.

1693

16 January	Betterton goes on salary again at his own request.
27 July	The Legard report is made public.
23 October	Alexander Davenant flees to the Canary Islands; Skipwith and Killigrew publicly ask Betterton to resume management (date uncertain).
ca. November	Doggett, Bowen, et al. mutiny; Betterton helps persuade and coerce them into coming back.
December	Rich takes over the financial aspects of management.

1694

January	Rich stops paying the fruit concession compensation.
by late November or early December	The Petition of the Players is submitted to Lord Chamberlain Dorset.
7 December	The 17 December meeting is scheduled.
10 December	The Reply of the Patentees is delivered.
12 December	The patentees get a government decree that no one receive a license to act or to build a playhouse without notice being given to Skipwith, Rich, and Charles Killigrew.
17 December	The hearing at Sir Robert Howard's chambers with Dorset resolves nothing.
22 December	Acting is suspended on account of Queen Mary's illness; this marks the termination of Betterton's employment with the Patent Company.
28 December	Queen Mary dies; the theatres remain dark until Easter Monday 1695.

1695

11 February	The patentees make an independent attempt at reconciliation; the rebels refuse it.
19 March	The Lord Chamberlain attempts a reconciliation without success.
in March	The rebels reconvert Lincoln's Inn Fields to a theatre.
25 March	A license is granted to the Lincoln's Inn Fields Company.
30 March	The mourning suspension of acting is lifted.
1 April	The Patent Company reopens with *Abdelazer*.
16 April	The Lord Chamberlain reasserts the old prohibition

against changing companies after Doggett and Verbruggen have done so.

29 or 30 April   Lincoln's Inn Fields opens with *Love for Love*.

In 1687 Alexander Davenant bought up his brother Charles's shares in
the United Company.[1] Alexander had served as treasurer of the Duke's
Company from 1674 or 1675 to 1683, so he had intimate knowledge of
the finances and profitability of a well-run theatre company. However,
his subsequent actions indicate that he bought purely on speculation,
with no interest in the artistic tradition or future of the company. Though
Betterton witnessed the sale between brothers, neither he nor Charles had
any hint from the legal papers that the purchase money was not Alexander's own. In fact, most of the money came from Sir Thomas Skipwith,
to whom the shares really belonged. Skipwith then secretly "farmed" the
shares to Alexander, who was entitled to the profits due on them in
return for a weekly rent he paid to Skipwith.

Alexander immediately began rearranging the management. A record
of the United Company's payments to its managers between 1682 and
1692 has been preserved, evidently as a result of the court suit begun by
Charles Killigrew over his share of the profits.[2] Betterton and Smith received their customary salaries through 29 October 1687; then beginning 5 November 1687 Thomas Davenant was paid £2 10s. a week for
managing. Hotson did not know these accounts, but apparently on the
basis of objections by several people to Thomas Davenant's management,
he concluded that Alexander had "deposed" Betterton and Smith and
put his younger brother in their place.[3] This idea has never been chal-
lenged, and in some ways it seems to make sense: Betterton, "deposed,"
sprang at the chance to regain authority in "his own" company in 1695.
But this is not the case, and I will try to show that while he gave up his
title in 1687, he did not lose his authority.

The facts are these. Indubitably Thomas Davenant began collecting a
high salary for managing in 1687, but this is not to say that he proceeded to "manage" as Betterton and Smith had managed. We could
expect a good deal of protest had he tried. At that time Alexander nominally owned four of twenty shares. The company was making good
money. Would either the outside investors or the actor-sharers have accepted the replacement of the revered and successful Betterton by a rank

and untried amateur without protest, or at least gossip? Contemporaries knowledgeable about such matters are strangely silent. They are vocal enough about tensions after 1691, but say nothing about problems in 1687. The reason seems to be that there was no deposition but rather a minor reorganization for which Betterton was well compensated and which cost him no real power.

Studying the various relevant documents, we can see indications that Alexander Davenant made Betterton a good offer—at the expense of the sharers' total profits, though not in ways that would damage the company's theatrical operations. Betterton was fifty-two years old in 1687. He was undisputed master of his profession and had been comanager for nearly twenty years. If Alexander had offered (1) to transfer some administrative duties to Thomas Davenant, while retaining Betterton as senior consultant and policy maker; (2) to compensate him for the salary loss with an additional portion of shares and a yearly "present"; and (3) to adjust matters with comanager William Smith—why should Betterton not willingly have agreed? The patentees charge that something of just this sort did indeed happen.

And as to ye Indirect means begun by Alexander Davenant tis well known Mr Alexander Davenant did nothing of Moment in ye Manageing of ye Theatres without Mr Betterton but from 1687 till Mr Davenant went off in 1693 all things were done as Mr Betterton would have it. . . . [Betterton had] one share & half a quarter & this half quarter was in parte of satisfaction for his care in ye Management. And Mr Smith had ye like when he was an Actor & Joint manager with Mr Betterton but when Mr Smith went out of ye house And Mr Thomas Davenant in 1687 came into ye Management & had 3*ll* 10*s* for his trouble then Mr Betterton had a quarter & half a quarter of a share Added to him by Alexander Davenant for what private Consideration is unknown to us.[4]

Alexander's offer of additional shares to Betterton need not have been underhanded. Charles Killigrew is the complainant who says he was not consulted about these and other changes. He was unhappy principally because the basis on which his profit was calculated had been reduced by Alexander's order.[5] But Killigrew did not take the matter to court until three years after the managerial change had been made (though he was certainly aware of it), not caring much about management as long as he got the money he expected. The significant sequence of events is hidden

in the second part of the quotation above. Alexander seems to have settled with the departing Smith for £100; promoted Betterton to senior
consultant, while transferring Smith's interest to him; and given his
younger brother the title and salary of the "managers." Smith's name was
written in the 12 January "1687/8" list of their Majesties' Comedians
but later canceled; and in his will of 17 November 1688 Smith declares
that he has drawn up the document because he is "going into the King's
Army" at his own expense.[6] At the time he wrote this will he was feeling
quite sentimental and positive toward his fellow actors. He provided that
Alexander and Thomas Davenant were to receive mourning rings, should
he die in service, and that Betterton, his oldest and best friend, was to be
guardian for his son. Thus the parting seems to have been amiable.
Smith is listed in two manuscript casts placed after 1687 by the editors
of *The London Stage*, but we have no other indication that he returned to
the stage. When he testified in reply to Charles Killigrew's share suit in
1691, he said flatly that he left both acting and managing in 1687.

The players charged in their 1694 petition that Christopher Rich had
refused to give them the £100 settlement customary for retiring shareholders, citing Smith as an example of a shareholder who collected the
money (article 2). Rich replied that "wee have been told that ye £100
given to Mr William Smith was upon an other consideration well known
to Mr Betterton," not the retirement settlement in question. The situation is obscure: Smith may well have been planning to retire before
Alexander moved in. His obituary says that he had come into money
which allowed him to retire comfortably, but the source is not identified,
and £100 does not seem large enough to fit that description.[7]

Whatever the details of the deal made with Smith, Alexander Davenant proceeded, irresponsibly, to give his brother both Betterton's and
Smith's salaries. Thomas was twenty-three years old, and so far as we
know he had no theatrical experience. Hotson asserts, without citing
specific evidence, that "young Thomas Davenant was counselled by Betterton in his handling of affairs, though Betterton received no compensation for this service."[8] I have found no clear source for this statement,
and am inclined to think it represents Hotson's interpretation of a period
during which Betterton and young Davenant shared managerial duties.
Thomas Davenant ran errands like taking the list of their Majesties' Comedians to the Lord Chamberlain 23 August 1689; hearing complaints
about "the management of the moneys" with Killigrew in 1691; and

collecting for royal playgoing.[9] The patentees refer to him as "deputy manager" in article 2 of their reply to the Petition of the Players.

Exactly what other responsibilities Thomas Davenant may have had is impossible to say. His cavalier treatment of a play by Shadwell's protégé Nicholas Brady in January 1692 led Shadwell to protest to his old friend the Earl of Dorset, now Lord Chamberlain, and *The Rape, or the Innocent Imposters* was promptly staged in February with a strong cast, including both Bettertons. Southerne remembered that the new manager had given Congreve "the privilege of the house" (a writer's free admission) half a year before *The Old Batchelour* received its premiere, which would have been about October 1692.[10] The only definite trace of Thomas Davenant as manager I have found after that is his name on a bill for royal playgoing through January 1694.[11] In the restructuring of the company after his brother Alexander fled (ca. October 1693), Thomas would almost certainly have been demoted. Article 8 of the Petition of the Players dates Betterton's return to official status as manager from "When Mr. Thomas Davenent left the management of the playhouse."

According to the patentees, throughout Alexander Davenant's nominal ownership of the company "all things were done as Mr Betterton would have it," and they say particularly that "he gave out which Plays he would during that time" (article 6). Betterton's day-to-day choice of what play to present clearly had an important effect on the company's success—a detrimental one, if we believe the patentees. During James II's uneasy reign new operas were out of the question, especially after the *Albion and Albanius* fiasco. But as soon as London had quieted down after the Glorious Revolution, Betterton's hand can clearly be seen guiding the company's endeavors. *The Prophetess*, *King Arthur*, and *The Fairy-Queen* blossom out from one another in ever-increasing complexity from 1690 to 1692. The first was Betterton's own adaptation; Dryden thanks Betterton for his work on the second; and the third is so complex and experimental that no one in London except Betterton would have been competent to stage it.[12] Even if Thomas Davenant were nominally "manager" at this time, Betterton obviously had considerable authority to dispose of company funds: *The Fairy-Queen* is said to have cost £3000. Without the approval of the management, he could not possibly have risked the kind of investment opera required, much less have done it for three seasons in a row.

The idea that Betterton was "deposed" from management has been too readily accepted. The authors of the *Biographical Dictionary*, for example, say that after the loss of his savings in 1692, "Betterton had good reason to consider afresh . . . his future. . . . He had been divested of his managerial position, . . . [and] he no longer had control over the company's destiny nor a secure financial situation for himself."[13] In fact, Betterton had as much control and as much security as were available to anyone in the United Company until Rich began to assert himself. Scholars have assumed too readily that Rich began interfering in company policy in 1690, when he bought Alexander Davenant's one remaining share. But Rich himself testified that he stepped in only after Alexander fled,[14] and article 1 of the Petition of the Players confirms the fact: one of the shocking things about Rich's take-over was that the actors had been unaware that outsiders owned deeds to Alexander's shares and the hereditary patents.

In light of this reassessment, we can see the conditions which led to the rebellion of 1694–95 much more clearly. The 1693–94 season was evidently spent in a power struggle between Rich and Betterton, which Betterton lost. In the fall of 1694 came the final insult. Cibber tells us that Rich attempted to replace some of the senior actors: the patentees, "under Pretence of bringing younger Actors forward, order'd several of *Betterton's* and Mrs. *Barry's* chief Parts to be given to young *Powel* and Mrs. *Bracegirdle*."[15] This violation of traditional rights to parts (discussed below) is confirmed by the Petition of the Players and admitted by the patentees in their reply. Probably the high-handed tactics were intended to force Betterton and Mrs Barry to retire. It is difficult to see how Rich could have tried such a policy much earlier—and it is impossible to believe that other actors would have tolerated it once the trend became obvious. Under the circumstances the only alternative to retirement was rebellion.

Two more points need to be made before we move on to the rebellion itself, both having to do with earlier attempts to break up the United Company. Early in 1689 Henry Killigrew tried to form a second company, hoping to get a patent from the newly established monarchs, William and Mary.[16] He evidently thought a second company could be made to pay. About November 1693 Doggett, Bowen, and other unnamed actors tried to break away from the company just shaken by Alexander Davenant's departure. The Reply of the Patentees says that "ye last Year when Mr Doggett Bowen & others Mutined Mr Betterton declared they

ought to be Ejected ye House & by his perswasions they were denyed to
be received till they Quitted ye Combination & each Man treated onely
for himselfe" (article 8). Betterton was managing again by this time, and
the rebels may not have wanted to work under him—though both those
named started out at Lincoln's Inn Fields in 1695, and Betterton included a paragraph on Doggett's unreasonably low salary in the 1694
Petition. Even if Doggett, Bowen, and friends felt, like Henry Killigrew
before them, that the audience to support a second theatre was available,
Betterton appears not to have favored the idea of competition, and he
quickly put a stop to this attempted breakaway by playing upon dissension within the group. In the fall of 1693 Betterton was very much the
company man. Conditions must have changed drastically to induce him
to lead a rebellion just a year later.

In December 1693 Rich and Skipwith made public the conveyance by
which they held the rights to Alexander Davenant's shares.[17] We have performance records only of new plays during the 1693–94 season, so it is
difficult to reconstruct in any order the tensions which split the company.
Betterton tolerated the encroachment on his powers by Rich for a year,
and then led a breakaway. Such details as we know about the immediate
causes come primarily from the Petition of the Players to the Lord Chamberlain (undated, but from late November or early December 1694) and
the Reply of the Patentees (10 December 1694). Both documents are
extremely biased; both overstate their case from time to time. The testimony represents viewpoints that were fundamentally irreconcilable, and
these differing approaches to the theatrical enterprise were to influence
the kinds of companies which resulted from the split. As long as shareholders had been content with modest profits, the actors could make a
comfortable living, secure in their employment. They could put relatively
large sums into new shows without upsetting their investors. When Rich
began new accounting practices in an effort to increase his profit margin,
the actors felt the squeeze enough to be willing to risk competition again
for the freedom of being self-employed. After the rebellion each company
pursued its own financial policy. Rich tried to operate for profit. Lincoln's
Inn Fields began as a cooperative, with the goal of providing its actor
members a decent living, not making large profits for an owner.

The Petition of the Players contains two basic complaints against the
patentees: that they are calculating the net profits unfairly and on a
different basis than was customary, and that they are in various ways

denying the actors frequent enough opportunities to perform for them to earn a living. The petition includes greater and lesser examples of both complaints. With regard to kinds of income, the disposition of after-money had been decided in Chancery in May 1692, and the patentees certainly had no right to touch it, as section 3 alleges they were doing. Furthermore, the patentees' threat to close the theatre was one which directly affected all the actors, whether on salary or paid by share. The patentees seem to have been harassing individual actors as well as the company at large. They had subverted the longstanding arrangements for Mrs Barry's annual benefit (section 7), and they coerced Doggett into accepting a lower salary than he had been promised (section 14). While salaries were obviously important to all the actors, the tactic of the patentees which particularly rankled was that of replacing established stars with younger actors. Section 6 outlines the practice:

When wee parted with Our shares the Managers promised to continue to us all the Customary priviledges of shareing Actors but now everything is taken from us, the whole Course & Method of the Dukes Theatre totally changed. All things are Ordered at the will & pleasure of the present Claimers severall [actors] turned out for noe crime & without warning & ignorant insufficient fellowes putt in their places . . . tending to the ruine & destruction of the Company & treateing us not as we were the Kings & Queenes servants but the Claimers slaves.

The actors had long been accustomed to self-governance. Rich's dictatorial methods both infuriated and frightened them.

Complaints which are not really germane to the issue take up some of the petition (e.g., sections 1 and 9), and a certain amount of trivia pads it. But even the trivia bespeaks the resentment of the petitioners: the new wig which Betterton expected annually as a traditional token of his rank stands on almost equal footing with the patentees' attempt to lessen his holdings by a share and a quarter (section 8). Much more important is a clue in section 11 to the high-handed methods Rich used to persuade his employees to accept his offers, however stingy. The patentees are alleged to have docked Williams's salary on account of some internal dispute without the warning and explanation which were customary. Such arrogance might or might not coerce an individual, but it indicates gross disregard for employees—to Rich, they were all expendable. Throughout the petition, abuses are cited which the Lincoln's Inn Fields cooperative specifically endeavored to avoid. Matters of long-range consequence in the Lincoln's Inn Fields articles, like the sum paid to a retiring sharer for his investment in company property or the graded arrangements for a sort of life and accident insurance, have their roots in the controversy represented in section 2 of the petition.

We do not know the exact date of the petition. It is not, however, a very accommodating document, even though it asks for a hearing of these grievances. Cibber says that at some early stage in "these Contentions," "the Actors offer'd a Treaty of Peace; but their Masters imagining no Consequence could shake the Right of their Authority, refus'd all Terms of Accommodation."[18] Only later, according to Cibber, were "their Grievances . . . laid before the Earl of *Dorset*." The Petition of the Players is not a very well argued document, but it is certainly a provocative one from the patentees' point of view. I would offer the guess that by the time the actors wrote this petition they had no thought of reconciliation, but hoped either to be allowed to set up on their own, or to win arbitration which would drive the infuriated Rich to sell his shares and leave the theatre. In essence, the petition threatens a strike if the Lord Chamberlain will not put an end to Rich's methods of management. The patentees, for their part, were threatening a lockout.

A close reading of the Reply of the Patentees must raise serious questions as to their good faith, not to mention their honesty. Even granting that Skipwith and Rich (a lawyer) had the training to present their case more effectively than the players might, some of their tactics are distinctly underhanded. By itself the tone of the reply would be grounds for outrage on the part of the players, and the intractability of the patentees may have hardened the actors' decision to set up another company rather than deal with Rich on any terms. In fairness, we should note that on many of the disputed points an unbiased legal opinion would favor the patentees. They could cite contract obligations, and often precedent, in support of most of their actions. They were, however, at a political disadvantage. Betterton and the Lord Chamberlain had been friends for at least twenty years. In fact, the patentees found themselves summoned to a meeting to discuss the dispute three days before they delivered their reply.[19] They seem to have realized that they could not expect an impartial hearing from the authorities, and hence they emphasized their indisputable legal rights, while making a systematic attempt to discredit Betterton. Obviously they regarded him as ringleader of the rebellion.

The Reply of the Patentees (in which Charles Killigrew tacitly joins Rich and Skipwith) begins with a recitation of the original patent grants. Key words are written in broad pen strokes and phrases are underlined, which, read separately from the rest of the text, summarize the rights included in the patents and in the indenture of the 1682 union. Even in this seemingly noncontroversial part of the reply, the patentees' strategy is clear. Having already recited the clause which directs that "all scandalous & mutinous persons should from time to time be . . . Ejected," they refer to "Mr Betterton & his Mutinous Companions (as ye Patent is pleased to term them)." The description is legally correct, but can scarcely be said to show a spirit of compromise.

The patentees then summarize each section of the Petition of the Players in turn and give their reply to it. They stress the large sums of money owed to them when Alexander Davenant absconded: their intervention was based on the desire to recoup their investment. The first ten sections of the answer are designed to refute the petitioners' allegations, but are phrased to discredit Betterton individually. The patentees take every opportunity to associate him with Alexander Davenant and to give the impression that he had colluded in defrauding both outside Adventurers and his fellow actors. They say that Betterton had known by 1690 that Alexander had sold his shares to Rich and Skipwith—though he did not sign or witness the extant forms of those agreements.[20] They imply that Betterton persuaded "divers other persons . . . to signe to ye same [petition] when severall of them hath since Declared that they neither read nor heard read ye Paper annexed . . . wherein those Sandalous [sic] words are mentioned," which indicates "what Sort of a Man Mr Betterton is" (article 1). This allegation is based on an interview with Mrs Bowman, who, when asked "why she signed ye Petition," "Answered onely because Mr Betterton whom she calls ffather desired her soe to doe."[21] Yet ultimately all but three of the signers stood by the charges: they must have had some basis in fact.

Deliberately or in ignorance the patentees confuse some issues. The much-disputed £100 payment to a retiring actor-sharer is not at all the same issue as whether the patentees can arbitrarily switch an actor from share to salary and vice versa (article 2). The retirement grant was one of many practices apparently not written into company contracts, and the patentees insist upon the letter of the contracts. Charles Killigrew's assertion that "he doth not know that he hath Obleiged himselfe to ye said pretension" of a retirement grant is simply untrue: in 1676 he had bribed two of his father's actors to get the rest to settle for £100 instead of £200.[22] Another of the patentees' tactics shows up in this article: the original Duke's Company sharers whose repayment the patentees so loudly doubt were conveniently dead by 1695 and could not testify; retired members still alive are not named. The reassignment of actors' shares in the Duke's Company had originally been controlled by Sir William Davenant, to whom they reverted at the death or retirement of the shareholder. By the 1690s, however, actors with seniority like Betterton and Bowman were accustomed to deciding for themselves whether to risk an income from profits or settle for a salary. These issues probably fused in the patentees' thinking when they tried to force the senior actors out and were met by demands for a large amount of cash in retirement payments.

Although they know that the questions of rent on the Dorset Garden theatre apartments (another unwritten custom) and rights to fine money and aftermoney are still under dispute in Chancery, the patentees treat each of these subjects as a new, personal affront. In answering this charge they do not mention the trust fund which the court had ordered set up with the money in question, for the purpose of paying off the company's debts and maintaining a supply of cash for future expenses. Such a fund would reduce shareholders' profits, though it would benefit the actors in terms of security and working conditions.

"Keeping Improper persons in partes & turning out putting in & advancing whom he pleased" were "arbitrary Acts" when done by Betterton, but the patentees maintain their right "to change their servants as they think fitt according to ye power given by ye said patents" (article 6). In the same section they allege that Alexander Davenant allowed Betterton "to brow beate and discountenance Young Actors as Mr Giloe Carlisle Mountfort & others." ("Young" means hireling in this context.) The significant point about this assertion is that all three actors named were dead by 1694.[23] Betterton had extensive contact with many other "young" actors—the patentees admit that he was in charge of rehearsals and teaching (though they hasten to add that he was lax in performing these duties—see article 8). As with Alexander Davenant, the patentees' strategy is to make charges which could be neither proved nor disproved, since the people involved were, we might say, unavailable.

The patentees hint darkly at "private Consideration[s]" and secret agreements "which wee shall not now discover unless he [Betterton] pleases" (articles 1, 2, 8). They regret that "to their sad Experience [they] find that a Man at 60 is not able to doe That which he could at 30 or 40," and claim that the company's losses have been due to Betterton's choice of repertory and the necessity of letting him rest several days between performances of his "great parts" (article 8). The fact that Betterton continued to act vigorously for ten years after this belies the charge. The attempt to blame him for the company's losses may come closer to the truth. He unquestionably believed in spending a lot of money on big shows, as witness the £3000 *Fairy-Queen*. Betterton put that much money into an opera which opened in 1692 just two months after the company had acknowledged an £800 debt. We should note, however, that two years later, even after Alexander had decamped, the company was only £189 in debt, by the patentees' own admission (article 6).[24] Betterton's theatrical instincts were sound, and he did not just look on the theatre as an investment, the way Rich and Skipwith did. I do not mean to imply that Betterton was scrupulously disinterested in all his managerial arrangements. He may well have set up a blind, or holding, company to receive his portion of the very high rent he had negotiated for the owners of the Dorset Garden theatre. The salary paid to his wife was, by this time, largely a "compliment," as the patentees complain. Certainly he helped his friends and did not hesitate to crush challenges to company authority like the Doggett-Bowen rebellion in 1693. But whatever his faults of bookkeeping or of pride, the important actors in the London theatre almost unanimously preferred to work with him rather than go back to Rich.

The patentees use three other ploys to avoid answering the players' charges. The amount of authority they recognize in Thomas Davenant varies from article to article as seems expedient (compare sections 2, 7, and 11). For some of the lesser points they assert that the problems have been solved (12, 14, and 15), though they rather ominously ask to be allowed to determine what salary any returning mutineer should be given. And they end with a list of actors who did not sign the players' petition, implying that the numbers are about equal. They do not, of course, mention that the nonsigners were for the most part very junior people, perhaps never even invited to participate in the rebellion.

By December 1694 feelings were obviously running high. The patentees appear to have been far more interested in having their authority confirmed than in bringing the rebels back into the fold. They would have been happy to force some of the older actors into retirement as a means of reducing the overhead. They had legal right on their side: no doubt they were astonished and infuriated to discover that public and government sympathy lay with the rebels. As Cibber says, the patentees had "a Monopoly of the Stage, and consequently presum'd they might impose what Conditions they pleased upon their People," without considering "that they were all this while endeavouring to enslave a Set of Actors whom the Publick . . . were inclined to support."[25]

Secession was probably in the actors' minds well before the reply. The patentees had not been given a hearing when the date for a meeting was set by the Lord Chamberlain's secretary. On 17 December Dorset and Sir Robert Howard would meet with the aggrieved parties. But even before this meeting the patentees hastened to defend their monopoly. On 12 December we find the following government order:

Patent for Erecting a New Play House Sir Thomas Skipwith Bart Charles Killigrew Esqr & Mr Christopher Rich, Interressed in the Patents of the 2 Theaters of the Play House desires, that nothing Passe concerning the Erecting a Play house or Acting in any House Erected for representing any Comedies Tragedys or any other Publick Entertainment, till Notice be first given to some of them. Whitehall twelfth December 1694.[26]

This tells us that the rebels were seeking political support for their own license—or at least the patentees thought they were. The meeting on the seventeenth was a stalemate, and acting ceased at the end of that week on account of Queen Mary's illness.

The death of Queen Mary on 28 December halted all acting until Easter Monday 1695. During January or early February the rebels presumably got the legal "Opinion" Cibber explains—"that no Patent for acting Plays, *etc* could tie up the Hands of a succeeding Prince from granting the like Authority where it might be thought proper to trust it."[27] They must have had some confidence that a royal grant would be forthcoming, since they promptly set about reconstituting Lincoln's Inn Fields as a theatre. By this time the patentees appear to have been thoroughly frightened: they had wanted to force the senior actors into submission or retirement, not have them established as a competing company.

On 19 March the patentees signified their "Submission" to the Lord Chamberlain's proposed resolution of the "Differences" between actors and patentees—a compromise which definitely favored the actors. Ignored by the rebels, the patentees again asked the Lord Chamberlain to help arrange "an amicable composure of matters"—for them, a restrained and undemanding position.[28] The contrast with the tone of the reply is remarkable. The patentees say plaintively that on 11 February they sent to Betterton and his fellows, requesting a private meeting, and were refused. They note that they have "submitted to your Lordships Proposalls in Confidence That your Lordship would unite us, and Settle all matters in difference between us, yet Wee find that they proceed in Converting the Tennis Court in Lincolnes Inn Feilds to a Playhouse." The patentees ask that "a Stopp . . . be putt thereunto," and suggest that if the "said Comedians" are still dissatisfied, the issues could be referred to former managers Henry Harris and William Smith for arbitration. But a proposal which might have been welcomed in November or December was now irrelevant.

Three days after the arbitration proposal, the Lord Chamberlain legitimized the rebels with a license.

> Charles Earle of Dorsett and Middlesex Lord Chamberlaine of His Majesties Houshold one of His Majesties most honorable Privy Councill and Knight of the most notable Order of the Garter &c.

In pursuance of His Majesties Pleasure and Command, given unto mee herein, I doe hereby give and grant full power Licence and Authority unto Thomas Betterton, Elizabeth Barry Anne Bracegirdle John Bowman, Joseph Williams, Cave Underhill, Thomas Doggett, William Bowen, Susan Verbruggen, Elianor Leigh, George Bright, His Majesties sworne servants and Comoedians in Ordinary, and the major Part of them, their Agents and Servants, from time to time, in any convenient Place or Places, to Act & represent, all and all manner of Comedyes & Tragedyes, Playes Interludes, & Opera's, and to performe all other Theatricall and musicall Entertaynments of what kind soever, But so, as to bee allwayes under my Government and Regulation from time to time, as hath been exercised by my Predecessors. And this Licence to continue untill further Order under my hand & seale. Given under my hand & seale this 25th day of March 1695. In the seaventh year of His Majesties Reigne.

Dorsett.

(P.R.O. LC 7/3)

What the actors received was not a "patent" but a "license" to perform. It was valid only at the pleasure of the monarch, but in contravening the patent monopolies it set an important precedent. Precisely how the actors wangled this license we can only guess. Downes mentions the help of Dorset and Howard (which seems plausible) and implies that they put the case to the King.[29] Cibber elaborates the connection into an audience with the King for the rebel leaders. Perhaps Dorset arranged an audience for the actors to thank the King, but the key point in the establishment of Lincoln's Inn Fields was a matter of legal opinion on precedents, not something the King could adjudicate. I belabor the point because Lowe, expanding on Cibber's effusiveness, says that "His Majesty, though he took little interest in theatrical matters, was yet curious to see at close quarters such notable artists as Betterton and Mrs. Barry." This appears to be a flight of fancy.[30]

At all events, the rebels had got what they wanted. Their license freed them from Christopher Rich, and from all obligations to outside Adventurers. They were also, however, without the rights to the only two decent theatres in London, and they had walked out, leaving behind their entire stock of costumes and scenery. They were free of Rich, but they were not without problems.

II
THE NATURE OF THE
RESULTING COMPANIES

The split left both companies in difficult positions. Lincoln's Inn Fields had a decisive advantage in personnel, but in buildings, equipment, and financial resources Rich still had the basis for a strong theatre company. Each party had a repertory problem. In surveying the resources of the two companies as they approached their first full season of competition in 1695–96, we need to see what the strengths and weaknesses of each were, and how they attempted to cope with their problems. The organizational structure of the two groups is decisively different, as an analysis will show. For the sake of convenience, I will sometimes use Rich's name to designate the Patent Company. Rich was the active participant; Skipwith averred that he himself had little to do with management after 1694, having left it all to Rich.[31] Before 1700 Lincoln's Inn Fields was not in any way officially "Betterton's" company, though contemporaries sometimes referred to it that way. Such a designation is misleading, and I have tried to avoid it.

From the beginning of the rebellion, the essential division in the United Company is clear: the established actors and actresses sided with Betterton against Rich. However, Betterton became their leader only in the sense that he was the principal actor in London in 1695. From the earliest document concerning the company, its license, the intention to organize it as a cooperative is clear. The rebels included several members of companies Betterton had previously run, a few stalwarts going back as far as the original Duke's Company. (For an annotated list of the two companies' personnel, see Appendix C.) These people had in common not only their repertory and training but the philosophy of company management inherited from Sir William Davenant, which put the good of the company above the profits of the owners. The Lincoln's Inn Fields Company had experienced actors to do virtually any play that had been mounted during Betterton's career, except for operas and farces. They were not burdened with the drunken, jealous Powell, and while they had a selection of comedians, they did not have a troublemaker like Jo Haynes. The company felt secure enough that they did not try to wipe Rich out—people who did not care for the terms Lincoln's Inn Fields was offering could go back to Rich without significantly damaging the rebel company. In fact Williams and the Verbruggens (and eventually Doggett) did just that.

Rich, in contrast, faced the prospect of energetic recruiting in order to build a troupe capable of doing much of anything. He had Powell, who was talented but unreliable; Cibber, who was promising but untried; Haynes, Pinkethman, and later Doggett for farce and low comedy; and Mrs Knight for his leading tragedienne. The addition of the Verbruggens (who were not satisfied with an offer from Lincoln's Inn Fields of a full share for John but only a salary for Susannah), gave the Patent Company an experienced leading man and a strong comedienne.[32] On April 10, 1695 Verbruggen signed with Skipwith for 20 percent of all profits to be divided among the Adventurers, and on behalf of his wife he signed another contract providing for (a) a £75 bonus payment immediately and (b) another 20 percent of the Adventurers' profits, with the provision that if this did not amount to £105 per annum, that sum would be made up to her. These alluring terms were not, however, realized. An annotation on Verbruggen's agreement states "That because a Share produced nothing, Sir Thomas Skipwith advanced £4 a weeke to Mr Verbruggen."[33] Obviously the Patent Company was in dire need of experienced performers. Many of Rich's troupe had been with the company two years or less. Rich had to buy back anyone he could from Lincoln's Inn Fields, and simply to stay in business he had to pay (or at least promise) exorbitant wages to the remnants left to him. Cibber gleefully records how the hirelings turned the situation to their advantage. "The Leavings of *Betterton*'s Interest . . . you may be sure, would not lose this Occasion of setting a Price upon their Merit equal to their own Opinion of it, which was but just double to what they had before."[34] The necessity must have galled Rich, but he was mad enough at the rebels to pay the double wages his weak and inexperienced actors were now demanding. The Patent Company also recruited outside London, and by the 1698–99 season they had a fairly serviceable collection of performers with the advantage of youth.

In the realm of theatres and equipment, Rich held both the elaborate machine house, Dorset Garden, and the plainer but more satisfactory Drury Lane. The theatres themselves should have proven a great advantage to him, but he lacked the technical skill to make them a potent factor in his favor. Dorset Garden was by this time in poor repair and seldom used—though routine maintenance would probably have kept it functional after a thorough overhaul. While he was unwilling or unable to make much use of his other theatre, Rich had reason to fear that Betterton could use either to his advantage if he could get it. The Earl's agent leased Dorset Garden to weight lifters, but not to the rebels, and the patentees contrived to block an attempt by Betterton to rent Drury Lane in 1702.[35] Along with the theatres Rich also held the United Company's entire stock of costumes, scenery, and miscellaneous equipment.

The rebel company, on the other hand, had not only to reconvert their old tennis court into a theatre, but outfit it from scratch. The Lincoln's Inn Fields Sharing Agreement begins with a passage explaining that the participating actors

have taken ye Tennis Court in Little Lincolns Inne Feilds and paid a greate fine and doe pay a Great rent for ye same and at an Extraordinary Charge & Expence have converted ye same into a Theatre or Playhouse where they now act Comedies Tragedies etc.

And further the said parties being necessited to provide every thing anew for the Carrying on soe Great an undertakeing as all variety of Cloaths Forreigne habitts Scenes properties etc. which must be paid out of the publique Receipts.[36]

So little is known about the three theatres that we have no way to compare their seating capacities accurately. Pictures of Edward A. Langhans's models of Drury Lane and Dorset Garden give a rough impression of how much larger stage Dorset Garden had, and all contemporary sources indicate that Lincoln's Inn Fields was considerably smaller than either of the others in both seating capacity and stage space.[37] Judging by the simplicity of the productions mounted at the "New Theatre" (as Lincoln's Inn Fields was called), the renovation did not include much machinery. The rebels lacked the time and also the capital to add expensive refinements to their makeshift theatre. Whether they viewed the place as a temporary or a permanent home for the new company we cannot tell. Perhaps they did not give the matter much thought to begin with. But in restricting themselves to actor-sharers the cooperative eliminated the traditional source of capital for new buildings. Both Davenant and Killigrew had needed outside help to finance new theatres in much more favorable times. The smaller seating capacity and comparatively primitive staging of Lincoln's Inn Fields cramped Betterton's style and hurt the company in the long run.

The vexed question of rights to plays reappeared with the dissolution of the United Company. Exclusive rights to plays from the Duke's and King's Company repertories had passed on to the United Company, but specific rights apparently remained vested partly in actors and partly in proprietors, as before the Restoration. No division of existing plays was made in 1695. No known documents contest rights to plays, both sides apparently foreseeing only a long and expensive legal battle, probably ending in compromise. The result was that each company did any pre-1695 play it chose, sometimes in direct competition. Rich made a practice of imitating some of Lincoln's Inn Fields's stock plays, but however amusing it might be to see Powell (or later, Estcourt) mimic Betterton, the senior actors' performances of their own parts had to be popular enough to make the mockery amusing. Rich knew he could not hope to sustain a company by doing mediocre productions of old plays. His actors were obviously going to be much better off doing lighter weight drama and farce to begin with than trying to meet the stars on their own ground. When he turned to new plays, he produced farce and scripts in the increasingly popular sentimental vein. The Lincoln's Inn Fields Company, perhaps remembering the Killigrew-Davenant competition, also mounted new plays to avoid stagnation, though they did not always read the new audience's tastes correctly.

Over the course of the years the factor which told most strongly against Lincoln's Inn Fields was financial resources. Rich had access to money—and when angry enough to spend it, could make good use of his buying power. He also had the strong central management (not to say dictatorship) which made him answerable to no one for his fiscal decisions. The New Theatre, in contrast, had no capital and no ready means of acquiring any. If Betterton had not lost his fortune in 1692 he might have contributed; probably none of the other sharers had that kind of money. Lincoln's Inn Fields maintained its independence, but at the cost of cutting itself off from the logical source of money—investors. Davenant's plan to reinvest profits in the company's productions was a logical one, but the cooperative system developed by Lincoln's Inn Fields as a reaction to Rich's tyranny did not make anyone responsible for enforcing such reinvestment.

A brief analysis of the sharers' agreement (preserved in LC 7/1, and printed in Appendix D) will show both how the actors attempted to protect themselves against a recurrence of the United Company's problems, and how they thereby made other, unforeseen difficulties for themselves. Comparison with the Duke's Company and United Company agreements shows how unusual the Lincoln's Inn Fields organization was. For simplicity, I will break my observations down into a numbered series.

(1) The license privileges and responsibilities weigh equally on all sharing members of the company. In practice they probably divided routine tasks, but officially they were all participants in decision-making. For the first time women are allowed to hold shares directly.[38] The Duke's Company agreement had given Sir William Davenant complete authority over his actresses, nor did women hold shares in the King's Company. When the Verbruggens returned to Drury Lane in 1695, John signed an agreement in his wife's behalf (discussed above). Perhaps the presence of several unmarried or widowed actresses in the "New" company forced an arrangement which would not otherwise have been tried.

(2) A great deal is made of the "Extraordinary Charge and Expence"

involved in converting and outfitting the theatre. Some of this cost was met by gifts. Cibber reports that "many People of Quality came into a voluntary Subscription of twenty, and some of forty Guineas a-piece, for the erecting a Theatre."[39] Testimony from the holder of an Adventurer's share in the Patent Company (who was suing for unpaid profits) confirms Cibber, and says that the rebel actors were able to set up Lincoln's Inn Fields because of "Subscriptions & Incouragement from diverse persons of Quality who were desireous of the Company."[40] Even this help was probably just enough to accomplish minimal renovations. If fifty persons of quality chipped in (probably a generous estimate), half of them paying £40 and half £20, the sum raised would have been only £1500. This would have been scant capital with which to refurbish a theatre, and it was strictly a one-time contribution. As the sharing agreement notes, the high cost of assembling a new stock of costumes, scenery, and props would have to be "paid out of the publique *Receipts*." In short, they had no capital and would have to rely on daily operating profits for any further outlay on new productions.

(3) Provision is made for payment of £100 to any sharer who dies or retires—the practice to commence five years after the establishment of the company.[41] Thus they propose to carry on a practice eliminated by Rich—but specify that the payment is to be in installments. To this company, £100 was a significant capital sum. Death and retirement benefits are naturally more important to these people than to Rich's fledglings: this is an *old* company, and its members need to be thinking about retirement and insurance plans. Two separate clauses deal with "fringe benefits," as we now call them. First, a special arrangement is made for anyone who dies within three years, acknowledging both the company's obligations and its lack of capital. Second, accident and disability insurance of a sort are provided. Any disabled sharer will be paid 40*s.* per acting week; those holding less than a full share will be paid proportionately less. This clause reinstitutes a practice Rich had attempted to end. The Duke's and United companies had apparently been generous with incapacitated actors. Philip Cademan, Davenant's stepson, is the celebrated case, though nepotism may have been at work in that instance. But the traditional pattern was to continue to employ actors as long as they could work, even when they grew old or physically infirm. Rich, bent on making money, had no interest in Cademan, Sandford, or anyone else who did not give him what he considered full value for salary.

(4) Provision is also made for sickness and accident insurance to cover the "hyred Servants" making 20*s*. per week or more. This clause presumably applies to technicians, the prompter, wardrobe staff, and other support personnel.

(5) The articles state that to be "received into share" any new sharer must sign this agreement. This requirement was evidently a means of excluding hidden participants: the actors wanted no more Skipwiths and Riches rung in on them.

(6) The agreement specifies that no more than ten full shares will ever be parceled out—an attempt to prevent excessive dilution of the profits; and further, that "no person shall have any proportion of above one share in consideration of Acting"—which should have put a ceiling on differences in income, an important issue in a cooperative. This provision also made strong central authority on the Davenant model impossible. From Verbruggen's Petition (printed in Appendix E) we know that Betterton was initially given an extra half share, presumably for functioning as superintendent of rehearsals. But on the whole the company was set up to be much more explicitly democratic than its predecessors.

The result really was a cooperative. In the original Duke's Company ownership was widely scattered, but the agreement repeatedly specified Davenant's *total* control of daily operations. The startling thing about the Lincoln's Inn Fields agreement is its silence about leadership. In the United Company agreement Charles Killigrew and Charles Davenant were titular heads, but day-by-day management was vested in Betterton and Smith; in the event of the principal owners' disagreeing, three senior actors were to be named as arbitrators. At Lincoln's Inn Fields Betterton was presumably the first among equals, but initially he was given no formal authority at all. The mess which resulted by 1700 is notorious. Another significant point to be noted is the lack of any provision for keeping and verifying the company's financial records—a sign of unity at first, but a matter which was ultimately to produce something close to civil war in the company.

In sum, the sharers' agreement was designed to protect actors—and even salaried help—against both disablement and the likes of Christopher Rich. In many ways it is a humane and democratic document. But it betrays, first, a desperate lack of capital and, more important, a fatal vagueness about precisely who would set policy and make the company run.

III
The Changing Audience

Although some vestiges of the old cliché about the coterie audience in this period remain current,[42] its inaccuracies have long been realized, and in recent years our understanding of audience composition has greatly improved.[43] Nonetheless, we must not discount the importance to the theatre world of royal patronage, both in prestige and money. Neither James II nor Queen Mary kept up Charles II's intimate acquaintance with the theatre, though they did occasionally attend and support the United Company. When Mary died in December 1694, active royal interest in the theatre died too. William III made no pretense of caring for English drama, and Queen Anne gave only token support—largely for the sake of maintaining Stuart prerogatives, not from any genuine enthusiasm.

Attendance by the Court circle was a thing of the past. And simply on the basis of life span, the original Restoration audience must have been significantly diminished by 1695. As early as 1688, Shadwell was saying in the prologue to *The Squire of Alsatia*, "Our Poet found your gentle Fathers kind." The new audience was a different generation; it also differed in composition. John Loftis points out that although the same terms continued to be used to describe sections of the audience—gentlemen, merchants, and cits, for example—the people composing those groups came from different classes than had earlier audience members. Hence, "the citizens recognized as such in the early eighteenth-century theater were not the leading members of the business community, the exporters and financiers, but rather the petty traders, the shopkeepers, and the apprentices."[44]

The new audience promoted the development of different moral and aesthetic standards in the theatre. One clear indication of changing preferences in the last decade of the century is the reception accorded various kinds of plays, and the resulting shifts in common play types.[45] The objections to earlier styles, coming as they did when two theatres were fighting for patronage from a very limited audience,[46] had much greater effects on drama than they might have had in a more stable situation. The timing proved unfortunate for the theatres and for the development of English drama.

Moral pressures had already affected the United Company before the breakaway. Indications of changing attitudes begin to appear shortly after William and Mary mount the English throne. Bishop Burnet, in his *History of his Own Time*, traces the development of the Societies for the Reformation of Manners back to the reaction against James II.[47] In 1689 the warrants to "Robin Hog" Stephens, Messenger of the Press, license him to report and seize "scandalous" (i.e., immoral) as well as "seditious" books and papers printed without the government's imprimatur.[48] These activities did not immediately affect the stage. But they resulted in prosecutions for the printing of obscene books, an issue which had appeared in court so seldom at that time that English jurisprudence had no clear precedent for judging cases.[49] The reform virus soon spread to members of the theatre audience and to others who simply found the theatre obnoxious. Pressure for outright closing of the theatres became significant for the first time since the 1660s. Narcissus Luttrell reports in December 1691 that "one of the bishops [in the House of Lords] moved to suppresse the playhouse, it being a nursery of lewdness, but the temporall lords were against it."[50] Certainly a large number of Londoners retained the Puritans' abhorrence of the theatre, and now once again this hostility was being given free vent—perhaps in part a sign of the diminution in royal patronage. All this is simply a reminder that the "Collier Crisis" was the climax of nearly two decades of change and protest.

Playwrights usually identify "the Ladies" as the principal source of approval or criticism on matters of decorum and morals in plays. John Harrington Smith notes the pattern of writers' entreaties and responses to the new arbiters beginning in the late 1680s: "Even before 1690 . . . the ladies had become a power to be reckoned with in the theater, and they continued so past that date. In the last decade of the century their influence is traceable in the prefaces of writers whose plays had offended. After 1700 the note of exculpation disappears from prefaces, but this is not because the ladies had ceased to exert pressure on the stage but rather because they had by then won their battle and were getting what they wanted."[51]

What the reformers' outcry ultimately produces is, of course, a move toward "humane" and even "exemplary" drama, but the "new" modes do not replace the "old" drama overnight, or even over the course of the decade.[52] Some part of the audience still favored the Carolean style of "hard," satiric comedy. Oddly enough, old plays with plots and language no new writers could hope to get away with—*The Country-Wife*, for example—continue in repertory at both houses, and reprints indicate no significant changes in the text. Plays of the new wave do not change directly to exemplary themes, but writers take pains to soften the old form. They clean up their language and make sure their rakes reform by the end of the play, however implausibly. Throughout much of the decade, Betterton supports Dryden's campaign to revive the old comedy by producing the works of such protégés as Congreve and Southerne. The audience, not yet entirely changed, reacts capriciously, liking *The Old Batchelour* but not *The Double-Dealer* (both 1693). As the next chapters will show, Lincoln's Inn Fields's indifference to "new" comedy is a clear sign that they were out of touch with part of their potential audience. Rich's company rarely puts on an "old" comedy, while Lincoln's Inn Fields mounts fewer "new" style comedies. Their disadvantage in this respect lies more in audience distaste for the old comedy than in real success of the new. The failure of most of the quasi-exemplary comedies played by both theatres masks the extent of Lincoln's Inn Fields's failure to keep pace with the times.

The search for a new audience has other effects on theatrical productions, both practical and aesthetic. The most obvious demonstration of an effort to suit the convenience of a different set of patrons is the change in curtain time. Like the alteration in play types, it comes about gradually, less by design than by accident and casual experimentation. At the beginning of the Carolean period curtain time is three or three-thirty in the afternoon. By 1695 it has drifted up to four or even later, and after 1700 the time runs between five and six.[53] This shift proves that the theatres were no longer able to rely on a leisured, Court-circle audience. To fill their houses the managers had to attract part of the working populace—people who were occupied in trade until the end of the afternoon. Obviously this brings a more middle-class, more Whiggish, more mercantile audience into the theatre, and contributes to the great shift in audience attitudes traced by John Loftis.

Both managements had to resort to extra features, first to entice nontheatregoers, then in the hope of retaining the interest of unsophisticated patrons after they had ventured inside. At first these features are merely extensions of theatre arts, such as additional dances and special songs. Indeed, a whole special class of performers develops—people who are hired specifically to appear in these extra features. The additions grow into short masques done as entr'actes and afterpieces. Betterton and the

Lincoln's Inn Fields actors, elitist by inclination, try to maintain professional standards and go to great, even ridiculous expense to import distinguished foreign singers and dancers. Rich does the same thing on a more reasonable budget, but he also discovers that less theatrical performers draw just about as well. The traditional distinctions between theatres and fairs vanish, and rope dancers, jugglers, and animal acts appear regularly. Lincoln's Inn Fields has to meet the competition, and so we find "Vaulting on the Manag'd Horse" in the intervals of *The Country-Wife*, 21 October 1701. The multitude of nontheatrical or semi-theatrical attractions after 1700—singers, dancers, animals, masques, double bills, variety shows, medleys of favorite scenes—is eloquent testimony that the theatres had to seek out customers who would not attend just to see a play.

As this chapter shows, the competition which was reestablished in 1695 began on a very different footing than the one between Davenant and Killigrew in the 1660s. Following rebellion and secession, détente would not be the order of the day. Instead, there would be bitter, and—on Rich's part—deliberately destructive competition. At the start of the battle most of the immediate advantages lay with the Lincoln's Inn Fields Company. They had everything they could want for immediate success except an adequate theatre: prestige, star actors, the support of the public. Rich's circumstances at the beginning of 1695 looked desperate. Indeed, Rich later testified in a court case that the patentees had considered closing their theatres, at least for a time:

it being debated between them . . . whether to carry on acting or to desist by reason of the said chief actors and others deserting as aforesaid . . . it was thought that if acting were not carried on under the authority of the Letters patents that the whole concern might be lost; And therefore it was resolved . . . to carry on acting with all possible vigor, and for that purpose to hire and entertain Actors and others, and to Endeavor to procure the Return of all (or so many as could be) of such as had deserted, and to use such means as should be advised for the Recalling or annulling of the said License granted . . . by the Earl of Dorset.[54]

In the early months of 1695, Rich had no expectation of profitable operations within any foreseeable future. His reason for struggling on against such odds, this passage makes clear, was a keen sense of the ultimate commercial worth of his patent. Rich held the rights descending from both the original patents of 1660, while the rebels merely had a license to act: Rich feared that the patent would become void in law if acting under its authority should cease.

Rich had one huge advantage in this confrontation with the rebels— money. He had the resources to make a fight if he chose to. For the sake of maintaining the patent, if nothing else, Rich was determined to do precisely that. Unlike Lincoln's Inn Fields, the Drury Lane company was not dependent on current receipts. So Rich paid a fortune for the troublemakers and nonentities left to him, bought back what actors he could from the New Theatre, recruited from Ireland and the provinces—and gritted his teeth. "We were assured," Cibber tells us, "that let the Audiences be never so low, our Masters would make good all Deficiencies."[55] The prognosis at this point is clear: either Betterton and the rebels would run the patentees out of business in short order; or the Patent Company would hang on, improve, and ultimately find itself in a position to capitalize on its potential advantages of youth and good theatres.

Chapter 4

The Success
of the Rebels,
1695–1698

THE remaining chapters will survey the competition between Lincoln's Inn Fields and the Patent Company at Drury Lane up to the new union of 1708. This period was a time of radical insecurity in the theatre. Heated competition, desperate experimentation, attacks by reformers, and demoralization about public taste and the future of drama characterized these years. Management policy and its effects are my subject here. In the broadest sense, I will be studying the life of the Lincoln's Inn Fields Company. The elements involved constitute a circle: the state of the company affected its offerings, and the reception of those offerings in turn affected the state of the company. Scholarly investigation of this interaction has been surprisingly meager. *The London Stage* offers a few passing observations but is a performance calendar, not a commentary. Nicoll prints some relevant documents, and Hotson ends his book with a sketchy account of the two companies, drawn mainly from legal records. No theatre historian has previously made use of one of our best sources of information about the circumstances of the 1708 union—the Coke Papers at Harvard.

Only very recently has anyone realized the importance of the theatrical competition.[1] Up to 1705, study is greatly impeded by the scantiness of performance records. Downes, Gildon, and the anonymous *Comparison between the Two Stages* (1702) provide miscellaneous, rather unchronological, information. Prologues and epilogues can be used—cautiously—and the prefaces to printed quartos contain a considerable amount of untapped material. This is especially true after the 1699–1700 season, since part 2 of *The London Stage* prints almost nothing from such sources. Cibber's *Apology*, written forty years later, has always served as the basis for histories of the stage: it is a gold mine of exciting but sometimes unreliable information. Overall, Cibber's picture is fairly accurate. After an initial success, Lincoln's Inn Fields floundered. But it did not stumble nearly as early as he implies, and it recovered—which he does not suggest at all. With a little effort, a much more accurate picture of Lincoln's Inn Fields's operations can be pieced together. In these years the whole course of English drama changed: the Carolean play types were left behind, and a new set evolved. The history of the theatre companies played a part in this: the prolongation of the careers of the Carolean actors, the dilution of the audience between two houses, the frenzied introduction of singers, dancers, jugglers, animal acts, and the like—all affected English theatre and drama for decades to come.

The survey which follows is designed to determine the changing condition of the Lincoln's Inn Fields Company and to isolate the factors which affected its success. At each phase in the company's history I will systematically examine the management, competitive devices, and repertory of each company. "Management" covers such intramural matters as personnel, leadership, company finances, morale, and signs of dissension. By "competitive devices" I mean short- and long-term strategies for attracting business away from the other house—added music and dancing, advertising, burlesque, double bills, variety shows, and so forth. Under "repertory" I will analyze the new plays mounted by each house, making an effort to determine their success or failure.

To judge the health of either company, we need to know how its offerings were doing. The relevant evidence is maddeningly sketchy until the advent of daily newspaper bills, which gradually catch on between 1702 and 1705. Part 1 of *The London Stage* includes much more gossip from contemporaries than part 2, but even in the years before 1700, serious errors are easy to make. For example, Shirley Kenny overestimates the damage done to the rebel company by Drury Lane's success with *The Constant Couple* because she does not take into account the success of "Betterton's" *Henry the Fourth* in January 1700. A play-by-play consideration will both alert us to trends in the drama, and help us see exactly how well or badly each company was doing. To check *every* play may sometimes be tedious, but is a vital safeguard. Kenny, working from a play here and a play there, is baffled by the bad state of Drury Lane in the 1697–98 season—but the reason is no further to seek than the catastrophe the Patent Company suffered with an expensive opera, Settle's *The World in the Moon* (June 1697), a play Kenny never mentions. The result of my very detailed survey of repertory, in conjunction with study of management and competitive devices, will be, I hope, a clear sense of the condition of the Lincoln's Inn Fields Company during each of four phases of the renewed theatrical competition.

I
MANAGEMENT AND PERSONNEL

As we saw in chapter 3, Lincoln's Inn Fields had an enormous competitive advantage when acting resumed in the spring of 1695. *A Comparison between the Two Stages* gives us the following picture:

'Twas strange that the general defection of the old Actors which left *Drury-lane*, and the fondness which the better sort shew'd for 'em at the opening of their *New-house*, and indeed the Novelty it self, had not quite destroy'd those few young ones that remain'd behind. The disproportion was so great at parting, that 'twas almost impossible, in *Drury-lane*, to muster up a sufficient number to take in all the Parts of any Play; and of them so few were tolerable, that a Play must of necessity be damn'd that had not extraordinary favour from the Audience: No fewer than *Sixteen* (most of the old standing) went away; and with them the very beauty and vigour of the Stage; they who were left behind being for the most part Learners, Boys and Girls, a very unequal match for them who revolted. . . . The *Theatre-Royal* was then sunk into a very despicable Condition: Very little difference appear'd between that and the Theatre at the Bear Garden.[2]

In all probability, the rebels expected Rich's remnants to collapse—upon which they would be invited to pick up the pieces and could resume operations in their old theatres. Indeed, by the fall of 1696 the Patent Company was reportedly on the brink of collapse. According to a commentator that November, "The other house [Drury Lane] has no company at all, and unless a new play comes out on Saturday revives their reputation, they must break."[3] Lincoln's Inn Fields's failure to do much recruiting for more than three seasons suggests that they considered the situation temporary.

Despite its makeshift theatre and management by committee, the Lincoln's Inn Fields Company seems initially to have run pretty smoothly.

In view of Betterton's nearly lifelong responsibility for management, one tends to assume that he controlled the business, but the sharers' agreement made him no more than first among equals. Verbruggen reported that he "ingaged himselfe as a sharing Actor & Manager" when he joined Lincoln's Inn Fields, and later in the same document he referred to himself as "assistant Manager to Mr Betterton" (see Appendix E). Testimony from authors, both happy and disgruntled, suggests that from the first Mrs Barry's contribution was especially important in the search for new plays. Cibber confirms this picture in general, while also suggesting problems to come in the "Commonwealth": "Many of them [the senior actors] began to make their particular Interest more their Point than that of the general: and though some Deference might be had to the Measures and Advice of *Betterton*, several of them wanted to govern in their Turn, and were often out of Humour that their Opinion was not equally regarded" (*Apology*, 1:228). We have no specific evidence who the disgruntled shareholders were. Like Davenant's company, the New Theatre kept its arguments to itself and appears to have been stable in the first years after the rebellion.

In contrast, the Patent Company was operating on the basis of a carefully defined hierarchy. Rich controlled finances absolutely, and employed George Powell as his "commanding Officer" (in Cibber's phrase) during the first three seasons after the rebellion, as might be expected from Powell's eagerness to replace Betterton.[4] He had charge of rehearsals and repertory and apparently tried to live up to the Betterton model, not only as leading man but as a script reviser and as the company's principal script reader. He had the unenviable job of keeping his actors at work when Rich could not—or did not—pay them. On one occasion (if Cibber's memory is accurate) this was a period of six weeks.[5] Powell was initially overjoyed by what he conceived as his victory over Betterton,[6] but he soon began to neglect his job. He had a drinking problem, and he suffered from the same kind of petty jealousy which caused Doggett to walk out of Lincoln's Inn Fields in 1696. Cibber says:

I have known in our own Company this ridiculous sort of Regret carried so far, that the Tragedian has thought himself injured when the *Comedian* pretended to wear a fine Coat! I remember *Powel*, upon surveying my first Dress in the *Relapse*, was out of all temper, and reproach'd our Master [Rich] in very rude Terms that he had not so good a Suit to play *Cæsar Borgia* in! though he knew, at the same time, my Lord *Foppington* fill'd the House, when his bouncing *Borgia* would do little more than pay Fiddles and Candles to it. (*Apology*, 1:228)

Cibber neither liked nor respected Powell, but other evidence seems to confirm his generally derogatory account. In 1702 "Critic" voiced the opinion that Powell was "an idle Fellow, that neither minds his Business, nor lives quietly in any Community."[7] Rich never functioned as an absentee landlord, however, and he kept his ragged company at work.

Even before competition resumed, both companies negotiated with people on the other side, as the crossovers in the spring of 1695 tell us. And despite the Lord Chamberlain's reiterated prohibitions of such meddling, both companies remained interested in talking with potential deserters from the opposition. The first major case involves the habitually malcontent Thomas Doggett. According to Cibber, Doggett "over-valued Comedy for its being nearer to Nature than Tragedy," and he "could not, with Patience look upon the costly Trains and Plumes of Tragedy, in which knowing himself to be useless, he thought were all a vain Extravagance: And when he found his Singularity could no longer oppose that Expence, he so obstinately adhered to his own Opinion, that he left the Society of his old Friends, and came over to us at the *Theatre-Royal*" (*Apology*, 1:229). This implies that the rebels did more tragedy than Drury Lane, but in new plays, at least, the evidence suggests otherwise. At any rate, on 3 April 1696 Doggett signed Articles of Agreement with Sir Thomas Skipwith, and a separate document which, in essence, offered him a descending scale of bribes for leaving the New Theatre by any one of several dates in the remainder of the 1695–96 season.[8] Doggett was unquestionably a valuable, experienced, and comparatively young comedian, a real loss to Lincoln's Inn Fields, and there are some indications that the rebel company went out of its way to keep him.[9] They presented Doggett's only play, a very lightweight farcical comedy, *The Country-Wake*, at just about the time he was signing articles with the Patent house. If Doggett had been agitating along the lines Cibber suggests, the company may have tried to pacify him by mounting his play, which had probably been refused by the United Company, since he admitted in the preface that he had written it three years before. Doggett was not appeased, however. He complained that his script "suffer'd in the Acting." The speaker called Sullen in *A Comparison* viewed the piece as typical of actors' efforts at writing, but reported that it was "Not then directly Damn'd, because he [Doggett] had a part in't."[10] Without his performance to carry it, the play dropped out of the repertory. Lincoln's Inn Fields may have considered itself well rid of him, despite his undeniable genius as a comic actor. He caused trouble at the Patent house almost immediately, and the Lord Chamberlain had to issue an order for his arrest for desertion on 23 November 1697.[11] He appears not to have worked in the London theatre again until he rejoined Lincoln's Inn Fields in 1700.

John Verbruggen also changed houses. A manuscript addition to the Clark Library copy of the *Post Boy* for 26–29 September 1696 reports: "Some say Mr Vanbrugen who abused Sir Tho. Skipwith and thereupon occasioned a quarrell between him & Mr Boile has not since appeared on ye stage." An undated and incomplete Lord Chamberlain's order from about this time says that "Mr Van Bruggen . . . hath violently assaulted [blank] Boyle . . . and hath with reproch full & scandalous words & speeches abused Sir Thomas Skipwith Baronet," and in consequence he is forbidden to act in any theatre until further order.[12] This suspension—if actually implemented—must soon have been lifted, since Verbruggen appeared in at least two new plays that fall. On 19 October he signed the preface to *Brutus of Alba* with Powell, and seems to have been serving as a member of the Patent Company, but on 26 October the Lord Chamberlain issued an order:

Haveing heard ye differences between ye Comoedians of both Theatres it appeared that both ye Companies had seduced Actors Mr Doggett from ye Theatre in Lincolns Inne feilds and Mr Vanbruggen from the pattentees Contrary to Theire owne Articles and my Orders pursuant thereunto I doe therefore hereby Order for this time onely that Mr Vanbruggen shall remaine to act with the pattentees untill the first day of January next (that they may in the meane time provide themselves of others to Act his Parts). . . . And for ye future my Orders [against seducing actors] . . . shall be punctually observed.[13]

For Verbruggen to create Loveless in the first production of *The Relapse* after he had signed a contract with Lincoln's Inn Fields was no doubt awkward. We have no indication who replaced him in the role.

Who made the first move in Verbruggen's "seduction" is an interesting issue. In his petition of 1703 he claimed that Lincoln's Inn Fields approached him as a replacement for William Smith, but this seems questionable. That document greatly overstates the rebels' immediate need for him: "Sheweth/That Mr William Smith One of the cheife Actors & Sharers of the Company in Lincolns Inn Fields dying about Michaelmas 1696 & the Company being in great distress for one to performe his parts your petitioner [Verbruggen] upon their extraordinary sollicitations & promises Withdrew himselfe by the Lord Chamberlains leave from the Company in Covent Garden" (see Appendix E). Smith's death is firmly dated December 1695 by a newspaper obituary. The New Theatre continued to act vigorously through the rest of that season, and they continued to rely on their standard repertory in the fall of 1696, without Smith. If the cooperative was so desperate to replace him that they had to make Verbruggen an offer too attractive to turn down, why did he wait until a new season had started before attempting to withdraw from the Patent Company? A more likely explanation is that in 1696 Verbruggen quarreled with Skipwith, was reprimanded, sought work with his old comrades at Lincoln's Inn Fields, and was released by the patentees on account of the riot he had caused. He was certainly more of a loss to Rich than a gain to Lincoln's Inn Fields, though his youth was good for the rebel company.

Colley Cibber was an off-season transfer—though he allowed himself to be bought back by Rich. Cast lists, official documents, and Cibber's own *Apology* give the impression that he was a faithful member of the Patent Company from the time he joined the London theatre until the protounion of 1706. The preface to his *Woman's Wit* (1697) indicates, however, that he had worked at Lincoln's Inn Fields during the summer of 1696. "During the time of my Writing the two first Acts, I was entertain'd in the New Theatre, and of course prepar'd my Characters to the taste of those Actors. . . . In the middle of my Writing the Third Act, not liking my Station there, I return'd again to the Theatre Royal." Rich apparently heard of this script in progress and was alarmed at the prospect of losing his most successful actor-author. On 29 October 1696, just three days after the Lord Chamberlain's ban on "seducing" actors and two days after Verbruggen had concluded an agreement with the New Theatre, Cibber signed a contract that bound him to write exclusively for the Patent Company as long as he remained a member of it.[14] This agreement was entirely separate from his actor's articles, except in coordinating the two obligations. The terms, while surprisingly generous in monetary matters, did prevent Cibber from having anything to do with the other company if he wanted to keep his job at Drury Lane. He agreed to give *Woman's Wit* to Drury Lane; not to publish it until at least a month after the production opened; to reserve first refusal on all plays he might write in the future to Rich; and finally, he agreed not to write anything for any rival company. That Rich would go to such lengths to retain his services as a writer on the basis of a first effort indicates how rare a commodity promising playwrights were at this time. Lincoln's Inn Fields had evidently made an effort to lure Cibber away, and Rich had to make it worth his while not to desert.

Several minor people switched companies between 1695 and 1697–98, apparently without the Lord Chamberlain's permission, since that officer kept reiterating his prohibition.[15] Mr Eldred moved from Lincoln's Inn Fields to the Patent Company during 1695–96, but seems to have quit within the year. Mr Pate also returned to the Patent Company; he was a popular singer, and hence was something of a loss to the New Theatre, but not a serious or irreplaceable one. Mrs Ayliff and Richard Leveridge sang at both houses to begin with, but later worked exclusively for Rich, who quickly came to realize the value of music as an attraction. Michael Leigh and Elizabeth Willis migrated the other direction, to Lincoln's Inn Fields. Both companies also lost or fired minor people, who then left the theatre altogether. Each lost a man by death: Smith died in December 1695; Horden was killed in a duel in May 1696. On the whole, the evidence indicates that both houses were at least willing to hear malcontents from the other side, and sometimes to make them an offer. How actively they tried to "seduce" actors from each other we cannot determine: Doggett's is the only absolutely clear case, and he proved little help to the Patent Company.

The core acting companies at both houses remained quite stable during these three seasons. One pattern at Lincoln's Inn Fields, however, plainly spelled trouble: the sharing actors were giving scant opportunity for advancement to their junior people. Minor actors were kept on call, and the theatre did employ special singers and dancers. But none of the junior people was allowed to move up to important roles in new plays (which are basically the only ones for which we have casts). Hirelings had traditionally been given Lenten plays and summer productions in which to learn their trade, and the best of them were gradually integrated into the main company. But there is no evidence that Lincoln's Inn Fields was looking out for its future this way: the elder actors were hanging onto their jobs with grim tenacity. This pattern of exclusion probably goes back to the last years of the United Company, and may have been one of the motives for the abortive mutiny led by Doggett and Bowen in 1693. For a brief time Lincoln's Inn Fields could get away with such stasis and complacency. But for the long-term future of an already elderly company, change and recruitment would be required. More immediately, such lack of opportunity was to create a morale and discipline problem: young actors had no lack of opportunity at Drury Lane. Unfortunately, the senior actors at Lincoln's Inn Fields had lost any sense of a future for the company beyond their all-too-mortal ends.

II
COMPETITIVE DEVICES
AND STRATEGIES

In the first hectic days of renewed competition in the spring of 1695 the Patent Company set about a campaign of harassment and burlesque. Cibber tells us how the company decided

to steal a March upon the Enemy, and take Possession of the same Play the Day before them: Accordingly, *Hamlet* was given out that Night to be Acted with us on *Monday*. The Notice of this sudden Enterprize soon reach'd the other House, who in my Opinion too much regarded it; for they shorten'd their first Orders, and resolv'd that *Hamlet* should to *Hamlet* be opposed on the same day. . . . When in their *Monday*'s Bills it was seen that *Hamlet* was up against us, our Consternation was terrible, to find that so hopeful a Project was frustrated. In this Distress, *Powel* . . . immediately called a Council of War, where the Question was, Whether he should fairly face the Enemy, or make a Retreat to some other Play of more probable Safety? It was soon resolved that to act *Hamlet* against *Hamlet* would be certainly throwing away the Play, and disgracing themselves to little or no Audience; to conclude, *Powel*, who was vain enough to envy *Betterton* as his Rival, proposed to change Plays with them, and that as they had given out the *Old Batchelor*, and had chang'd it for *Hamlet* against us, we should give up our *Hamlet* and turn the *Old Batchelor* upon them. . . . The Curiosity to see *Betterton* mimick'd drew us a pretty good Audience, and *Powel* (as far as Applause is a Proof of it) was allow'd to have burlesqu'd him very well. (*Apology*, 1:204–7)

Such carryings-on would not long sustain the Patent Company, but they were a beginning.

At the outset of the 1695–96 season the Drury Lane group seems once again to have tried stealing a march—in this case, I would infer, by hurriedly mounting a production of Thomas Scott's *The Mock-Marriage*. The prologue to Lincoln's Inn Fields's first play of the fall, *She Ventures and He Wins* (acted by 19 September) says:

> We promis'd boldly we wou'd do her [the novice author]
>   Right,
> Not like the other House, who, out of spite,
> Trump'd up a Play upon us in a Night.
> And it was scarcely thought on at the most,
> But Hey-Boys, *Presto*! conjur'd on the Post.

Another example of the aggressiveness of the Patent Company seems to be a clear case of theft. Mrs Pix asked George Powell to consider her play, *The Deceiver Deceived*, for Drury Lane. Powell claimed that she withdrew it, reneging on a definite commitment for a production; her version of the incident implies that he refused the play. In any case, early in the fall of 1697 Drury Lane mounted Powell's *Imposture Defeated*, a play so much like hers that Powell attempted in his preface to deny having stolen it. The resemblances of plot and even character names are too close to be a coincidence. Lincoln's Inn Fields reacted to this piece of skulduggery with some tough tactics of its own. According to an anonymous pamphleteer, the rebel actors, led by Congreve, tried to make a faction against the play. Congreve "was seen very gravely with his Hat over his Eyes among his chief Actors, and Actresses, together with the two She Things, call'd Poetesses, which Write for his House . . . they fell all together upon a full cry of Damnation, but when they found the malicious Hiss would not take, this very generous, obliging Mr Congreve was heard to say, We'll find out a New way for this Spark, take my word there is a way of clapping a Play down."[16] In the event, neither play did very good business.

Sparse records prevent our analyzing competition on a day-to-day basis, but we can see a number of exchanges by looking at the types and timing of new plays. A lighthearted comedy with a generous dose of music, like *Love's a Jest* (Lincoln's Inn Fields, ca. June 1696), might provoke a reply like *The Cornish Comedy* (Patent Company at Dorset Garden, ca. late June 1696). The exceptional success of *The Relapse* at Drury Lane (by 21 November 1696) may well explain why the rebel company mounted *The City Lady* so hastily in December.[17] Rich's response to the popularity of a masque, *The Loves of Mars and Venus* (Lincoln's Inn Fields, by 14 November 1696) was to mount *Cinthia and Endimion* the next month. Exotic locations are a part of the heroic play and naturally reappear with its revival. *Ibrahim* (Drury Lane, May 1696) matches the Near Eastern setting of *The Royal Mischief* (Lincoln's Inn Fields, ca. April 1696).

Competition meant war, and both companies scrambled to find ways to pull in an audience. Drury Lane exploited burlesque; Lincoln's Inn Fields developed the double bill. Since Powell considered the senior actors' style dated, personal burlesques of Betterton and Mrs Barry (in particular) were a natural continuation of his alternating attempts to imitate them or surpass them. The personal burlesque combined with the rehearsal play gave Drury Lane actors a chance to show off in their own persons, as well as a chance to distort and exaggerate their rivals' habits. *The Female Wits* (ca. September 1696) capitalized on the uproar Mrs Manley caused by taking *The Royal Mischief* away from Drury Lane when it was already in rehearsal the preceding spring. Part 2 of Vanbrugh's *Aesop* is another burlesque of the senior actors.

Drury Lane was counting on two factors to make these shows work. Obviously a clever satire by impudent youngsters could amuse the town in passing. The burlesque approach also reinforced another Drury Lane strategy—promoting its actors' personalities. Audiences went to Lincoln's Inn Fields to see Betterton and his comrades play their roles, but they could also be induced to come to Drury Lane to see Jo Haynes play himself. Flippant references to Powell's drinking or Mrs Lucas's love of coffee have little to do with their talents or abilities as actors, but such bits of information do impress on the audience the persona of a Powell or a Haynes. This sort of publicity seeking can be valuable to a company, and it is less directly parasitic than the old King's Company burlesques. The drawback to it, at least in the form of full-length plays, is that as their topicality fades, so do those parts of the repertory. When Doggett walked out of the London theatre, or Haynes died, their personae did not get passed out to the actors who inherited their roles.

Why did Lincoln's Inn Fields not reply in kind? The answer is simple: the rebels seem to have adopted the pose that they were ignoring the Patent Company's existence. Not only did the young rivals offer fewer objects to satirize, but to make fun of them would have given them more attention than the New Theatre cared to bestow. In fact, of course, both houses were acutely aware of the competition.

The specialty that Lincoln's Inn Fields developed during these first years was the double or multiple bill, represented by *The Anatomist*, played with *The Loves of Mars and Venus* (November 1696), and Motteux's combination of one-act pieces, *The Novelty* (June 1697). The veteran actors may have recalled the success Davenant had had with such ventures early in the Restoration. Why the patentees did not immediately copy this inexpensive, popular form of show remains a mystery, except that Motteux, who had a knack for integrating music with his comedies, worked for the rebels at this time. The pattern these combinations established was easily stretched to include "great scenes from favorite plays" on a single bill and the "short plays plus concert" format that turns up in the next few years. This tendency toward fragmentation did English drama no service—but as a stopgap, multiple bills brought in immediate profit from a small investment.

A number of elements in the turn-of-the-century theatre lent themselves readily to use as competitive devices. Prologues and epilogues, song and dance, and scenery were all exploited. Moreover, during the difficult 1697–98 season, Rich initiated a new tactic—use of animal acts and circus performers.

A survey of prologues and epilogues to new plays in this period is one way of gauging the rivalry between the two theatres. The Patent Company made a habit of referring to a state of "warfare." The prologue to "Powell's" *Bonduca* is an example of the fad:

> Between us and the other Theatre
> There is proclaim'd, and still maintain'd a War,
> And all, but knocking out of Brains, is fair.

Oroonoko and *Neglected Virtue* have such prologues, and the epilogue to
Cinthia and Endimion carries on the theme.[18]

In contrast, during 1695–96 the senior company put on an air of
being shocked by the rudeness of Drury Lane's approach to what they
imply should have been gentlemanly competition. Part of their superior
pose included derogatory remarks about the operation of the Patent Company. But the rebels maintained their aloof attitude by restricting their
comments to the sorts of plays their rivals produced, and the quality of
their productions; they seldom descended to personal references. Thus
the tone of the prologue to *She Ventures and He Wins* (quoted above)
managed to convey both the unsportsmanlike conduct of the reported
Drury Lane maneuver and the ludicrousness of the idea that a quickly
"trump'd up" show could compete with Lincoln's Inn Fields. Other prologues with similar references are those to *The Anatomist*, *The Innocent
Mistress*, and the commendatory poem printed with *Heroic Love*. Such
sophisticated thrusts were maddeningly difficult to parry, and Drury
Lane responded childishly, belittling the senior actors in the prologue to
Bonduca, for example:

> To us, Young Players, then let some Smiles fall:
> Let not their dear Antiquities sweep all.
> Antiquity on a Stage? Oh Fye! 'tis Idle:
> Age in Good Wine is well, or in a Fiddle.
> Ay then it has a little Musick there;
> But in an Old, Decrepid, Wither'd Player;
> It looks like a stale Maid at her last Prayer . . .
> . . . .
> Therefore divide your Favours the right way,
> To th' Young your Love, to th' old your Reverence pay.

The best-known example of vitriol from Drury Lane was spoken by Powell before *The Fatal Discovery*:

> We pluck the Vizor off from t'other house:
> And let you see their natural Grimmaces
> Affecting Youth with pale Autumnal faces.
> Wou'd it not any Ladies Anger move
> To see a Child of sixty five make Love.

Oh! my Statira! Oh, my angry dear,   (Grunting like Betterton.
Lord, what a dismal sound wou'd that make here.
                                            (Speaking like a Christian

The play referred to is Nathaniel Lee's *The Rival Queens*, which Cibber tells us Betterton revived with great success after the death of Mountfort and played until he found that the role was too much strain for his advancing age. Even if this derogatory picture were an accurate account of Betterton in the mid-nineties, we must not overlook the fact that he continued to play this role and others for which he was overaged, apparently to the satisfaction of his audience.

A remarkable number of epilogues delivered by female members of both companies hold out the fairly explicit, if teasing, promise of sexual favors in return for approval of a play. Mrs Bracegirdle, a professional virgin, used this ploy at the end of *The She-Gallants* (December 1695) to try to sell an old-style comedy. However much the "Sparks" she addressed may have enjoyed her challenge, the play, "offending the Ears of some Ladies who set up for Chastity," soon "made its Exit."[19] Both houses proceeded to increase the titillating effect by having their "little girls" prattle about what audience member should someday have their maidenheads. Miss Howard at Lincoln's Inn Fields spoke such an epilogue to *The City Lady* (December 1696). Miss Cross regularly delivered these pieces at Drury Lane.[20] The smutty epilogue, though not a new device, had quite a vogue in these years—a peculiar convention to flourish side by side with Jeremy Collier.

Song and dance made up an increasingly large part even of regular plays at the end of the century.[21] A large—though unfortunately undeterminable—number of employees of both houses were hired primarily or exclusively for their talents in these areas. Their names appear in records and in cast lists for masques and similar pieces, but not in *dramatis personae* of regular plays. For these specialties the theatres began importing foreign artists. Both Downes and incidental records indicate that the practice became standard around this time. *The London Stage* lists a Mr Sorin in the Lincoln's Inn Fields company roster for 1695–96 and the next season, calling him "dancing-master." The *Biographical Dictionary* cites the negotiations with this Frenchman as the beginning of what later turned into an enormous financial drain on the rebels.[22]

Competition became fierce in this area only in 1697–98 and thereafter, so I will deal with the subject further in chapter 5. Most singers early in the renewed competition were homegrown and home-trained, but as Italian music became better known in London, more and more performers attempted it and sought the training to handle it. The increasing popularity of concerts outside the theatre and the availability of special performers inspired the use of much more music and dance in regular plays than had hitherto been customary. Powell added their drawing power to his *Cornish Comedy* and *Imposture Defeated*—indeed, he says that the latter was "purely design'd for the Introduction of a little Musick." Both companies also used their singers and dancers in masques. *Love's Last Shift*, *Imposture Defeated*, and *The Relapse* all have short masques interpolated or tacked on at the end. Lincoln's Inn Fields also presented commemorative masques. As a special attraction in the fall of 1695 they did a short "Musical Entertainment" called *The Taking of Namur and His Majesty's Safe Return* to celebrate King William's victory.[23] Their contribution to the entertainment at Court on the King's birthday in November 1697 was a masque called *Europe's Revels for the Peace*. Neither of these pieces is as long as one act of a standard play, so that if they were performed in the public theatre (as apparently they were), they must have constituted only part of a bill.

These elements, in addition to the full-length masques, are important signs of a division of interests between music lovers and drama patrons. Managers used larger and larger amounts of music in the hope of attracting concertgoers back to theatre. Imported compositions, techniques, and eventually performers also helped educate the audience toward the interest in Italian opera which developed after 1700.

Scenery, which should have helped make up for some of the Patent Company's deficiencies, instead appears to have hurt them. Rich first attempted to reuse stock pieces—as had been the custom—but lacking a good showman who could combine and retouch them effectively, he got only shoddy results. The best that can be said for productions like *Philaster*, *Bonduca*, and *Brutus of Alba* is that they were cheap to put on. The rebels sneered at this travesty of the great Betterton style: "what we call a Masque some will allow/To be an Op'ra, as the World goes now."[24] Somebody's criticism must have stung Rich, because he then swung round to the other extreme. In late June 1697 the Patent Company made its first serious attempt to capitalize on its right to Dorset Garden by mounting a new opera. Settle's *The World in the Moon* was advertised (with some exaggeration) as having revolutionary scenery (*Post Boy*, 12–15 June). The script itself is an interesting experiment: it combines the rehearsal play and the city comedy mode, rather than being a solemn tragicomedy, as most previous operas had been. About specific differences in the design and presentation of the scenery we know little, except that the designs were clearly meant to top Betterton's last efforts at Dorset Garden. The epistle dedicatory says, "the Model of the Scenes of this Play, are something of an Original: I am sure I have removed a long Heap of Rubbish, and thrown away all our old *French* Lumber, our Clouds of Clouts, and set the Theatrical Paintings at a much fairer Light." Sybil Rosenfeld has speculated that the great innovation might have been a variety of the new form of perspective like that which Andrea Pozzo illustrates in his *Prospettiva dei Pittori e Architetti* (1700). She also demonstrates that the dimensions quoted in the libretto are not significantly larger than for other Dorset Garden operas.[25] Some parts of the scenery are reminiscent of Betterton's great shows, and some costumes may have been reused, no great claims having been made for new clothes.[26] In a great burst of patriotism, the epilogue claims that the piece is "All from an *English* Web, and *English* Growth."

Regardless of the exaggerated claims made in its behalf, the opera appears to have done much more poorly than it deserved. Part of the reason, Settle concedes, was the summer premiere. Less experimental productions had often taken longer to build and paint than anticipated, and if the designs were truly revolutionary—or even if the construction began from scratch—the scenery may have delayed the opening. In dedicating the published play to Rich, Settle goes out of his way to excuse the timing: he says he wishes "to tell the World, That never was such a Pile of Painting rais'd upon so Generous a Foundation; especially under all the Hardships of so backward a Season of the Year (our Misfortune, not Fault)." At least two Lincoln's Inn Fields comments make fun of the production, so it apparently did not appeal enough even to be revived profitably in the fall.[27] Moreover in the spring of 1698 with much less fanfare, we find the Patent Company using Drury Lane, not Dorset Garden, for a transplanted French opera, and no more is heard of "native" English scene design.

Both the experiment and, later, the return to French styles cost the Patent Company money, and these losses may well explain why in the fall of 1697 we get from Lincoln's Inn Fields the first cries of amazement and shocked disbelief over circus acts in the theatre. The prologue to *The Unnatural Mother* (ca. September 1697) says:

> The Stage is quite debauch'd, for every Day
> Some new-born Monster's shown you for a Play;
> Art Magick is for Poetry profest,
> Horses, Asses, Monkeys, and each obscener Beast,
> (To which *Egyptian* Monarch once did bow)
> Upon our English Stage are worship'd now.

Referring in part to the theft of Mrs Pix's play, the prologue to *The Deceiver Deceived* (November 1697) says:

> Deceiv'd Deceiver, and Imposter cheated!
> An Audience and the Devil too defeated!
> All trick and cheat! Pshaw, 'tis the Devil and all,
> I'll warr'nt ye we shall now have Cups and Ball; [i.e., jugglers]
> No, Gallants, we those tricks don't understand;
> 'Tis t'other House best shows the slight of hand:
> Hey Jingo, Sirs, what's this! their Comedy?
> *Presto* be gone, 'tis now our Farce you see.

Doubtless these transplants from Bartholomew Fair cost less than French dancing masters, and they obviously appealed to part of the audience.

An unnoticed reference to advertising practices deserves some mention here, since it suggests that competition raged in playbills as well as on the stage. In a commendatory poem printed with Granville's *Heroic Love*, Dryden makes several derogatory remarks about the state of theatre in general but includes a slap at Drury Lane in particular. To the aspiring playwright he says:

> thy blooming Age
> Can best, if any can, support the Stage:
> Which so declines, that shortly we may see,
> Players and Plays reduc'd to second Infancy.
> Sharp to the World, but thoughtless of Renown,
> They Plot not on the Stage, but on the Town,
> And in Despair their Empty Pit to fill,
> Set up some Foreign Monster in a Bill.[28]

Had Drury Lane followed Lincoln's Inn Fields's usual practice and ignored the poem, we would be little the wiser. But George Powell was sufficiently stung to reply to what he describes as "a late notoriously famous piece of Rhime." Powell points out that "If it be any suck [*recte*, such] Capital Blot in a Play-house Bill to set up a great Name, to help a small Audience, I would fain ask him, if his Ancient Spectacles, so Critical upon Our House Bills, are not a little oversighted at Theirs," since, he says, the other company has used patrons' names, and specifically that of the Comptroller of the Temple.[29]

Powell's outburst is of some interest because of the practice it implies, and we can identify the "monster" in this case. A coy report in the *Post Boy* for 13–15 January 1698 announces *The Prophetess* at Dorset Garden, "at the request of a Nobleman; they will not tell us who, but we presume for the Entertainment of a very great Foreigner." And Luttrell duly notes that Peter the Great "is this night at the playhouse incognito to see the Prophetesse acted."[30] Thus only six months after the revolutionary *World in the Moon*, the Patent Company had returned to Betterton's landmark production, the showpiece called for by courtiers detailed to entertain Peter the Great.

Here we find the playhouse managers seizing on extraneous attractions—even members of the audience—to try to fill their theatres. Curiously enough, neither house had yet thought of advertising on their posters the authorship of the plays they performed—an omission which tells us something about the unliterary way in which plays were still then regarded.[31]

III
WRITERS AND REPERTORY

The advantage in old plays clearly rested with Lincoln's Inn Fields. The Patent Company had to fill huge gaps in casts and re-rehearse almost any play they wanted to perform. Lincoln's Inn Fields was under less immediate pressure to mount new plays: in these three years they did about nine new shows each season. The Patent Company began with *seventeen*, then dropped to ten, then to eight—in addition to working up an unknown number of old plays. A disturbing number of the new plays failed at both houses. The division of 1695 provided the first real market for new plays since 1682, and no new generation of professional play-wrights had grown up to replace the Carolean generation. Etherege, Shadwell, Otway, Behn, and Lee were dead. Dryden and Wycherley were no longer writing plays. Crowne was sick; Banks and Settle were tem-porarily inactive. Southerne was in the process of retiring. Durfey and Ravenscroft were elderly hacks. Motteux was a promising young Hu-guenot refugee with a knack for pastiches and musical additions. Con-greve was the only tested, professional playwright fully active as of the 1695–96 season—and he was to write just two more plays.

Both companies were forced to accept plays refused by the United Company years earlier, since neither had a satisfactory source of supply. For the first time in many years the recreational efforts of gentleman amateurs and women had a real chance of production. Women writers tended to favor the New Theatre, especially after Drury Lane ridiculed them in *The Female Wits* (ca. September 1696). Lincoln's Inn Fields also benefited from the Barry-Bracegirdle tandem, which encouraged writers to produce villainess-and-pathetic-heroine vehicles for them. Vanbrugh was the first major dramatist to appear after the rebellion. His basic allegiance before 1700 was to Drury Lane, Skipwith being a patron of his; but he also gave the rebel company one of its most important plays.[32] Both houses mounted so many scripts tacked together by actors that to mention the fact became a condemnation. Powell wrote and cribbed for Drury Lane, and Jo Haynes probably supervised *The Female Wits*.[33] Dog-gett and Joseph Harris each had undistinguished works done by Lincoln's Inn Fields. Colley Cibber was the one actor who went on to produce durable scripts for his company, but he also had several failures in the first years of his career.

Scholars have tended to assume that part of the rebels' difficulties acquiring scripts resulted from their cavalier treatment of writers. The most damaging single complaint, that of David Craufurd in 1700, will be dealt with in chapter 5. However, we may observe at this point that neither company treated second-rate authors well. Mrs Manley's play, *The Royal Mischief* (ca. April 1696), was in rehearsal at Drury Lane when outbursts of temper from both actors and author resulted in her with-drawing the play. The comparatively young actors at the Patent house, who had not cut their teeth on seventies horror and heroic plays, found Mrs Manley's piece hard to take seriously. Feelings hurt, she stormed out, vowing never to work for them again. Powell's copying *The Deceiver De-*

ceived when he read it for Mrs Pix is hardly the way to encourage a writer. The record of one other instance of Drury Lane's mistreating a writer comes from *A Comparison between the Two Stages*.[34] Abstract and jesting, it nonetheless reflects something of the attitude toward amateurs held by both companies. The gist of the story is that the actors contrived to make an unidentified gentleman amateur spend a great deal of money on food and drink to convince them to present his play. By the time he had jollied them along through rehearsals and paid incidental expenses, the production had cost him nearly as much as he made on his benefit night—so he took his next play to Lincoln's Inn Fields, where he made six times the profit. The anecdote may be an exaggeration of a true story, or as much a joke about gullible authors as about Drury Lane. Would-be writers were not always reasonable, of course. Robert Gould's satiric poem "The Play-House" had referred abusively to Betterton and Mrs Barry in the 1680s, but he assumed good will on their part when he offered them a play in 1695. When "The Mighty Actress" told him she was "not so good a Christian as to forgive" him, he was surprised and indignant, and went away to revise the poem to be even more scathing.[35]

As the following survey makes painfully clear, both companies suffered from the lack of good new plays. Judging the success of a play is difficult before the institution of daily ads. Contemporary commentary is sparse at best. Downes is some help with Lincoln's Inn Fields plays, but we have no comparable source for Drury Lane. Authorial pride or pique can make prefaces and dedications tricky guides. Evidence of performance after the initial run is a great help if we have it: plays which did not do passably well simply did not enter the repertory. Sparse records make evaluation of head-to-head competition difficult. One of the few cases in which we have a clear example of response to a successful production concerns Congreve's *The Mourning Bride*. The thirteen-day original run specified by Downes lasted from ca. 20 February to ca. 11 March 1697. An enthusiastic audience member reported to the future Vice-Chamberlain Coke that the house "was full to the last."[36] The Patent Company countered with four plays. *The Triumphs of Virtue* is a tragicomedy similar in type to Congreve's play and seems obviously intended as a rival. *A Comparison* tells us that it was a flat failure. Rich then turned to satire, adding the second part of Vanbrugh's *Aesop* to his bills—a direct hit at the senior actors. Its success is unknown, but apparently it did not pull people away from *The Mourning Bride*. Around the end of the run we find performances of *The Prophetess* and the operatic *Indian Queen*, both Dorset Garden spectaculars. We have no way of knowing just when the Patent Company worked up *The Prophetess*, but there is a fine irony in their running Betterton's own show against him. As in the sixties, a popular attraction at one house could empty the other of audience. However bad the available new plays might have been, the two companies had little choice but to mount them.

My survey of repertory is confined to new plays after the first season of competition, because records of revivals are too incomplete to tell us much. In distinguishing genre I have followed Hume's categories, especially his distinction between the old "hard" comedy of the Carolean period and the "new" styles (humane and reform comedy) which flourished at the end of the century. Where there is any evidence to suggest success or failure I have used it, but in some cases we simply have no way to tell how a show did.

1695

Lincoln's Inn Fields opened in April 1695 with *Love for Love*. Downes says of it, "this Comedy was Superior in Success, than most of the precedent Plays . . . being Extraordinary well Acted . . . it took 13 Days Successively." Cibber adds that the rebels "had seldom occasion to act any other Play 'till the End of the Season."[37] Lincoln's Inn Fields probably mounted *Troilus and Cressida* (for which Eccles, their house composer, reset a song), and *Tyrannick Love* (for which Purcell wrote songs sung by Mrs Ayliff and Bowman) about this time. If a reprint of *The Conquest of Granada* in 1695 is associated with a revival, the rebel company was probably the venue, since it is a kind of drama despised by Powell.

The Patent Company's offerings for the tag end of this season are less certain. All we can say with assurance is that there are no signs of a success comparable to Congreve's play. According to Skipwith and Rich's answer to Sir Edward Smith's suit in 1704, the treasurer's records indicate the company performed eighty-four times between March and July 1695.[38] Cibber tells us that they opened with Mrs Behn's *Abdelazer* (1676). He also implies that *Hamlet*, *Julius Caesar*, and *Othello* were among the classics immediately essayed by Drury Lane. "*Shakespear* was defac'd and tortured in every signal Character—*Hamlet* and *Othello* lost in one Hour all their good Sense, their Dignity and Fame. *Brutus* and *Cassius* became noisy Blusterers, with bold unmeaning Eyes, mistaken

Sentiments, and turgid Elocution!"[39] *Hamlet* and *Othello* were reprinted in 1695, which strengthens the likelihood that Cibber was not collapsing time in this case. Among other reprints not entered in the *London Stage* calendar for lack of a specific date, *The Devil of a Wife* was probably a Patent Company show: Griffin and perhaps Freeman of the original cast belonged to that company. A song for Mrs Cibber ties Otway's *Don Carlos* to the Patent Company, as does a song for Miss Cross in *The Tempest*.[40] From Cibber we also learn that Powell's ambition to replace Betterton extended to *The Old Batchelour*, a script more appropriate on the whole to the younger company. The bills reportedly advertised "The Part of the *Old Batchelor* to be perform'd in Imitation of the Original."[41] Since Drury Lane had to learn and rehearse productions, and since Lincoln's Inn Fields had to dress every show, probably not much variety was offered at either house that first spring.

1695–1696

The pattern of productions in 1695–96 is instructive, despite all its gaps. Lincoln's Inn Fields relied heavily on stock plays, while searching for promising—or even possible—new scripts. The Patent Company, by contrast, had to take whatever plays it could find and mount them in a hurry. Plays which were reprinted this season are in most cases not assignable to either company.

The New Theatre mounted seven new comedies in 1695–96. *She Ventures and He Wins*, a comedy of example written by a woman who remained anonymous, was sponsored by Mrs Barry. It failed so completely that the company stopped playing temporarily.[42] *Lover's Luck* is a comedy in the "mixed" mode, the first play written by Thomas Dilke. He bubbles over with enthusiasm in his epistle dedicatory at "The Generall Approbation the Town has been pleas'd to afford me," but as far as we know, the play was a one-season success. Downes says it "fill'd the House 6 Days together, and above 50*l*. the 8*th*, the Day it was left off."[43] *The She-Gallants*, a play George Granville claimed to have written as an exercise twelve years earlier, is a dated, hard-style comedy—which probably contributed to its failure. As a favor to an old friend, the company mounted *The Husband His Own Cuckold*, by Dryden's son, John Jr., who was also encouraged by Sir Robert Howard. The play has the spirit of Carolean comedy, with a new reform-style ending grafted on. We have no record of its reception nor of a revival. Two actors had comedies staged at Lincoln's Inn Fields this season. Joseph Harris's *The City Bride*, a lightweight adaptation from Webster, was "Damn'd" according to *A Comparison*. Doggett's *The Country-Wake* is an old-fashioned sex farce which was a moderate success during the brief period Doggett remained with the house. He played the show in his tours, but it was not a stock play in London. The most interesting of the New Theatre's comedies is Motteux's experimental *Love's a Jest* (June 1696), basically a new-style play, but with a great deal of interpolated music. Motteux claimed in his preface that it was an "extraordinary Success," and he is confirmed by Downes's report that it "got the Company Reputation and Money."[44]

Lincoln's Inn Fields mounted only two new tragedies. Banks's *Cyrus the Great* was a United Company reject, described by Hume as "the worst of the late heroic love-and-drivel mode." When William Smith died on the fourth day, Downes records that the play closed, never to be acted again.[45] The company seems to have retreated to stock tragedies until Mrs Manley transferred *The Royal Mischief* from Drury Lane. An extravagantly histrionic villainess, exotic Near Eastern setting, and complex staging (by the standards of their theatre) would probably have attracted the veteran actors even if they had not showed up their rivals by doing the play. The mystery is that Mrs Manley ever offered it to Drury Lane. Though it had a reasonable first run, it was not revived.[46]

Christopher Rich and his financial partner Skipwith operated the Patent house 214 days in 1695–96, for which we have only a few identifiable productions.[47] Of seven new comedies at Drury Lane, only Cibber's play, *Love's Last Shift* (January), was a real success. Thomas Scott's *The Mock-Marriage* and Mrs Pix's *The Spanish Wives* probably had adequate initial runs, and the latter got into the repertory: we have performances recorded 2 February 1699 and 14 July 1703. Four of the comedies were flat failures: *Don Quixote*, part 3 (a play so coarse it may have helped draw an official censure);[48] Powell's *The Cornish Comedy; The Younger Brother* (an attempt to trade on Aphra Behn's name);[49] and Mrs Manley's *The Lost Lover*.

The Patent Company tried seven new tragedies, of which only Southerne's *Oroonoko* became a stock play. That Dryden's protégé should give a play to the company with which his mentor was feuding was an unexpected piece of luck: with *Love's Last Shift*, it saved their season. Mrs Pix's *Ibrahim*, in the heroic-pathetic verse mode, brought them moderate success, but Norton's stoic *Pausanias* failed. Robert Gould says that *The Rival Sisters* "was kindly receiv'd," but the play was not revived, and he is a particularly unreliable reporter where his own work is concerned. For Mrs Trotter's *Agnes de Castro* we have no records. We do know that the company also revived Lee's *Caesar Borgia* and Banks's *Vertue Betray'd*.[50] *Neglected Virtue*, brought to the stage by Hildebrand Horden, is said in the dedication to have had an "unpleasant" reception, run down by "those wide-mouth'd Curs, the Criticks." Thomas Scott's adaptation of Fletcher's *A Wife for a Month* as *The Unhappy Kindness* is said in the preface to have met with "little Encouragement."

Trying to capitalize on its theatres, the Patent Company mounted three "operas." *The Indian Queen*, long-delayed, is the kind of Dorset Garden show to which visiting dignitaries were treated in the nineties: it was performed regularly for some time.[51] *Bonduca* and *Philaster* are cheap adaptations which did not flourish. Powell brags that *Bonduca* was "studied up in one Fortnight." The prologue tells us that Rich, or at least his actor-manager, understood their competitive advantages and disadvantages:

> Besides, though our weak Merit shines less Bright,
> Yet we'ave the Advantage, a Fairer Light,
> Our Nobler *Theatre's*. Nay we are bringing
> Machines, Scenes, Opera's, Musick, Dancing, Singing;
> Translated from the Chiller, Bleaker *Strand*,
> To your Sweet Covent-*Garden's* Warmer Land.

However, something fancier than these retreads was needed.

The senior actors had plenty of old shows in repertory to ease them through the expensive first season, and while none of their new offerings made remarkable returns, stock plays ought to have given them decent receipts. Their biggest success, *Love's a Jest*, was a harbinger to be followed in the coming years. The Patent Company experimented far more than its rival, both in the number and kinds of plays produced—seventeen new productions as against nine. The combination of new forms and new actors naturally resulted in some failures. But *Oroonoko* and *Love's Last Shift*, brilliant successes, and the operatic *Indian Queen*, proved Rich's company a viable operation. The prologue to Settle's adaptation of *Philaster* turns their circumstances into a plea for tolerance:

We're tender Buds, till you the Lords o'th' Soil
Warm us to Life by your Auspicious Smile.
The Elder Heroes of the other Stage
Were Striplings once of our young Beardless Age;
And to Perfection did not leap, but climb:
Merit's the Product of long Growth and Time.
Who push for Fame by fair Degrees must strike;
A General in the Field has trail'd a Pike.
Grant us this first our Tryal-Year alone;
Eexpect [*sic*] Performance when our Wings are grown:
Let our Pen-feather'd Strength this Favour borrow,
Only to Creep to day, and Soar to morrow.

1696–1697

Comedies again constituted the majority of new productions at Lincoln's Inn Fields. Indeed the company tried only two new tragedies. Filmer's stoic *The Unnatural Brother* lasted just three days, according to the preface, which adds that the author's friends told him French sparseness was out of fashion. Congreve's one essay into serious drama, *The Mourning Bride*, immediately became a stock play. The company attempted five new comic productions. They refurbished Fletcher's *Rule a Wife*, which had been a staple of Betterton's early career, though according to the edition of 1697 he did not act in the revival. Dilke's *The City Lady* (ca. December 1696), a lively new-style comedy, written and produced in haste, ran into unexpected trouble. The dedication tells us that "The tedious waiting to have the Curtain drawn, after the Prologue was spoke, occasion'd by Mr. *Underhill*'s violent Bleeding, put the Audience out of Humour." Presumably his indisposition was sudden, and the audience did not know what was happening, since he had not appeared in the prologue. The hemorrhaging was serious enough to keep Underhill from performing, and the rest of the company was so unnerved that "scarce any thing was done but by Halves, and in much Confusion." Dilke singles out Mrs Barry as having maintained her poise and given a good performance in spite of the situation. But the disgruntled audience damned the play out of hand, and it only limped through a third night.[52] Underhill had recovered from whatever ailed him by May, but for four months during the height of that season the company staged no new comedies.

Vanbrugh contributed *The Provok'd Wife* to the New Theatre's stock comedies in April 1697. The play is a type which appealed to the veterans, an old-style satirical investigation of marital discord. Durfey's *The Intrigues at Versailles*, which marks Underhill's definite return to the stage in May, is another old-style wit comedy, though a very talky one. Like *The Provok'd Wife*, this play probably reflects the preferences of the elder actors, but it was not revived so far as we know and must be accounted a failure. Mrs Pix gave Lincoln's Inn Fields a successful new-style comedy, *The Innocent Mistress,* which Gildon calls a "good Success, tho' acted in the hot Season of the Year."[53] The company also did well with some experiments following the pattern of *Love's a Jest* the previous season. An odd double bill, Ravenscroft's farce, *The Anatomist*, and Motteux's masque, *The Loves of Mars and Venus*, appealed to both theatre and concertgoers. Gildon credits "the Advantage of the excellent Musick" with the "extraordinary Success" of the experiment.[54] Then just before summer heat and the Long Vacation emptied the City, Motteux fitted together a pastiche called *The Novelty—Every Act a Play*. He took short pieces from a couple of friends, condensed the last part of the failed *Unnatural Brother*, and added a masque of his own. The preface implies a run of at least six days, since the author got two benefits. This suggests that Sullen's "every Word stolen, and then Damn'd," in *A Comparison*, may be a misleading exaggeration; but we have no record of revivals.

By contrast, the Patent Company offered few comedies and managed only one success in three tries. *The Relapse* saved the house in November 1696 and became a perennial favorite. Their other comedies failed. Despite the brave front Cibber puts on in the preface to *Woman's Wit, A Comparison* says "Damn'd"; Cibber left the script out of his *Collected Plays*; and it was apparently never revived. James Drake felt that his *Sham Lawyer*, however poor a play, did not get a fair chance: he published on the title page the legend: "As it was *Damnably* Acted at the Theatre-Royal."

Rich also offered one new tragedy and a tragicomedy this season. Gildon's *The Roman Bride's Revenge* came and went quickly. An anonymous tragicomedy, *The Triumphs of Virtue,* forms part of Rich's efforts to counter the success of *The Mourning Bride*. We know of two and probably three other plays running opposite Congreve's tragedy, so we may assume that this piece did not survive the contest.

The theme of the Patent Company's miscellaneous works this season is satire and self-promotion. *The Female Wits* ran six days, but then, the preface implies, the New Theatre used its Court leverage to have the mock-heroic piece suppressed. It was not published until 1704, and we know of no later performances. *Aesop*, a series of tableaux to frame the fables, opened in the fall and generated a topical second part by spring. *A Comparison* calls *Aesop* one of the three "Masterpieces" that sustained the Patent Company in its early years.[55] Finally, John Dennis contributed a play that uses Drury Lane and the Patent Company's own actors as part of its setting. *A Plot and No Plot* made a good vehicle for Jo Haynes, even if Dennis did not carry out his idea with much imagination. Hot weather reportedly lowered attendance, and although the play did well initially, there is no further record of it.

In the fall the patentees mounted another cheap opera, Powell and Verbruggen's reworking of *Brutus of Alba*. The dedication confidently invites "visitors" for two benefit performances, but the next month the prologue to Lincoln's Inn Fields's *The Anatomist* implies that *Brutus* failed. Speaking of the typical amateur playwright, it says:

> With that, he writes a thing, which we refuse,
> Then, wondring how we durst affront his Muse,
> Strait in a huff he gives it t'other House;
> Who either slight it, or 'twill be its Lot
> To get as much as their last Op'ra got.

Rich had cut corners by reusing scenery, machines, and costumes from *Albion and Albanius, Psyche*, and even *The Tempest*;[56] but the attempt is further evidence that the Patent Company was aware of the potential value of Dorset Garden. However, their next opera, *Cinthia and Endimion* did not use much machinery. A line on the title page claims that it had been designed for Court presentation before the death of Queen Mary, which would account for its fairly plain staging. (The Court theatre could not match Dorset Garden in scale or equipment.) *A Comparison* makes fun of Durfey's pretensions and concludes with its usual judgment, "Damn'd." The Patent Company's major experiment of the 1696–97 season (discussed above) was a bravura attempt to replace the French-derived Betterton style of scene design in opera. *The World in the Moon* opened late in June and failed, and the company spent the next season struggling to recoup their losses.

This season the score card adds up even more in favor of the rebels than last: they had more successes and fewer failures than the Patent Company. Lincoln's Inn Fields added three successful plays to their repertory as compared with two for their rivals, and they made no foolish investments like the Settle extravaganza. An unhealthy sign at the New Theatre is the company's apparent reluctance to encourage a replacement for Underhill. The patentees did well with two Vanbrugh plays, *The Relapse* and *Aesop*, but played only two hundred days between October and July.[57] Overall the Drury Lane Company is the one in trouble after two full seasons of competition. The rumors of collapse in November 1696 concerned them, not Lincoln's Inn Fields, and it was Drury Lane which risked a disastrous speculation at the end of the 1696–97 season.

1697–1698

In this season Lincoln's Inn Fields clearly shows a dangerous inclination toward stasis. Only two new plays appear to have succeeded, yet the company mounted only nine. Whether by chance or as a reflection of taste, two were comedies, seven tragedies. The first of their new comedies was Mrs Pix's *The Deceiver Deceived*. Her preface complains, not directly of Drury Lane's alleged piracy, but of a libelous faction against her play which spoiled its reception. The prologue, which outlines the theft, apparently had not succeeded in drawing her the sympathy of the audience. Dilke's *The Pretenders*, a light satire akin to the country comedy mode, also seems to have failed.

The veterans mounted a villainess tragedy set in Siam, *The Unnatural Mother*, a showpiece for Mrs Barry. By Lincoln's Inn Fields's standards, the production was elaborate, but the play was apparently not very well received. We have no record of the success of Ravenscroft's brief *The Italian Husband* or Mrs Trotter's *Fatal Friendship*, but lack of revival suggests little success. *A Comparison* reports failure for Motteux's *Beauty in Distress* (his first venture into serious drama), and Mrs Pix's historically inclined *Queen Catharine*. On the plus side of the tally Downes tells us that Granville's *Heroic Love*, a pseudoclassical tragedy, was "Superlatively Writ; a very good Tragedy, well Acted, and mightily pleas'd the Court and City."[58] Downes and *A Comparison* agree that Charles Hopkins's heroic tragedy *Boadicea* did well. The prologue to that play suggests, however, that Lincoln's Inn Fields was feeling a bit haunted by the failure of so many new productions.

Do you not wonder, Sirs, in these poor Days,
Poets should hope for Profit from their Plays?
Dream of a full Third Day, nay, good sixth Night,
(Especially considering how they Write.)
But so it is; and thus I go to show it,
Wo to us Players, every one turns Poet.

. . . .

Though you hate Blood-shed, out of pure good Nature,
As Poets, Criticks, or as Fops hate Satyr
Be not to Day afraid to see us Bleed,
But let for once, a Tragedy succeed.

Beneath the bantering tone there is a sour sense of growing problems.

Playing 202 days, the Patent Company was having its troubles too.[59] It offered only two full-length new comedies. Durfey's *The Campaigners* failed, if we may believe *A Comparison*, despite a carefully laundered ending. Powell's supposedly plagiarized *Imposture Defeated* lasted more than 5 days, according to its preface, but then sank from view. The one lasting comic success at Drury Lane was *The Country House*, a two-act farce translated from French by Vanbrugh—testimony to the move toward double bills. In tragedy the Patent Company tried *The Fatal Discovery*, a cheap shocker full of incest, rape, murder, and suicide. Audience reaction is unknown, but it was not revived. Crowne's predictably stoic *Caligula* was not very successful. Gildon refurbished an old French opera, *Phaeton*, which his dedication admits was something less than a wild success; *A Comparison* says "damn'd." Phillips's *Revengeful Queen* appears to have failed. William Walker, a gentleman amateur, caused gossip by appearing in an old-fashioned heroic tragedy he had written himself, called *Victorious Love*. Interestingly, he speculates in his preface that Lincoln's Inn Fields might have given it a better production.

This was a bad season for both houses. The Patent Company was recuperating from its fiasco with *The World in the Moon*. Lincoln's Inn Fields simply appears lethargic. Perhaps, as Cibber suggests, the elder actors were increasingly resting on their reputations. Neither company had a major success or added a stock mainpiece to its repertory—a depressing return on fifteen new shows. Nonetheless, it is important to notice that the two most successful new plays of the season—*Boadicea* and *Heroic Love*—were both Lincoln's Inn Fields productions.

Cibber tells us that after the initial triumph of *Love for Love* the rebels' fortunes quickly declined: "they went on with Success for a Year or two."[60] And by early 1697, he reports, the Drury Lane Company "began to be look'd upon in another Light; the late Contempt we had lain under was now wearing off." The success of *Love's Last Shift, The Relapse,* and *Aesop* had indeed kept Drury Lane alive. But the implication of a quick shift in the balance of power is misleading—a product of Cibber's complacent hindsight. The New Theatre had no reason to be unduly troubled about Drury Lane's successes: with a tremendous advantage in the standard repertory shows, the veterans were much less dependent on finding popular new scripts immediately. Conversely Rich, better capitalized, could better afford to ride out hard times and failures (though his employees suffered).

The key to the whole theatrical situation is simple: Drury Lane *survived*, and Lincoln's Inn Fields was forced to revamp and plan for a longer haul—a process which will be analyzed in the next chapter. By hook and crook Rich held his group together. Cibber reports that he

would laugh with them [his actors] over a Bottle, and bite them in their Bargains: He kept them poor, that they might not be able to rebel; and sometimes merry, that they might not think of it: All their Articles of Agreement had a Clause in them that he was sure to creep out at, *viz.* Their respective Sallaries were to be paid in such manner and proportion as others of the same Company were paid; which in effect made them all, when he pleas'd, but limited Sharers of Loss, and himself sole Proprietor of Profits; and this Loss or Profit they only had such verbal Accounts of as he thought proper to give them. 'Tis true, he would sometimes advance them Money (but not more than he knew at most could be due to them) upon their Bonds; upon which, whenever they were mutinous, he would threaten to sue them. (*Apology*, 1:252–53)

Rich also managed not to give any dividends to the other Patent Company proprietors and even succeeded in not paying rent to the owners of Dorset Garden between 1695 and 1704.[61] The consensus, both then and now, is that he was salting away a good bit of money during at least part of this time. Initially the venture cannot have been profitable, but he did keep the patent alive during the years in which his company was growing up. By 1699–1700 they achieved ascendancy. Nonetheless their reputation was not really secure as of the 1697–98 season. The "warfare" between the theatres, as we have seen, initially existed largely in the minds of Patent Company writers and actors. The stream of belittling prologues came mostly from one direction. The burlesque in *The Female Wits* and the habit of "mimicking" Betterton are good evidence for the dominance of Lincoln's Inn Fields.

A great cliché requires examination at this point. The New Theatre is supposed to have suffered, almost from the start, from the effects of decrepitude and dissension. The charge of overripeness is based on such comments as Aston's that Betterton played Hamlet too long, and Powell's prologue to *The Fatal Discovery* in which he sneers at the old actors' "Affecting Youth with pale Autumnal faces" (1697). The image of Betterton, aged seventy-four, tottering through the 1709 benefit *Love for Love* as the youthful Valentine, is so grotesque to modern readers it tempts us to see his last fifteen years this way.[62]

No one seems to have remarked, heretofore, that the new plays at Lincoln's Inn Fields contain rather few old characters. Betterton and his leading ladies, themselves no teen-agers, could thus appear to best advantage, establishing the age range themselves, not having to look young in comparison to much younger actors. Until about 1700, when the older men in the company began to retire, and Betterton had to appear more and more with actors thirty and forty years younger than he, the problem was relatively well disguised.

For the other charge, we can say only that through the 1697–98 season there are no signs of dissension at the New Theatre. The previous year had brought successes in *The Anatomist, The Provok'd Wife,* and *The Mourning Bride*; the failure of most new plays in 1697–98 was not encouraging to a shoestring operation, but if anyone was in real trouble that season, it was Drury Lane. The Patent Company had found their bent with *Love's Last Shift* in the first winter. Contrary to Cibber's suggestion, they seem by November 1696 to have been in desperate straits, until *The Relapse* saved the house and *Aesop* gave them a further boost. In this context Rich's mounting an operatic extravaganza looks like a sign, not of prosperity, but of the gambler's heavy plunge—the sort of thing we saw the United Company do in the early 1690s when it was in trouble and hoped to recoup with one great triumph. Rich's instinct may not have been wholly wrong. The town was running mad after concerts,[63] and spectacle was the one area in which the Patent Company had a potentially insuperable advantage. But the expensive and embarrassing failure of *The World in the Moon* rocked what little stability the company possessed. The 1697–98 season brought no good new plays, and we can see signs of basic insecurity. The prologue to *The Fatal Discovery* (February 1698) contains not only Powell's disparagement of the veterans but also this telling admission:

> Now you must know, I've heard some people say,
> Should this House fail, where do you think to Play?
> Why thus, in short, my answer I declare,
> If we must be o'ercome, I will take care
> Never to be their Prisoner of War:
> Nor Tug an Oar at the New Theatre.

Had the company been reasonably prosperous, Powell would not have been referring to its possible collapse. Later that spring when William Walker had his play staged at Drury Lane, he felt constrained to defend himself for doing so. "I am blamed for suffering my Play to be Acted at the Theatre-Royal, accus'd of Foolish Presumption, in setting my weak Shoulders to Prop this Declining Fabrick, and of affronting the Town, in Favouring whom they Discountenance."[64] This scarcely suggests that Drury Lane was taking the lead.

A most interesting (and hitherto unnoticed) sign of trouble is the appearance of the "distress benefit" at Drury Lane in June 1698. For example, *The Plain-Dealer* is advertised on 2 June, "the Profits of the Play being given for the Release of a distressed Gentleman from Prison." When this custom begins to show up regularly at both houses in the spring of 1700, *The London Stage* editors conjecture that it represents an effort at public relations, designed to counter legal and moral attacks on the theatre. This is very likely—but probably only a partial explanation, in view of the seasonal nature of the phenomenon. Houses tended to be thin in May and June. When a manager did not expect to make his expenses (£30–£35 a performance by this time), a benefit cost him nothing. If the charitable enterprise drew a good audience, he lost only a profit he would not have made otherwise—and he saved himself an anticipated loss. If receipts covered only house charges, then the object of the benefit got nothing, and the manager was none the worse for having advertised it. Thus the distress benefit can be construed as insurance against loss. The company had to operate: better operate gaining nothing than expecting to run at a loss.

The whole country was in poor financial shape in the mid-nineties.[65] As usual, the theatres' fortunes reflect social-political stress. And by the spring of 1698 moral reformers were concentrating their efforts against the stage. Scholars since Joseph Wood Krutch have known better than to suppose that Jeremy Collier came out of nowhere to smite the theatres. His *Short View of the Immorality, and Profaneness of the English Stage* was only the high point in a rising clamor of protests. But the number of individuals who responded to his book in prefaces and pamphlets shows just how threatened the writers and actors felt. They had reason to panic. On 12 May 1698 Luttrell reported a "presentment" by the justices of Middlesex, not only against the playhouses and their actors, "but also [against] Mr Congreve, for writing the Double Dealer; Durfey, for Don Quixot; and Tonson and Brisco, booksellers, for printing them." For the first time since the 1660s, there was serious talk of closing the theatres altogether.[66]

In the midst of these excitements, trends in the drama became obscured. But the degree to which a phase of English drama was over will become increasingly plain in the course of the next three chapters. The Stuart Court theatre was dead, although this fact was not comprehended by either writers or managers in the late 1690s. The upsurge of interest in new plays when competition resumed in 1695 appears to be a sign of renewed vigor—until one sees how very few of these plays managed a decent inaugural run, let alone survived into another season. When Rich started adding animal acts to his offerings he was admitting that plays alone were not enough. Betterton's company held out for a season, but in the spring of 1699 they imported the French dancer Balon: not even the veteran actors were filling a theatre any longer. The audience of habitual theatregoers proved too small to support both houses, and the managers had to turn to special attractions, medleys, and circus acts.

Chapter 5

Cutthroat Competition, 1698–1702

THESE years represent the darkest period for the English theatre since the Commonwealth. Neither house enjoyed financial or artistic success. The movement to reform the stage gained widespread support within the audience; simultaneously, the theatres suffered an active campaign of legal harassment from reforming groups like the Societies for the Reformation of Manners and the Society for the Promotion of Christian Knowledge. Talk of closing the theatres altogether was in the air. More immediately, the increasingly tense political situation had an adverse effect on theatrical business, prompting discussion of a new union. Under these circumstances expensive competition naturally damaged both houses, and it comes as no surprise when, after the 1701–2 season, signs of a *modus vivendi* start to appear.

I
Management, Theatre Buildings, and the Climate of Public Opinion

The Lincoln's Inn Fields Company literally went to pieces in these years. At some point between 1698 and 1700 (impossible to determine exactly) the cooperative management lapsed into chaotic dissension, and Betterton had neither the authority to restore order nor the ability to reason the company back into concerted effort. Cibber reports that

[Barton] *Booth*, who was then a young Actor among them, has often told me of the Difficulties *Betterton* then labour'd under and complain'd of: How impracticable he found it to keep their Body to that common Order which was necessary for their Support; of their relying too much upon their intrinsick Merit; and though but few of them were young even when they first became

113

their own Masters, yet they were all now ten Years older,[1] and consequently more liable to fall into an inactive Negligence, or were only separately diligent for themselves in the sole Regard of their Benefit-Plays; which several of their Principals knew, at worst, would raise them Contributions that would more than tolerably subsist them for the current Year. (*Apology*, 1:315)

This selfishness was the opposite of cooperation, and by April 1699 the company was publicly admitting the results. In the epilogue to *The Princess of Parma* Mrs Bracegirdle spoke of the fallen fortunes of the company and described a "frightful Dream": the New Theatre reconverted to a tennis court.

> I Dreamt, this House, for want of due Support,
> Once more was turn'd into a *Tennis Court*;
> Methought—
> Our Neighbouring Foes Unrivall'd now Commanded,
> And most of the Stage Forces were Disbanded:
> Some of the Men, to Strole, were gone together;
> Some of the Women to Act—Heaven knows whither;
> Stage Wars were ceas'd, both Houses shrunk to One,
> And all Expensive Foreigners were gone.
>
> . . . .
>
> For want of Choice, methought some Curs'd the Players;
> Some went to Puppet Shews—Nay, some to Prayers:
> No Rake cou'd Jaunt from House to House for Doxies,
> And what was worse, No Beaux cou'd Bilk the Boxes.
> But Drudging Players were Bilk'd of half their Pay,
> All Poets of their Sixth, and some of their Third Day . . .
>
> . . . .
>
> How think you this wou'd please the Town?
> Tis what you must Expect, if we go down.

Such warnings served no practical end. The actors continued their slovenly ways, and the audience increasingly favored Drury Lane. Betterton himself acknowledged the preference in the prologue he spoke to Gildon's adaptation of *Measure for Measure* (February 1700):

> To please this Winter, we all Meanes have us'd;
> Old *Playes* have been Reviv'd, and New Produc'd.

But you, it seems by *Us*, wou'd not be Serv'd;
And others Thrive, while we were almost Starv'd.
Our *House* you daily shun'd, yet Theirs you Cram'd.
And Flock'd to see the very *Plays* you Damn'd.
In vain you Prais'd our Action, and our Wit;
The best Applause is in a Crowded Pit.
In vain you said, you did their *Farce* despise;
Wit won the *Bays*, but *Farce* the Golden Prize.

Sneers at the quality of the opposition's scripts did not make up for laziness and dissension in the veteran company.

The most notorious instance of demoralization at Lincoln's Inn Fields can be dated about May 1700. David Craufurd's preface to *Courtship A-la-mode* tells us that he took the play to Lincoln's Inn Fields, but after six weeks of "sham Rehearsals" with insolent and inattentive actors he withdrew it and took it to Drury Lane, where it was "Plaid in less than twenty days." The chaos at Lincoln's Inn Fields described by Craufurd suggests that the company was in a deplorable state by the summer of 1700. We should probably note that the play was a poor one, and that according to *A Comparison* the company only accepted it under pressure from "a certain *Scotch* Lord."[2] Nonetheless, the situation as Craufurd reports it sounds intolerable, and early in the next season outside intervention was required.

Lord Jersey took office as Lord Chamberlain in June 1700, and by November he felt obliged to step in and restore some semblance of order at the New Theatre. At whose behest he inquired into the company's circumstances we do not know. The move was most unusual and bespeaks the inability of the members of the cooperative to come to any workable agreement by themselves. On 11 November Jersey issued the following "Orders for ye Play house in Lincolns Inn Fields:"

Whereas I am informed there are frequent disorders among ye Actors of his Majesties Company of Comoedians in Lincolns Inn Fields, to ye great prejudice of ye said Company, for want of sufficient Authority to keep them to their Duty: For ye better Government thereof of [*sic*] ye said Company for ye time to come I do hereby appoint Mr Thomas Betterton to take upon him ye sole management thereof, with power to reward those who are diligent, and to punish such as he finds negligent in their business, according to ye Orders which are & shall be made for ye good Government of that House, and to direct everything in ye best manner he can, for ye benefit, and advantage of ye said Company: Provided that all money to be laid out for cloths, scenes &c be ordered only by the Consent, and agreement of ye Majority of Sharers as formerly, except where it shall happen, that for ye immediate service of ye Company, any thing may be found wanting, that then Mr Betterton may in such cases, be att Liberty to lay out any sum not exceeding forty shillings. (P.R.O. LC 5/153, fol. 23)

The importance of this official intervention and the significance of some of the details have not been understood even by those scholars who know about the order. Neither Lowe nor Nicoll deals with the implications.[3] The authors of the *Biographical Dictionary* do not take its date into account, and they weigh Craufurd's testimony heavily against Betterton. Professor Kenny says dismissively that the "change . . . did not improve the management notably because of his [Betterton's] incompetence as a manager."[4]

As we will see, this conclusion is inaccurate. In assessing what Betterton was and was not able to accomplish, we should take into account the exact nature of the powers bestowed on him. Basically, the Lord Chamberlain gave him the right to fine negligent actors and give bonuses where deserved. He was *not* given sole authority to choose and mount new productions, and he was explicitly forbidden to make large financial commitments without the sharers' permission. The pitiful state of the company is clearly shown in the Lord Chamberlain's insistence that Betterton be "att Liberty" to lay out two whole pounds when immediately necessary. All larger sums still required "Consent, and agreement of ye Majority of Sharers as formerly." Apparently the actors could not agree to put current funds back into productions, and so the group was suffering from an acute shortage of capital. The ludicrousness of the forty-shilling limit is reinforced by recollecting that Betterton had been able to pour as much as three and four thousand pounds into his United Company opera productions. No doubt that had been foolhardy, but what condition is a theatre in if sums under two pounds are grounds for dispute? What Betterton gained in November 1700 was power to insist on discipline, not overall direction and control of the sort he had once exercised over the Duke's and United companies.

Although the powers granted him were thus limited, Betterton evidently set to work immediately to use the carrot and stick of bonuses and fines to straighten out the mess. By December 1701 (a year later) Mrs Bracegirdle could speak the epilogue to Rowe's *Tamerlane*, confidently acknowledging that though the house had nearly sunk, it was now reviving. In the intervening year the company mounted only eight new plays, none of them a major success. The basis of whatever solvency Betterton could claim in December 1701 must have come from better handling of the standard repertory and improved discipline.

We have too little evidence about the repertory even to speculate on what the company did, much less how it arrived at those decisions. We should note, however, that the Lincoln's Inn Fields company roster had undergone marked attrition in the years 1698–1700. The core of the company (the original sharing actors) remained intact: the major actresses continued to shine, and even the roster of minor women remained surprisingly stable, considering that they were of childbearing age. Other groups show considerable changes. Adjunct employees, the singers and dancers whose names appear in only one season, either left the stage by choice or simply were not rehired. (Very few of them changed companies.) Singly, these people were probably not paid much, but cumulatively their departure must have meant some saving. More important, the old guard and some promising younger men among the supporting actors had retired or gone to Dublin by 1700–1701: Scudamore, Thurmond, Trefusis, Kynaston, and Sandford all were gone. The next season Joseph Harris and John Hodgson disappeared. Whether this was due to inadequate pay or old age we cannot always determine.

These retirements necessitated extensive recasting and a certain amount of type shifting. As I pointed out in chapter 4, Mrs Barry had already begun to play mature and older women. Between 1698 and 1700 Betterton too at last turned to older parts—for example, in *Love's Victim*, *The Ambitious Step-Mother*, and *Henry the Fourth*. To maintain any balance at all in casts, he had to take some senior roles. To replace the seven men who had left by 1700 Betterton had on hand William Bowen, long a major supporting actor, and four other reliable minor actors: Arnold, Bailey, Freeman, and Knapp. These men already had parts in the stock plays. As Betterton turned to older roles, the greatest weakness in this company was young dramatic leads. Evidently the second-string males were just not up to such roles. In the fall of 1700, by contrivance or happy coincidence, Betterton acquired exactly what he needed to stabilize the company. Barton Booth came over from Ireland, young, eager, and tractable. Simultaneously, Powell decamped from the Patent Company, where Wilks (who had come from Dublin the previous year) was gaining on him fast. Powell was not the most desirable personality to bring into the house, but he had experience, he was the right age, and he had talent, if he could be persuaded to use it. Betterton may have, in legal parlance, "seduced" Powell from the Patent Company, but Powell was ready to move. Cibber says he left in a temper on account of Wilks.[5] We have no way of knowing what salary Betterton offered Powell (Cibber implies he was supposed to be making at least £4 per week from Rich), but neither do we have any recorded complaints on the subject. Printed casts prove Cibber wrong when he says that Powell stayed at the New Theatre only one year (1: 239): he did not rejoin Drury Lane until June 1704.

With Powell's arrival, Lincoln's Inn Fields once again had a workable range of ages and abilities. However, certain financial adjustments were necessary. Even with dead wood cut and retiring actors not replaced, the shrunken company was having trouble making a living wage. Powell surely did not come cheap. The newly promoted third-rank actors almost certainly expected to be paid more, while the original sharers naturally held fast to their shares and control of the profits.

Some of these readjustments were already in process by the fall of 1700, and we may guess that the turmoil which caused the Lord Chamberlain to step in that November was in part connected with disputes concerning rank and pay in the reshuffled company. We possess no back-stage gossip on details (Cibber being a member of the other house), but one piece of evidence is suggestive. William Bowen, a volatile actor of Irish descent, was one of the few people named in the Lincoln's Inn Fields license who had remained with the company as a hireling, not a sharer.[6] For ten years he had played fops like Witwoud in *The Way of the World* and fools like Francis the Drawer in *Henry the Fourth*. In mid-November 1700 he abruptly left the theatre. The *Post Boy* of 14–16 November reported: "We hear that this day Mr. William Bowen, the late famous Comedian of the New Playhouse, being convinc'd by Mr. Collier's Book against the Stage, and satisfied that a Shopkeeper's life was the readier way to Heaven of the two, opens a Cane Shop . . . in Middle-Row, Holborn. . . . This sudden Change is much admir'd at." We may doubt the sincerity of this supposed conversion, since he was acting again by March. Significantly, however, this withdrawal occurred within days after

Betterton had been granted operational control of the company. Bowen probably felt that his pay and status ought to be higher, but evidently he overvalued himself, for his holdout brought him no concessions. Rather surprisingly, he was allowed a benefit at Lincoln's Inn Fields in March. The *Post Boy* of 1–4 March says: "We are informed that the famous Comedian Mr. William Bowen, who has for some months discontinued acting on account of some Difference between him and the rest of the Sharers of the New Theatre, is to have the Committee . . . play'd at the said theatre for his benefit. . . . It is reported that after this performance which is to be his last on the English Stage, he designs for Ireland." After the benefit, and after various rumors or announcements that he would go to Ireland, Bowen instead moved to Drury Lane in June 1701. Why would the shaky New Theatre let a good actor go over to the opposition? Two reasons seem likely. John Bowman played a similar line, so Lincoln's Inn Fields could spare the temperamental Bowen, though they would miss his youth. Second, from their viewpoint Bowen would not greatly benefit Drury Lane, since Cibber already reigned as fop supreme in that company. From the patentees' side, Bowen may have been able to convince Rich that he was capable of a greater range of parts than he had been allowed; and even if he proved to be limited, taking a well-known actor from the rebels was still something of a coup.

Lincoln's Inn Fields reached its lowest point in the spring of 1701. Betterton even inquired discreetly whether the Patent Company would entertain the thought of a new union. The discussions, if the proposal got as far as discussion, must have taken place in February and March 1701. Both houses mention the possibility. The prologue to Mrs Trotter's *The Unhappy Penitent* (premiered 4 February 1701 at Drury Lane) says:

> But now the peaceful Tattle of the Town,
> Is how to join both Houses into one,
> And whilst the blustering hot-brain'd Heroes fight,
> Our softer Sex pleads gently to unite.

The epilogue "Sent by C. V." for Mrs Pix's *The Double Distress* (Lincoln's Inn Fields, ca. March 1701) likewise supports the proposal and works the idea of a union into an elaborate metaphor of commerce. The passage quoted above suggests that Drury Lane gave the idea some attention. We may guess though that most writers, mindful of hard times under the old United Company, viewed the notion with disfavor. In "A *Prologue* on the propos'd Union of the Two Houses" Farquhar objects:

> If we grow one, then Slavery must ensue
> To Poets, Players, and, my Friends, to you.
> For to one House confin'd, you then must praise
> Both cursed Actors, and confounded Plays.

He concludes by saying, "leave us as we are."[7] For whatever reason, the possibility of a new union came to naught. Because the suggestion is buried in obscure prologues and epilogues and nothing came of it, many stage historians have overlooked the incident.[8] In context it has rather more importance. For Lincoln's Inn Fields to contemplate the idea indicates just how bad the situation had become at that house. Betterton had officially held control for only three and a half months, scarcely time to redirect the energies of a willing troupe, much less those of his quarreling partners.

When Betterton reassumed such power as he was given in November 1700, he must have seen that active measures would be necessary. Discipline had to be restored, but beyond that the company could no longer afford to rest complacently on its glorious past. Betterton evidently tried to cut basic operating costs where possible, but as we will see in section II, he also persuaded the company to spend a great deal of money on guest artists—entirely too much, no doubt. The most spectacular example is Mme Subligny of the Paris Opéra, who danced briefly at Lincoln's Inn Fields in the early months of 1702, commanding the same extravagant price her fellow celebrity Balon had received in 1699, four hundred guineas. The company could not really afford that rate, whatever corners were cut. Mme Subligny proved a great attraction, but not great enough to offset her price.[9] Partly as a means of covering such expenses, Betterton hired almost no new actors during the next two seasons. The company agreed to restrict itself to inexpensive productions, and they depended on stock plays for the bulk of their repertory. To some extent the company's new casts would have revitalized its old productions, reducing the necessity of staging new plays. In 1701, however, Lincoln's Inn Fields's problems remained obvious and acute.

By 1700 the veteran company must also have realized their dire need of better quarters. The Patent Company had not expired in confusion and vacated its theatres, as the rebel actors had probably once expected, and the increasingly shaky cooperative was in no position to finance a new building. Theatre historians except Hotson have had little to say about this situation, but around the turn of the century the Lincoln's Inn Fields Company had a chance to return to Dorset Garden, and they also made a serious effort to lease Drury Lane.

The patentees seem to have lost legal control of Dorset Garden in July 1699, a fact which has hitherto escaped notice.[10] Dorset Garden stood on ground owned by the Earl of Dorset. The patentees paid the 1696 ground rent to his agent, a Mr Shepheard, nearly a year late. Around the end of 1697 Shepheard refused (as it were) to extend them further credit. When the Earl realized that the rent was in arrears, he immediately got a court order evicting the patentees from the theatre, which in fact they seldom used, and on which they were paying no building rent. In July 1698, after they had failed to vacate, Dorset "caused an entry to be made on the premisses," and placed an agent there to watch the building for him. Objections on both sides were heard by the Court of King's Bench in Easter Term, 1699, and Rich later conceded that a judgment was found against the patentees. The last performance they admitted to giving at Dorset Garden was 19 July 1699. By 12 September, Tom Brown was writing his friend in the country that the strongman William Joy had taken over Dorset Garden—a comedown for the theatre also commented on in the prologue "By a Friend" to Farquhar's *The Constant Couple* that fall. Rich negotiated an agreement with Dorset in early December 1699, which renewed the old lease at the same rent on the condition that he would make up the arrears by Christmas. This, however, he reported he had failed to do. He did not state specifically that he lost possession of the theatre; but until 1706 we have no documentable performances there by the Patent Company.[11]

This raises an obvious question. Why did the Lincoln's Inn Fields Company not jump at the chance to move to Dorset Garden? After July 1699 the Earl of Dorset could presumably have agreed to let the building sharers (who had long gone unpaid by Rich) rent the theatre to the rebel company—and Dorset was their old friend and protector. The answer is probably a combination of three factors. First is timing. The veterans were in a state of demoralized disorganization in 1699 and 1700. Second, Dorset Garden had not been used regularly for theatre performances in many years, and was by this time in a state of poor repair. To make the theatre truly functional would have cost a good deal of money. This brings us to the third factor: the Lincoln's Inn Fields Company was in no financial position to incur such expenses. Had Dorset Garden been available in 1695, they might have included in their company structure some investors willing to underwrite the remodeling. But in 1700 they had no means to take on so large a project themselves, nor any easy way to include capitalists from outside. By the latter part of 1701 the company was shakily back on its feet—but by that time Betterton had his eye on a greater prize than Dorset Garden.

The Union of 1682 had included a nineteen-year lease on Drury Lane, which was due to expire 9 November 1701. Although Charles Killigrew's interests had clearly lain with the patentees in 1695, by 1700 he was suing them for back rent, and relations between them had grown less cordial.[12] Whether Betterton approached Killigrew or vice versa is not clear from the subsequent lawsuits, but Killigrew later testified that in the fall of 1701 he got an offer from someone other than the patentees to rent Drury Lane. He carried the offer to Rich, who refused

to take a new lease of the said Theatre and to pay such rent for the same as they [the stockholders] were offered by other persons and thereupon your Orators have entered into a treaty and are come to an Agreement which is duely executed under hand and Seale with T. Betterton gent and John Watson Citizen and Draper of London to lett a Lease of the said theatre to them for the Terme of ffive yeares to comence from Midsumer 1702 at and under the yearely rent of ffive pounds per diem for every day that any play shall bee acted in the said theatre.[13]

Killigrew naturally preferred Betterton's offer of £5 per acting day to the £3 Rich was in arrears with, but the patentees flatly refused to vacate Drury Lane even after their lease expired. Killigrew charged angrily that the patentees adopted stalling tactics and threatened countersuits "to make them [the stockholders] spend as much or more moneys then their demands shall amount unto before they shall recover [Drury Lane], and doe goe about to persuade the said Betterton & J. Watson not to performe the said Agreement." During the spring of 1702 Killigrew seems to have tried to buy up stock in the Drury Lane Company. He evidently hoped to arrange a controlling interest in the company: Rich was the principal stockholder and "managing partner," but he did not himself have a majority holding.

Killigrew may well have turned first to the actors. Cibber reports a very curious incident at just this time. Rich, he says, rarely paid his actors even half the money due to them, but

> I remember . . . he once paid us nine Days in one Week: This happen'd when the *Funeral*, or *Grief à la Mode*, was first acted, with more than expected Success. Whether this well-tim'd Bounty was only allow'd us to save Appearances I will not say: But if that was his real Motive for it, it was too costly a frolick to be repeated, and was at least the only Grimace of its kind he vouchsafed us; we never having received one Day more of those Arrears in above fifteen Years Service. (*Apology*, 1:263–64)

This burst of unwonted generosity was not the inexplicable event that Cibber's narrative makes it seem. Steele's first play had its successful run in late November or early December 1701—just at the time Rich had reason to fear that he might be turned out of his theatre or have his actors "seduced" away by the angry Charles Killigrew.

By March someone—probably Killigrew—was propagandizing the Adventurers. The *Post Man* for 5–7 March 1702 carried the following advertisement:

> If any Persons who have any Interest in the Joint Stock of the Playhouse in Drury Lane by any grant or purchase under the Patents granted from the Crown to Sir William Davenant or Mr. Killigrew, are willing to sell their said Interest, whether shares or part of shares arising by Profits of Acting in the said Playhouse, this is to desire all such persons to enter their names, their lodgings, what shares they have and the lowest price they will set at, with Mr. Thomas Hay near the Pump in Chancery Lane, and they shall be treated with for the same.

The results were apparently unsuccessful or inconclusive, but on 11 June 1702 a formal lease on Drury Lane was signed with Betterton and John Watson—which the patentees ignored. Less than a week after Betterton's lease was supposed to begin, Killigrew took the patentees to court, suing not for eviction but for rent due since the expiration of their lease. The distinction is important: Killigrew wanted his money, and he was entirely indifferent as to how he got it or from whom. Had he wished to force the issue, he could probably have seen Rich turned out of Drury Lane.

In the event, however, Rich cannily reviewed the claims of the various complainants, and bought off some of them (to whom he admitted arrears were owing), while refusing to pay the rest on the ground that their claims were unproven.[14] On 20 September 1703 Rich negotiated a new ground lease with the Earl of Bedford, the previous one having expired at Christmas 1702.[15] This put him in a position where he could force the building owners to remove their building if he wished. Rich had no desire, however, to erect his own building on the ground, and such radical measures proved unnecessary. Whether Killigrew ever got the rent due him is unclear, but obviously Betterton's lease on Drury Lane was useless. Nonetheless, Betterton's aggressive attempt to acquire a better theatre after he had been made manager suggests that he thought the company could be revived and that he expected it to stay in business.

Meanwhile the Patent Company had been through some tribulations of its own. Rich did not believe in paying full salaries, and though he made all financial decisions, he preferred to relay them through a manager, usually a leading actor, who could serve as a shield between himself and the rest of the company. An unpopular move like a salary reduction could thus be relayed through a fellow sufferer, and not come straight from Rich. Half pay was about the best Rich's actors could ever hope for, and he made a habit of playing one off against another. Cibber implies that this strategy was very much on Rich's mind when Powell returned to Drury Lane in 1704: Wilks's popularity and arrogance had increased, and Powell would serve to counterbalance him. Before 1700 when Powell was manager, he had also been a useful actor.

But *Powel*, it seems, had a still greater Merit to him, which was, (as he [Rich] observ'd) that when Affairs were in his Hands, he had kept the Actors quiet, without one Day's Pay, for six Weeks together, and it was not every body could do that; for you see, said he, *Wilks* will never be easy unless I give him his whole Pay, when others have it not, and what an Injustice would that be to the rest if I were to comply with him? How do I know but then they may be all in a Mutiny, and *mayhap* (that was his Expression) with *Powel* at the Head of 'em? (*Apology*, 1:255–56)

Rich's ability to trick and bamboozle his actors is made abundantly plain in 1699 and 1701 when the company was evidently convinced of the desirability of mounting operas—in the first instance to compete with an operatic success at Lincoln's Inn Fields. Rich seems to have been happy to allow them to proceed—but mindful of the expensive fiasco with *The*

World in the Moon in 1697, he declined to ante up the cost, and so we find his luckless actors signing contracts to have the necessary scenery painted at their own risk and expense for *The Island Princess* (1699) and *The Virgin Prophetess* (1701).[16] Bad as things were at Lincoln's Inn Fields, the Drury Lane actors were scarcely in clover.

During the worst of Lincoln's Inn Fields's troubles the Patent Company took the lead in competition. By this time, as Cibber says, they had become a force to be reckoned with. However, they never gained a commanding lead, and comments in the prologues to their new plays show that the Patent house was just as baffled by the capricious audience as were their competitors at the New Theatre. The prologue to *Love at a Loss* asks, "What must be done to make a Play succeed? / The common Methods are all over try'd" and any number of others echo the sentiment.[17] Two forces from outside the theatre affected both companies profoundly in these years. The first was the reform movement which, spurred by Collier, had grown into a serious menace. The other was the crisis in international politics in the years 1701 and 1702.

Reformers worked both from inside the theatre and outside it. Audiences readily damned plays on the least pretext. Durfey reported in his dedication to *The Bath* that the play was stopped "by Superiour command" for two or three days because someone objected to the phrase, "Best in Christendom." Some writers consciously tried to avoid censure, and restricted their plots and language accordingly. Others piously declared the reform long overdue and puffed their attempts to aid it. Mrs Trotter came out strongly for reform in the epistle dedicatory to *The Unhappy Penitent* (Drury Lane, February 1701). She might well have been puzzled by audience reactions—the year before she had produced a workmanlike comedy called *Love at a Loss* (Drury Lane, November 1700), which failed in spite of (or perhaps because of) the extremity of its new reform style. In the main plot, after a suitable period of delay the rake Beaumine repents and cheerfully marries Lesbia, the heroine he had deserted. But in the epilogue (perhaps by another hand) Lesbia acknowledges that the plot is just so much wishful thinking and cautions girls not to count on life's being like the play, for "tho' ten thousand LESBIAS may be seen, / Where is that Man alive would act BEAUMINE?"

Determined reformers made increasing use of legal pressure against the theatres. Plays had to be licensed to be acted as well as to be published, as the Lord Chamberlain had regular occasion to remind both companies.[18] His admonition of 24 January 1696 specifically extended to prologues and revived plays, and under Queen Anne songs and epilogues were also checked on. Some scripts were heavily censored: for example, the whole first act was cut out of Cibber's *Richard III*, and his protests moved no one at the Master of the Revels' Office. To make sure that performances remained free of incidental additions and blasphemy, "informers" bought tickets to the pit, and finally grew so obvious in their note-taking that the actors began to make a joke of them. The epilogue to *Tamerlane* (Lincoln's Inn Fields, December 1701), in one of many references to these earnest gentlemen, ridiculed them:

> Now sow'r Reformers in an empty Pit,
> With Table Books, as at a Lecture, sit,
> To take Notes, and give Evidence 'gainst Wit.

Informers were no laughing matter. They testified against individual actors and entire casts, and caused a great deal of trouble. Under a statute passed in the reign of James I (but apparently not hitherto enforced), if

any Person or Persons doe or shall in any Stage play Interlude Shewe Maygame or Pageant jestingly or Prophanely speake or use the holy Name of God or Christ Jesus, or of the Holy Ghoste or of the Trinitie . . . [he or they] shall forfeite for everie such Offence by hym or them comitted Tenne Pounds, the one Moytie thereof to the Kings Majestie his Heires and Successors, the other Moytie thereof to hym or them that will sue for the same in any Courte of Recorde at Westminster.[19]

On 29 November 1700, John Hodgson was so fined, and many other actors were prosecuted, although the outcome of many of these cases remains obscure. From time to time plays mention the situation—the gentleman in the opening scene of *The Different Widows* (November 1703) amends his oaths to include classical deities, since he has just been fined for swearing by the Trinity. Surprisingly, no theatre commentator accuses informers of being in the business to make money. The Societies for the Reformation of Manners always urged members to turn their "moytie" over to charity, or not to accept it at all. No informer was ever prosecuted for taking a bribe, and it appears that none of the few convictions brought into question was reversed.[20]

An informer or group of informers would attend performances at each theatre now and then, doing a sort of spot check. Then the players would be hauled into court to answer charges about dates they could not possibly remember.[21] Joseph Wood Krutch gives some account of a number of specific cases. Accusations of blasphemy covered specific lines and ad libs delivered on any number of occasions.[22] Krutch deduces from the fragmentary records that the actors' main strategy in these cases was simply to delay the hearings as long as possible. But they also had their lawyers quibble over semantic points—such as whether the alleged offence took place in "Lincoln's-Fields" or "Lincoln's-Inn-Fields."[23] More important in the long run was the argument that actors should not be liable to arrest and prosecution for speaking lines in plays which had been licensed by the Master of the Revels. Some of these cases were decided for the Crown, some for the defendants. But the actors finally petitioned Queen Anne to protect them so long as they mounted plays which had been approved by her chosen officials, and she consented.[24]

However irritating censorship might have been, it did not actually prevent the theatres from functioning. Some writers complied gracefully with the censor's mandates; the cuts in Betterton's version of *Henry the Fourth* are clearly an attempt to anticipate his objections. Other writers, like Durfey, found audience responses too capricious to predict. More serious were a number of efforts to close the theatres entirely. The *Post Man* for 17–19 December 1700 carried an ominous presentment:

We the Grand Jury of Middlesex, do present that the Plays which are frequently acted in the Playhouse in Drury lane and Lincoln's Inn Fields in this county are full of prophane, irreverent, Lewd, indecent and immoral expressions, and tend to the great displeasure of Almighty God, and to the corruption of the auditory both in their Principles and Practices. We also present that the common Acting of Plays in the said Playhouse very much tend [sic] to the debauching and ruining of the Youth resorting thereto, and to the breach of Peace, and are occasions of many riots, routs, and disorderly assemblies, whereby many murders and other misdemeanours have been frequently done . . . and further that the Common acting of Plays at said Playhouse is a publick Nuisance. As also the Bear Garden at Hockley in the Hole . . . to be of the like Nuisance. We hope this Honourable Court will use the most effectual and speedy means for the suppressing thereof.

Although nothing came of it, the reformers were numerous and well organized: the situation was definitely threatening.

Besides the constant frontal attacks from preachers and legislators calling for the playhouses to be shut, a more insidious campaign was waged
by some powerful and straitlaced merchants. They argued that playbills,
posted in various places throughout the town to advertise the day's offerings, were a dangerous nuisance and should be banned.[25] In the years
before daily newspapers, this move struck at the theatres' principal means
of advertising. The most eloquent objections to the proposal and its implications are found in the dedication of Cibber's *Love makes a Man*, dated
16 January 1700 (i.e., 1701), just after the Middlesex Grand Jury presentment. Deeply concerned, Cibber wrote an essay quite unlike his
usual string of flatteries to a patron. With his livelihood threatened, he
fought with every weapon at hand, pointing out acidly, "I think the last
time they pull'd down the *Stage* in the City, they set up a *Scaffold* at
Court." He suggested that merchants were behind the campaign against
playbills, and that they were looking for space for their own advertising.
He scoffed at the idea that they really cared about moral reform, and
said they were jealous of the players' influence at Court.

The upshot of this contest is unclear. On 1 July 1703, the Grand Jury
of London complained to the Queen that "the Playhouse Bills are again
Posted up throughout the City, in contempt of a former presentment,
and a positive Order of the Lord Mayor and Court of Aldermen to the
contrary."[26] Whether earlier orders had been uniformly ignored, or not
enforced, or whether they applied only to some areas of London is not
clear. Voluble complaints about such an ordinance might be expected in
prefaces, prologues, or broadsides, but I have not found them. Apparently the threat came to nothing.

The extremely quiet season of 1701–2 which ends this period of my
survey resulted in part from the cliff-hanging state of international politics.[27] In August 1701 William III concluded the Grand Alliance of the
Hague, allying England with other European countries against France.
Parliament was also busy providing for a Church of England successor
to the throne beyond Princess Anne, who was now without a living
child. When James II died in exile in September, Louis XIV recognized
the "Old Pretender" as the King of England. Ogg traces the next war
from the declaration, saying "it was a gross violation of the most important clause in the treaty of Ryswick; and to Englishmen it implied that
the choice of their king rested with Versailles." Williamites and Jacobites
might quarrel bitterly over the virtues of each side's proposal for the

succession, but they expected to settle the affair among themselves, not have it taken out of their hands by Louis XIV. The issues of government, religion, and class allegiances involved in these events claimed the attention of a broader spectrum of the English public than had ever before concerned itself with politics. A "keenly contested general election" was held in the winter of 1701–2. Ogg compares both the interest and the tension generated to the years of the Popish Plot, with the difference that in 1701 the population, through an assertive Parliament, had much more immediate say in the government than they had in Charles II's day.

Ogg's parallel with the 1680s is instructive, but does not entirely explain the effect of this new crisis on the theatre. As in the earlier situation, energies once devoted to playwriting were now employed in pamphleteering. However, in this instance the theatre did not become a medium for the dissemination of propaganda. Except for *The Generous Conqueror* (December 1701)—a piece of thinly disguised Jacobite wishful thinking—almost none of the new plays can really be called "political." The "political allegory" in Rowe's *Tamerlane* (ca. December 1701), for example, is really just a paean to William III.[28] Politics entered few of the plays in these years; rather the political stresses and strains of the times helped contribute to a period of quiescence in the theatre.

II
COMPETITIVE DEVICES

Until the season of 1701–2, competition remained both bitter and destructive, but increasingly we will find each company preoccupied with its own survival. Even during the most heated exchanges Drury Lane could not seem to follow up its hits, and so did not exploit its advantage when Lincoln's Inn Fields was in turmoil.

The most devastating example of genre competition is the victory Drury Lane scored with *The Island Princess* over the New Theatre's *Rinaldo and Armida*. The Lincoln's Inn Fields Company had evidently made a special effort to mount an "opera" in their cramped little theatre. Their production of John Dennis's recension of Tasso (early December 1698) "surpriz'd not only *Drury-lane*, but indeed all the Town, no body ever dreaming of an *Opera* there. . . . And not a Fop but ran to see the *Celebrated Virgin* in a Machine."[29] Drury Lane was obviously hurt by this success: speaking the epilogue to *Love and a Bottle* around the same time, Haynes said:

> Royal Theatre, I come to *Mourn* for *thee*.
> And must these Structures then untimely fall
> Whilst the other House stands and gets the Devil and all?

Drury Lane riposted with an opera of its own—Motteux's revision of Tate's version of Fletcher's *The Island Princess* (early February 1699).[30] *A Comparison* suggests that this was a gamble for the younger company: "the House look'd like a brisk Highway-man, who consults his Perruke-maker about the newest Fashion an Hour before his Execution." The prologue also documents Rich's no-risk financing:

> Perhaps too, when you know we've our Pay
> At our own Cost t'adorn these Scenes to day,
> In Pity to the Players, you'll kindly use the Play.

Not only was *The Island Princess* designed as a response, but the adaptation was done by Motteux, who had previously worked for Lincoln's Inn Fields (save for an occasional prologue or epilogue). No contemporary left us a direct statement as to why Motteux suddenly switched over to Drury Lane. The epilogue to his first effort for the Patent Company makes clever use of the situation, but does not explain it.

> In altering Plays, there's an ungrateful Curse:
> Some still will say they're alter'd for the worse.
> If ours be so, sure 'tis a Plot on us;
> For he that did it, writes for t'other House:
> Perhaps he does so now two several ways;
> Those write for them who bring us wretched Plays.
> If with his Stuff he mean our House to break,
> To disappoint him, kind Sirs, let it take.

The motivation is probably no further to seek than Motteux's chronic pennilessness. But the epilogue and the tone of his note "To the Reader" indicate that he was on probation, as it were. Aware that he would not be welcomed back at Lincoln's Inn Fields, he credits the musicians and performers with the success of *The Island Princess*, a politic gesture.[31] However, he found Rich's methods none too congenial. According to a pamphlet printed after Motteux's death,

"The Island Princess" was altered, and musical words made to it by Mr. *Motteux*. The Patentee or *sole* Governor denied to give him a *third day* according to custom, the alterations being but few; but the Patentee proferred him a certain sum of money, in consideration of his musical words; which not satisfying Mr. *Motteux*, he summoned him before the Lord Chamberlain, where, by the Mediation of the then Lord Chamberlain's Secretary, the matter was compromised, and the dispute ended, to the satisfaction of the Poet.[32]

The success of *The Island Princess* set Drury Lane "in some eminency above the *New* [Theatre]," and "was a sad mortification to the old Stagers," according to *A Comparison*. Princess Anne even commanded a public performance, 29 April 1699. The eclipse of their special effort was a serious blow to Lincoln's Inn Fields.

Another direct clash occurred a year later, when Drury Lane tried to subvert its rivals' production of another Dennis play, *Iphigenia* (December 1699) by mounting Abel Boyer's *Achilles, or Iphigenia in Aulis* directly against it. The former follows the Tauris version of the story; the latter simply translates Racine. Lincoln's Inn Fields's modest success was indeed destroyed, but only at the cost of both houses being "losers by their *Iphigenia's*."[33] How often they went to the extreme of running the same stock play at approximately the same time we have no way to determine, but evidently the practice continued. One documented example is *The Rival Queens*, performed at both houses in the winter of 1698–99.

When new scripts regularly proved disastrous, both companies hit on a comparatively inexpensive solution. Competition in the spring of 1700 rested heavily on new productions of old plays. *A Comparison* offers a whimsical description of the exchange:

Batterton, being a cunning old Fox, bethought himself of a Project [to retrieve the losses of *Iphigenia*] . . . he enters his Closset, and falls down on his Knees, and Prays. O Shakespear, Shakespear! *What have our Sins brought upon us! We have renounc'd the wayes which thou has taught us, and are degenerated. . . . Look down from thy Throne . . . let thy Spirit dwell with us, . . . let the Streams of thy* Helicon *glide along by* Lincolns-Inn-Fields, *and fructifie our Soil. . . .* He rose, and rose much comforted: With that he falls to work about his Design, opens the Volume and picks out two or three of *Shakespears* Plays. (P. 25)

The New Theatre did present a number of Shakespeare revivals and adaptations, most notably Betterton's *Henry the Fourth* in January 1700, but we have no evidence outside this facetious treatment that they were planned as a series. More likely the productions were separate attempts to follow a pattern that was working at the moment. *A Comparison* continues:

This lucky hit of *Batterton's* put *D. Lane* to a non-plus: *Shakespear's* Ghost was rais'd at the New-house. . . . What's to be done then? Oh, says *Rich* I'll pray as well as he—What? Shall a *Heathen Player* have more Religion than a *Lawyer?* . . . with that Mr. R—— goes up to the Garret . . . and taking *Ben. Johnson's* Picture with him, he implores—. *Most mighty* Ben! . . . The Picture seem'd to Nod, which was a token of consent, up he rose, and very devoutly return'd the charitable Image to its place in his own *Theatre.* Then they fell to task on the *Fox*, the *Alchymist*, and *Silent Woman* . . . they drew up these in Battalia against *Harry* the 4th and *Harry* the 8th, and then the Fight began. (P. 26)

Recorded performances do not entirely match the picture drawn here, but they come close enough to make the conceit believable.[34] On the other hand we must not take the report too literally. By hindsight in 1702 Betterton is given credit for running Lincoln's Inn Fields at a time when he did not have sole legal control of it. And on the other side, although prefaces and gossip indicate that Rich usually left repertory choice to his manager, here he not only sees the strategic solution to the problem but knows which of Ben Jonson's works to recommend. Moreover, Cibber's version of *Richard III* and other Elizabethan-Jacobean revivals predate the alleged competition.

Insofar as matching old plays was a pattern consciously followed, the contest was ended by Vanbrugh's adaptation of *The Pilgrim*, then advertised as a Fletcher play.[35] The passage in *A Comparison* concludes:

The Battel continued a long time doubtful, and Victory hovering over both Camps, *Batterton* Sollicits for some Auxiliaries from the same Author, and then he flanks his Enemy with *Measure* for *Measure.* . . . Nay then, says the whole party at *D. Lane*, faith we'll e'en put the *Pilgrim* upon him—ay faith, so we will, says *Dryden*, and if you'll let my Son have the Profits of the *Third Night*, I'll give you a *Secular Mask*: Done, says the House, and so the Bargain was struck. (*A Comparison*, pp. 26–27)

That Dryden, who had once scorned them, should agree to work for Drury Lane is an index to the changing status of the two houses. Vanbrugh's adaptation (though not Dryden's masque) entered the repertory and was acted regularly for thirty years. More immediately, it seems to have ended the exchange in Drury Lane's favor.

Singers and dancers, always adjunct performers in the London theatre, became a major focus of competition after 1695. Richard Leveridge and Mrs Ayliff sang for both companies during the first full season of competition, but after that season allegiance was apparently expected from singers and dancers, just as from actors. In his 1974 Harvard dissertation, Curtis A. Price shows how the interpolation of more and more music into plays distorted the spoken drama without ever quite developing into a satisfactory form of opera. Separate staging of additional music in masques, for example, could help isolate these distractions from the main plot of the drama. But masques were expensive and usually did not use actors, so the theatres regarded them largely as a necessary enticement and a nuisance. In addition to "featured" solos or duets in masques, singers and dancers were given more and more prominence during act breaks, expanding upon the established custom of playing instrumental music during these periods. Two other distinctions came to be emphasized during the 1690s: actors who could sing versus singers who could act, and native training versus Italian training. Furthermore, the status of singers gave them a kind of leverage not available to actors. They could make money at separate concerts and did not need to be totally dependent on theatrical employment. The tensions set up by these conflicting interests complicated the struggles between theatres at the turn of the century.

Singers do not appear to have been imported specifically for the theatre until 1698–99, but foreign training had gained attention earlier. In his *Diary* for 30 May 1698 Evelyn recorded a petite musicale at Mr Pepys's, where he "heard that rare Voice, Mr Pate, who was lately come from Italy, reputed the most excellent singer, ever England had: he sang indeede many rare Italian Recitatives, &c."[36] Pate had started out with Lincoln's Inn Fields but moved to Drury Lane in 1695–96. Whether he went abroad to improve himself at his own expense, or whether Rich subsidized him, the patentees lost no time in employing him when he returned to England.

Lincoln's Inn Fields in particular courted financial disaster by paying

Continental artists enormous salaries for brief engagements. Downes tells us that "In the space of Ten Years past, Mr. *Betterton* to gratify the desires and Fancies of the Nobility and Gentry; procur'd from Abroad the best Dances [*sic*] and Singers, as, Monsieur *L'Abbe*, Madam *Sublini*, Monsieur *Balon*, *Margarita Delpine*, *Maria Gallia* and divers others" (*Roscius Anglicanus*, p. 46). These foreign stars certainly had a vogue, and wealthy patrons like Lord Cholmondeley contributed lavish presents to them,[37] but the fees Lincoln's Inn Fields handed out were incredible. Luttrell recorded that Balon got 400 guineas for just five weeks in 1699, and that rate set a precedent. Vanbrugh reported another excessive figure: 120 guineas paid to "the Emperors Crooked Eunuch . . . Francisco" for five performances in December of the same year.[38] In the winter of 1702 Mme Subligny of the Paris Opéra commanded £400 for a few weeks at Lincoln's Inn Fields. As early as 14–17 May 1698 the *Post Boy*, chatting about happenings at Court, mentions that "The Frenchman [L'Abbé], who is lately come over and Dances now at the Play-house," danced for the King. His first engagement was short, but in 1700 he signed a three year contract with Lincoln's Inn Fields, according to a petition he later filed with the Lord Chamberlain preserved in P.R.O. LC 7/3.[39]

The importation of such novelties apparently did fill the theatre. But Downes sourly comments that Betterton found these people so "Exorbitantly Expensive" that in the long run they "produc'd small Profit to him and his Company." Betterton's complaint about the cost of L'Abbé, Balon, and Subligny, reported by Gildon, bears this out.[40] Cibber recalled that such novelties worsened the situation by creating in the audience an appetite for novelty, with the result that "a Play without a Dance" was "less endur'd than it had been before."[41]

Drury Lane felt constrained to reply to imported talent in kind, at least initially. The *Post Boy* for 13–15 April 1699 announced: "As both the Theatres have been very industrious to Entertain the Town with several eminent Masters in Singing and Dancing, lately arrived, both from France and Italy, as Monsieur Balon, Signior Fideli, &c. we are now assured that the Masters of the Theatre Royal have engag'd Signior Clementine, the famous Eunuch . . . for the short time of his stay in England." But the patentees soon found ways to economize. They used less expensive foreign artists and local imitators. Harlequins and Scaramouches, used to playing at the Fairs, must have considered an invitation from Drury Lane a step up in the world. And they earned their keep:

Cibber says for example that his play *Love makes a Man* (December 1700) initially "only held up its Head by the Heels of the *French Tumblers*."[42] As late as 25 March 1701 Drury Lane advertised an unidentified Boy "to perform equal to Monsieur Ballon," and in April 1703 their bills made a big point of the "Devonshire Girl's" imitation of Mme Subligny. Foreign artists inevitably became a joking matter. In the prologue for part 1 of *Massaniello*, the low comedian Pinkethman says he will do almost anything to entertain the Town—except become a eunuch!

In a much-quoted letter of 12 September 1699 the roving reporter Tom Brown accused both theatres of lowering their standards to the level of the Fairs:

But tho' Bartholomew-Fair is dead and buried for a twelvemonth, yet it is some consolation to us, that it revives in both the play-houses. . . . They set so small a value on good sense, and so great a one on trifles that have no relation to the play. By the by, I am to tell you, that some of their late bills are so very monstrous, that neither we, nor our forefathers, ever knew anything like them. . . . For, not to mention the Bohemian women, that first taught us how to dance and swim together; nor the famous Mr Clinch of Barnet, with his kit and organ; nor the worthy gentleman that condescended to dance a Cheshire-rounds, at the instance of several persons of quality; nor t'other gentleman that sung like a turky-cock; nor, lastly, that prodigy of a man that mimick'd the harmony of the Essex lions; not to mention these and a hundred other notable curiosities, we have been so unmercifully over-run with an inundation of Monsieurs from Paris, that one would be almost tempted to wish that the war had still continued. . . . Shortly, I suppose, we shall be entertain'd here with all sorts of sights and shows, as, jumping through a hoop; (for why should not that be as proper as Mr Sympson's vaulting upon the wooden-horses?) dancing upon the high ropes, leaping over eight men's heads [etc.].[43]

Although Brown made no distinction between theatres, Lincoln's Inn Fields had clearly plunged more consistently on foreign performers with theatrical backgrounds than had Drury Lane. At the same time, when a native attraction could be found, the New Theatre was not above employing him or her. In the same fall as Tom Brown's account, two other letter writers mentioned how serious the loss of the dancer Miss Evans would be to Lincoln's Inn Fields.

Even with due allowance for Tom Brown's exaggeration—part of his stock-in-trade—we may deduce that both theatres tried to attract customers before Term time by presenting the kind of mixed bill well documented after daily newspapers become available to us. For instance, in the *Daily Courant* for 6 and 7 July 1702 (a slow time of year), Drury Lane advertised a benefit for the dancer Mrs Campion: "*Oronoko*; being the last time of Acting it till Winter; with New Musick set to Flutes; and to be perform'd by Mr *Banister* and his Son, and others, and some of Mr *Weldon*'s New Songs, perform'd in his last Consort; with several Dances by Mrs *Campion* and others: Also vaulting on the Horse; and Mr *Pinkeman* will present the Audience with a *New Vacation* Epilogue never yet spoken by him." Increasingly in the years after 1702 plays became only the longest part of a variety show.

Unfortunately for both theatres, foreign stars and local talent found they could get bookings on their own. This independence probably raised their prices for theatre engagements, and certainly drained audiences away from the theatres when some rival entertainment caught their fancy. In the fall of 1699 someone rented Dorset Garden to William Joy, the "English Samson," for entertainments involving displays of strength. Joy is known to have performed at least four times (probably far oftener), and his last exhibition was attended by the King.[44]

Prologues from both theatres indicate that Mr Clinch of Barnet, whose vocal tricks made him practically a one-man circus, was infringing on their territory in 1700–1701. In the prologue to *The Ambitious Stepmother* (ca. December 1700) Betterton wishes for a time when "*Clinch* and his Organ-Pipe, his Dogs and Bear, / To native *Barnet* might again repair," and the prologue to *Love at a Loss* mentions him with irritation the previous month. Rich finally booked him into Drury Lane just before Bartholomew Fair in 1702, which indicates how popular he remained. His act was part of a bill with Brome's *The Jovial Crew*, French dancing, vaulting on the horse, and a Harlequin-Scaramouch Night Scene.

The tightrope walker or "rope-dancer," Mrs Finley, better known as Lady Mary, also caused quite a stir. The epilogue to *The Bath* (May 1701) gives a clear picture of the extra attraction such acrobatic women offered, at least to male members of the audience. In mock despair Pinkethman complained:

> 'Gad, I began to think my Charms decay'd;
> And that the Beaus resolv'd a new Vagary

To go and live and die with Lady* *Mary*.
I ne'er consider'd what a Charm there lies
In dear Trunk hose, when quivering Legs and Thighs
Feed with conceipt the fond Spectator's Eyes.
To empty Benches here, I made grimace,
When on the Rope her Buttock with a Grace
She thump'd—Gadzooks, what signified my Face?
* The Nick-name of a famous Female Rope-dancer in the Fair.

Compared to the elaborate costume for tragedy, or even to male attire in "breeches" roles, trunk hose displayed far more of the female figure than was usually seen in public. The epilogue to *The Jew of Venice* (ca. January 1701) chides the audience for not appreciating money spent on costume and decor—"At vast Expence we labour to our Ruine, / And court your Favour with our own undoing"—and ends on a minatory note: " 'Tis *Shakespear's* Play, and if these Scenes miscarry, / Let [the fighter] *Gormon* take the Stage—or Lady *Mary*."[45]

Tom Brown's letter of 1699 is the only comment associating Lincoln's Inn Fields with nontheatrical enticements (by his definition) during the regular season until 1701. Two bits of evidence hitherto unnoticed suggest that around March of that year they swallowed their pride and employed a performing monkey. The prologue to *The Double Distress* (ca. March) says glumly, "Well, we've shew'n all we can to make you easie, / Tumblers and Monkeys, on the Stage to please you." If the epilogue to Drury Lane's *The Humour of the Age* the same month may be believed, the innovation appealed to the crowd. "Once *Dryden, Otway, Fletcher,* pleas'd the Town; / Now nothing but *The Monkey* will go down." This reference is particularly interesting because its tone is not one of jeering at Lincoln's Inn Fields for demeaning the stage, but of bewilderment at the tastes of the audience.

The rise of singers, dancers, jugglers, and worse as adjuncts to plays overlapped the decline of some older attractions. The number of masques fell off sharply, and most of the new ones were not received well enough to enter the repertory. Neither part of the New Theatre's double bill called *Love's a Lottery* (1699) succeeded, and Drury Lane soon dropped *The Secular Masque* from its popular revision of *The Pilgrim* (1700), in spite of the potential drawing power of Dryden's name. Music and scenery, the two principal elements of the masque form, did retain popularity in operas. Drury Lane's success with *The Island Princess*, hasty and relatively inexpensive production though it was, encouraged Rich's actors to try a fancier opera, again at their own expense. Quite unwisely, they engaged poor old Elkanah Settle to challenge the glories of Betterton's *Prophetess*, which for a decade had served as the ultimate standard in operatic extravagance. The advance publicity for *The Virgin Prophetess* promised great things. The *Post Boy* (14–16 May 1700) was puffing the piece a whole year before the company actually managed to perform it: "Great Preparations have been making for some Months past, for a new Opera, to be Acted next Term at the Theatre Royal, which for Grandeur, Decorations, Movements of Scenes, &c will be infinitely superior to Dioclesian [i.e., *The Prophetess*], which hitherto has been the greatest that the English Stage has produced. . . . The Musick is composed by the Ingenious Mr. Finger, and the Paintings made by Mr. Robinson." Around 12 May 1701 the opera finally received its premiere.[46] Sybil Rosenfeld calls it "almost a compendium of devices in use on the English stage," and adds, "We shall find no spectacles more elaborate in the 18th century."[47] The key word here is "compendium": this Trojan War opera risked no design experiments. We have a contract for scenery "for a New Opera Written by Mr Settle," dated 18 March 1699 (i.e., 1700), which is generally accepted as referring to *The Virgin Prophetess*. Hotson seizes on one clause in the contract to document preparation time for turn-of-the-century operas, since both parties agreed that Robinson was "to finish the Scenes . . . within Seaven Weeks of ye date hereof." But the show was not finished within seven weeks of 18 March 1700, a fact Hotson ignores.[48] Even allowing for unforeseen postponements, a year's delay and a late premiere seem unpropitious. Some of the scenery passed into stock,[49] and the "dome scene" became a popular extra attraction; but the opera itself seems to have been another expensive failure, though it does not appear to have been a catastrophe of the magnitude of Settle's *The World in the Moon* four years earlier. It marks the last serious venture into opera before 1705.

   "Warfare" prologues and epilogues fell off after 1700: both sides admitted that neither company could reliably please the town. The vogue for smutty epilogues also tapered off—no doubt an effect of Collier and more rigorous censorship.[50] The playwrights' sense of the state of the theatre was expressed in a recurring food image. The epilogue to *Feign'd Friendship* (ca. May 1699) deplored the fact that the meat of drama must now be dressed with expensive sauces—Balon and Clementine. The idea was picked up in prologues and epilogues to such plays as *The Double*

Distress, The Humour of the Age, and *The Inconstant*. Cibber harks back to that image when he says in his *Apology* that Balon, L'Abbé, and Subligny were "brought over at extraordinary Rates, to revive that sickly Appetite which plain Sense and Nature had satiated."[51] The hard fact was that plain, unadorned plays were no longer filling the theatres.

III
THE REPERTORY

Until 1702–3, performance records are exceedingly scanty, so again we have very little knowledge of daily competition for the years covered in this chapter. *The London Stage* can date most of the new plays only by publication. Known performances represent only a fraction of theatrical activity: Rich claimed his company was playing over two hundred nights per season in these years, and Lincoln's Inn Fields presumably had similar totals. More performances are known for Drury Lane than for Lincoln's Inn Fields because the Patent Company did more new plays and advertised more, and because the 108 performances (1696–1701) listed in the Morley lawsuit are all Patent Company productions. Despite the lacunae, some interesting patterns emerge.

1698–1699

The number of new plays at each house dropped again this season, and the pattern of new productions suggests an alarming decline at Lincoln's Inn Fields. The major event of the season was the great opera collision, discussed above. Lincoln's Inn Fields made a special effort with its production of Dennis's *Rinaldo and Armida* (early December). On 5 January Mrs Barry wrote to Lady Lisburne: "As for the Little affairs of our house I never knew a worse Winter only we have had pretty good success in the Opera of Rinaldo and Armida."[52] Even that success was spoiled a month later when Drury Lane mounted its revamping of *The Island Princess*. The triumph of Motteux's "opera" was a debilitating setback for the New Theatre. One hint of Lincoln's Inn Fields's struggle to attract an audience is to be found in a letter from Dryden to Mrs Steward dated 4 March 1699: "This Day was playd a reviv'd Comedy of Mr Congreve's calld the Double Dealer, which was never very takeing; in the play bill was printed,—Written by Mr Congreve; with Severall Expressions omitted: What kind of Expressions those were you may easily ghess; if you have seen the Monday's Gazette, wherein is the Kings Order, for the reformation of the Stage: but the printing an Authours name, in a Play bill, is a new manner of proceeding, at least in England."[53] Someone had finally realized the potential appeal of an author's name in published advertisements.

Lincoln's Inn Fields's other new plays this season were lacklustre and met with little success. The actor Joseph Harris concocted a double bill of a farce and a masque, entitled *Love's a Lottery* (March). He apparently hoped to draw on the current fad for lotteries, but his dedication indicates that the play failed. The timing may not have helped: it was a Lenten play, and the season of penance hardly seems the time to use gambling as a theme, especially since the city fathers regarded lotteries and the theatre as equally debauched.[54] Bringing Balon over from Paris in April seems to have been an act of desperation in a season when everything went wrong. The veteran actors tried an anonymous comedy in the "new" mode, *Feign'd Friendship*, later in the spring, but it failed. Crowne's last play, *Justice Busy* (never printed) was probably performed this spring. Downes informs us that "'twas well *Acted*, yet prov'd not a living Play."[55] Their tragedies fared even worse. Despite the ironclad appearance of the contract discussed in chapter 4, the New Theatre mounted Cibber's *Xerxes* (ca. March). Rich exercised his right of first refusal and wisely turned it down. According to the admittedly prejudiced *Laureat* (1740), "our young Professor cou'd not prevail on his Brethren in the same House where he was, to perform it, and therefore hired the Stage where Roscius presided, and pawn'd his Credit for Money to answer the Charges, if it shou'd not succeed."[56] Even ten years after the abortive one night stand of Cibber's tragedy, the mock inventory of the theatre's holdings published in the *Tatler* included "the imperial robes of *Xerxes*, worn but once."[57] Pix's *The False Friend* was beyond even the power of Mrs Bracegirdle in pathetic tragedy. Henry Smith's *The Princess of Parma*, a tragicomedy proudly touting the triumph of virtue, also failed that spring.

Drury Lane's season was every bit as bad, except for the lucky triumph of *The Island Princess*. Farquhar's first play, *Love and a Bottle* (December), was too close to the old hard comedy to be very popular, though it may have been playing as late as April or May, when a prologue at Lincoln's Inn Fields sneers at Irish-English farce.[58] A reform-style comedy, *Love without Interest* (ca. April), had "but indifferent Success and Reception," Pinkethman explains in the preface: "Its being hurried up a little too hastily, made it appear to some Disadvantage in the Performance." Durfey provided Drury Lane's only new tragedy, *The Rise and Fall of Massaniello*, a two-part "Tory play written while Whiggery was in power," in Eric Rothstein's phrase.[59] Between its unusually outspoken politics and a summer premiere, it had little chance of success, though Hume and Rothstein both regard it as a fascinating portrait of the mob. The prologue to the second part describes with painful accuracy the debilitating effort of playing to thin houses:

> We strut alas, who cease no Pains nor Care,
> To empty Boxes, and to Benches bare:
> Hear what a Dismal sound from Hollow Walls,
> Fills our sad Ears when a fierce Hero bawls.
> Thus when y'are absent our own Knells we Toll,
> And loss of you is our departed Soul.

Overall, this was a discouraging season for both companies.

1699–1700

The major event of this season was the immense success of Farquhar's *The Constant Couple, or A Trip to the Jubilee* at Drury Lane. Both companies resorted to Fair attractions in the fall; during the season Lincoln's Inn Fields mounted nine new plays, the Patent Company seven. The two Iphigenia plays sometime early in December, plus the great popularity of *The Constant Couple*, put the New Theatre on the defensive almost from the beginning. Vanbrugh's letter of 25 December 1699 tells us that "Miss Evans the dancer at the New Playhouse is dead . . . a feaver Slew her in eight and forty hours. She's much lamented by the Towne as well as the House, who can't well bare her loss; Matters running very low with 'em this Winter; if Congreve's Play don't help 'em they are undone."[60] This picture is a bit exaggerated, since Vanbrugh goes on to say that "Dogget was here last Week, they gave him thirty pounds to act Six times, which he did and fill'd the house [Lincoln's Inn Fields] every time." But guest artists do not sustain a company, nor is Christmas the end of the season.

Tragedy continued to be unpopular. The New Theatre tried Hopkins's rhymed heroic horror play, *Friendship Improved*, in November without success. Dennis's *Iphigenia* ran six nights in December, and his preface gives the impression that it was at least moderately successful from his point of view; but Downes says it "answer'd not the Expences they were at in Cloathing it."[61] Late in the spring they tried Southerne's stoic tragedy, *The Fate of Capua*. Despite the best professional attention, Downes reports that it "answer'd not the Companies Expectation," and concedes that it is "better to Read then Act."[62] Of Lincoln's Inn Fields's new comedies only *The Way of the World* was even a moderate success. Although it was being planned when Vanbrugh wrote his letter at Christmas, the play did not receive its premiere until March, and then its run was shorter than the company had hoped. Congreve's last script was not a commercial failure, in the sense of running for fewer than three days or failing to recoup costs. But in context we can see it was a *competitive* failure: it neither offset Drury Lane's success with *The Constant Couple* nor did it top the success *Love for Love* had garnered for the New Theatre originally. Given the internal troubles of the company that spring, no wonder Congreve was discouraged. Another element that made *The Way of the World* look less than successful was Betterton's acting version of *Henry the Fourth* (9 January 1700). A letter by Villiers Bathurst the twenty-eighth of that month says it "has drawn all the town, more than any new play that has bin produced of late," and it a became a stock play.[63]

Corye's *A Cure for Jealousy*, a routine humane comedy, seems to have been crushed by *The Constant Couple* before Christmas.[64] Manning's *The Generous Choice*, a Lenten production in the revived Spanish romance mode, failed flat. The anonymous *Beau Defeated* (traditionally credited to Mrs Pix), expired quickly in mid-March despite a new-style ending. Gildon's adaptation of *Measure for Measure*, with an interpolated masque, was apparently a fair success in February.[65] But for Congreve's play not to shine by comparison was a blow both to him and to the company.

The actors could still muster some enthusiasm for a new production, especially if a friend or copartner (Betterton, Southerne, Congreve) were its source. On the other hand, the Craufurd debacle also occurred at the end of this season. In his angry preface to *Courtship A-la-mode* (July 1700), David Craufurd gives this report of his experience at Lincoln's Inn Fields:

Mr *Betterton* did me all the Justice I cou'd indeed reasonably hope for. But that Example he gave, was not it seems to be follow'd by the whole Company. . . . Mr *Bowman* . . . kept the first Character of my Play six weeks, and then cou'd hardly read six lines on't. How far that way of management makes of late for the Interest and Honour of that House, is easie to be judg'd. Some who valu'd their reputations more, were indeed rarely or never absent. To these I gave my thanks; but finding that six or seven people cou'd not perform what was design'd for fifteen, I was oblig'd to remove it after so many sham Rehearsals, and in two days it got footing upon the other Stage.

The poor quality of the script and weariness at the end of a disappointing season combined to turn some actors against the project. Outside pressure to produce Craufurd's script may have generated another kind of resistance. No one had the authority to make the company behave. The incident is not attractive, but in context it is more understandable and less typical than it is sometimes made to seem.

The Patent Company had miserable luck with its two tragedies. Boyer's *Achilles; or Iphigenia in Aulis* was too dry and French to stand up even against Dennis's *Iphigenia*: evidently it expired in four nights. Cibber's *Richard III* (late December) had little chance of success after the censor "expung'd the whole first Act without sparing a Line." Cibber later admitted that his author's benefit made him less than £5, a pitiful return for so much work.[66] In comedy the Patent Company scored one triumph, plus one moderate but lasting success, one moral victory, and one flop. Farquhar's humane comedy, *The Constant Couple*, gave them the kind of overwhelming success that *Love for Love* had provided the rebels in 1695, and must have been an enormous boost to company spirit. Vanbrugh's adaptation of Fletcher's *The Pilgrim* had only an adequate initial run, but did enter the repertory, and was revived regularly for thirty years. Drury Lane's July production of *Courtship A-la-mode*, a mediocre humane comedy with some libertine talk, was primarily a slap at the New Theatre. With Craufurd's preface it turned out to be an effective public relations gesture in print, if not onstage. The one real failure was Burnaby's attempt at intrigue with a new-comedy ending, *The Reform'd Wife*. Its Lenten premiere probably indicates the company's lack of confidence in it. There is some possibility that a revival was attempted the following fall: the author kept working at his script, and added a new scene to a reissue of the first edition.[67] Drury Lane did try another cheap musical show, this time in a pastoral vein—Oldmixon's *The Grove* (February), an operatic tragicomedy which quickly failed. The preface implies that Drury Lane mounted a sloppy production: "Persons who were not so generous . . . will now see if what he had writ had been spoken, every thing wou'd have appear'd clear and natural, which, to shorten the Entertainment, had been before broken and disorder'd."

By the end of this season Lincoln's Inn Fields was in a terrible state. Only the great popularity of *The Constant Couple* kept Drury Lane from having an almost equally poor year, though that house was not suffering the discipline and morale problems which sent the New Theatre to the brink of disaster. The slightly larger number of new plays this year makes the season seem less moribund than the previous one, but neither house was in comfortable circumstances.

1700–1701

Nothing decisive happened this season. Lincoln's Inn Fields mounted no new plays until after the reorganization of 11 November. Drury Lane acted two hundred and seven days in all, and mounted nine new plays to the New Theatre's seven.[68] Drury Lane lost Powell to Lincoln's Inn Fields, but had Wilks to replace him—a fact which may help account for the heavy preponderance of comedies among their new plays.

The first play mounted by Lincoln's Inn Fields after Betterton's appointment as leader was Rowe's *The Ambitious Step-mother* (ca. December), an intrigue play with an oriental setting in the old Settle manner. According to Downes, it was "very well *Acted*, especially the Parts of Mr. *Betterton*, Mr. *Booth* and Madam *Barry*; the Play answer'd the Companies expectation."[69] Mrs Pix claimed as much for her *The Double Distress* (ca. March), a pathetic tragedy with a happy ending, though it does not seem to have been revived. *The Czar of Muscovy* (ca. March), another effort from Mrs Pix, is unusual in being a heroic tragedy in prose. It did not enter the repertory. With help from Betterton and inspiration from Otway's plays, Gildon provided Mrs Bracegirdle ample pathos in *Love's Victim* (April). According to the dedication "the greater Part of the Town" applauded the play, but it was never revived.

The first new comedy mounted under Betterton's guidance shows his preference for the Carolean satiric style. *The Ladies Visiting Day* (ca. January) has an unusually large cast for a Lincoln's Inn Fields play of the time, and apparently the company had great hopes for it. Burnaby says in his epistle dedicatory that his friends raised expectations too high before the play opened, with the result that it disappointed the audience. Nonetheless, *A Comparison* uncharacteristically observes that the play was "very popular," but was "a lose unjoynted huddle of Intrigue and De-

scription; partly Humour, partly Satyr, very little Wit, and no Moral."[70]
In *The Jew of Venice* (ca. January), a Shakespeare adaptation, Granville
attacked the speculators known as "stock-jobbers." Hazelton Spencer
calls this version successful because it was the one played until Macklin
returned to Shakespeare's text in 1741,[71] but it does not appear to have
enjoyed immediate popularity. Th last comedy of this season was Johnson's *Gentleman Cully* (ca. August), a humane play whose libertinism is
all talk. The preface indicates a summer production by the "Young Company" and says that the play did better than one might expect at this
time of year.

Drury Lane had moderately good luck with comedies this season,
though no outstanding successes. Experiment was the keynote. Mrs
Trotter felt that the audience had censured her new comedy, *Love at a
Loss* (November), unfairly, which (she says) "endear'd it to me, made me
earnest to have it clear itself in Print." Cibber tried the Spanish romance
mode in *Love makes a Man* (December), but later admitted that the play
"lagg'd on the Fourth Day."[72] Baker says his *The Humour of the Age* (March),
a preachy new-style comedy, met with an "extraordinary Reception," but
there is only one record of any revival, and the play was named in a court
suit for profanity—which may have dampened the company's enthusiasm for it.[73] An anonymous adaptation of Shirley's *The Sisters*, called *Like
to Like* (March), vanished without a trace. Farquhar tried to follow up his
"Jubilee" hit with a sequel to *The Constant Couple*, but not even Wilks's
popularity as the title character could support *Sir Harry Wildair* (April).
The company may have had slightly better luck with Durfey's *The Bath*
(May), a humane comedy treatment of marital discord, which "had
generally the good fortune to please," according to the dedication. Drury
Lane mounted only three new tragedies. Mrs Centlivre's *The Perjur'd Husband* (October) "only wanted the Addition of good Actors, and a full
Town, to have brought me a sixth night," according to the author's
grumpy preface. Mrs Trotter's *The Unhappy Penitent* (February), a pathetic love tragedy showing the domestic side of court life, seems to have
lasted only three nights. Settle's Trojan War opera, *The Virgin Prophetess*
(May) was evidently a humilating failure.

1701–1702

This was a pretty dismal season for both companies. Contrary to Emmett L. Avery's statement that "a great many new plays" were staged this

season,[74] we will find that there were significantly fewer than in any season since the Lincoln's Inn Fields breakaway.

	LIF	DL	Total
1695–96	9	17	26
1696–97	8	10	18
1697–98	9	8	17
1698–99	7	5	12
1699–1700	9	8	17
1700–1701	7	9	16
1701–2	4	6	10
	53	63	116

The totals for the next three seasons continue to fluctuate: 14 in 1702–3; 9 in 1703–4; and 9 again in 1704–5 prior to the opening of the Haymarket. The tiny number of new plays in 1701–2 reflects the distraction of the audience by a tense international situation and political turmoil—and also an extended stoppage of acting during the period of mourning for King William's death after 8 March.

Lincoln's Inn Fields rather oddly concentrated on tragedy in its new productions. Jane Wiseman wrote of her *Antiochus the Great* (November), "The Reception it met in the World, was not kind enough to make me Vain, nor yet so ill, to discourage my Proceeding." Charles Boyle revised his grandfather's *The Generall* (1664) as *Altemira* (ca. November). He claims that "it had the good Fortune to meet with Justice from the Actors, and Applause from the Audience," but it was not revived. Rowe's *Tamerlane* (December), a heroic play with a heavy dose of pathos, qualified as a "stock play" to Downes.[75] The parallel between William and the legendary conqueror appealed to the town and provided a handsome elegy when the King died. Lincoln's Inn Fields tried only one comedy, Mrs Centlivre's *The Beau's Duel*, late in the season. Despite its avowed morality, the play was not a success either in the summer or after revision the following fall.

The Patent Company, in contrast, emphasized comedy. Unpropitious as the title sounds, Steele's quasi-exemplary comedy called *The Funeral* (December) seems to have done very well. Even *A Comparison* says so.

The audience would have none of Burnaby's satiric *The Modish Husband* (ca. January), a complete failure for which the author blamed an organized faction. Vanbrugh tried the Spanish romance mode in his adaptation called *The False Friend* (ca. January), but with little success. *A Comparison* tells us that Cibber was hurt the fourth day and could not perform after that, but adds that this was not the "only reason" for the play's failure.[76] The initial run of Farquhar's *The Inconstant* (early February) was spoiled by Mme Subligny. Though Farquhar's preface says he got two benefits from the play and expected it to be revived after Lent, King William's death intervened, and so far as we know it was not acted again until 1716. John Dennis attempted to ride Betterton's coattails with a Falstaff play, *The Comical Gallant* (May). As always, Dennis blames the production, not his script, for the failure. According to his epistle dedicatory, "*Falstaffe*'s part . . . was by no means acted to the satisfaction of the Audience." Both author and management were begging for unfavorable comparison when they mounted a play about a character so recently associated with Betterton. Drury Lane's only new serious play, *The Generous Conqueror*, had strong overtones of Jacobite propaganda which ruined its chances completely. In his dedication Bevil Higgons says naïvely, "I believe no Play that was so well received the first Day, ever attracted so few Spectators afterwards." In 1701–2, Jacobite sympathies did not draw crowds.[77]

The death of King William would have ruined a far better season than this one. A letter of 11 March 1702 comments: "None will suffer by the King's death but the poor players, who are ready to starve; neither are they to act till the coronation. One cannot pass by the Play-house now when it is dark but you are sure to be stripped. I accidentally met yesterday the box-keeper, who swore to me he had not drunk all day, for that now they are all out of pay, none will trust them so much as for a pot of ale."[78] During this spring Betterton was trying hard to get his hands on Drury Lane, without success. Still, after six seasons of renewed competition some kind of equilibrium was being reached. We find also that a new generation of playwrights had grown up. Cibber, Centlivre, and Farquhar had served their apprenticeship, and though their judgments were by no means infallible, they could be relied on to turn out competently crafted plays. That all three usually worked for the Patent Company after 1700 is significant.

At the end of the initial phase of competition, in 1697–98, we found a good deal of confidence at both houses. The Patent Company actors had survived hard times and inexperience to become worthy challengers; the veteran actors (though dangerously complacent) could still feel secure in their established reputation with the town. Surveying the state of the theatres at the end of the 1701–2 season, we find uncertainty about what to try next.

A variety of factors contributed to the decline of confidence after 1698. The Collier crisis and the reformers' campaign of legal harassment, plus political distractions, hurt attendance and unsettled the actors. Internal dissension, particularly at Lincoln's Inn Fields, was probably a more immediate cause of difficulty. The stormy state of the King's Company around 1676 and 1677 is an instructive parallel in some respects. The important point to observe, however, is that although Lincoln's Inn Fields indubitably tore itself apart, Drury Lane (unlike the Duke's Company in the seventies) was not flourishing either. The problem, overall, was that the audience damned new plays and turned out sparsely for old ones.

Speaking Oldmixon's prologue to *Measure for Measure* in February 1700, Betterton complained about audience taste and scolded them for their hypocrisy: "In vain you said, you did their *Farce* despise; / Wit won the *Bays*, but *Farce* the Golden Prize." To this Farquhar retorted in a "Prologue In *Answer* to . . . Mr *Oldmixon*": "Our *PLAYS* are *Farce*, because our *House* is Cram'd; / Their *PLAYS* all Good: For what?—because they'r Damn'd."[79] There is some truth in this reply. Writers certainly tended to wail after any failure that great drama was no longer appreciated. (Dennis specialized in such complaints.) But in retrospect we can see that most of the failures were pretty poor stuff. Creating a great bogey, Farce, the elder actors expressed irritation at the lasting triumph of Farquhar's *The Constant Couple*. When *The Way of the World* ran only a few performances, the New Theatre was unlikely to compliment the audience on its taste. But farces like *Love's a Lottery* were neither popular nor profitable in these years. The rise of farce—mostly in afterpiece form—is a post-1702 phenomenon.

Nor, despite the durable critical formula, was the audience determined to see nothing but moral plays, new-style reform comedies. As the survey of repertory shows, reform comedy was not doing well either. The real problem was that nothing seemed to please the audience consistently. Both companies were having more and more trouble filling their houses.

The steady advance of afternoon curtain time, moving gradually from three or three-thirty forward to five, five-thirty, and even six o'clock, has long been recognized as an attempt to draw a working audience in a period when the Carolean Court circle had ceased to exist. Sir Charles Sedley and his friends could take any and every afternoon off; a busy merchant or shopkeeper (even if he were willing to indulge in ungodly pursuits) could not. Starting later meant ending later, a circumstance which brought problems too. Hence we find an ad in the *Post Boy*, 5–7 December 1700, which says: "The Actors of the Theatre Royal, finding the Inconveniency to the Gentry of Playing so late at night, are resolved to continue, beginning their Plays at the Hour of Five every Day, as exprest in their Bills." Continued tinkering with curtain time indicates that no very satisfactory compromise was found for a number of years.

Rich evidently felt that a well-papered house was better than an empty one. Cibber tells us that to offset the preference of "People of Quality" for the New Theatre (ca. 1697–98), Rich

resolv'd, at least, to be well with their Domesticks, and therefore cunningly open'd the upper Gallery to them *gratis*: For before this time no Footman was ever admitted, or had presum'd to come into it, till after the fourth Act was ended: This additional Privilege (the greatest Plague that ever Play-house had to complain of) he conceived would not only incline them to give us a good Word in the respective Families they belong'd to, but would naturally incite them to come all Hands aloft in the Crack of our Applauses: And indeed it so far succeeded, that it often thunder'd from the full Gallery above, while our thin Pit and Boxes below were in the utmost Serenity. This riotous Privilege, so craftily given, and which from Custom was at last ripen'd into Right, became the most disgraceful Nusance that ever depreciated the Theatre. How often have the most polite Audiences, in the most affecting Scenes of the best Plays, been disturb'd and insulted by the Noise and Clamour of these savage Spectators? (*Apology*, 1:233–34)

Early references to this practice appear in the prologues to *The Island Princess* (1699) and *Sir Harry Wildair* (1701), and in *A Comparison* (1702; p. 32). Lincoln's Inn Fields seems to have resisted the practice. The *Post Boy* (27–30 December 1701) reported: "On Saturday night a Footman was killed at the Playhouse door in Little-Lincoln's Inn Fields by a Centinel that guarded the door who shot him as he was endeavouring to get in by force. There were some others wounded."[80] With this lower-class element becoming a decidedly vocal part of the audience, we cannot be too surprised at the growing taste for entertainments which, many contemporaries remark, were once confined to Bartholomew Fair.

Given his background and prejudices, Betterton was not the man to cater skillfully to this changing audience. Nonetheless, he did get Lincoln's Inn Fields back on its feet. In this chapter we have seen both its disintegration and a partial restoration of order. The King's sudden death in 1702 closed both theatres and raised all sorts of questions about their status and influence under the new sovereign.

Chapter 6

The Years of
Uncertainty, 1702–1705

T HEATRE historians have generally passed lightly over these years,
perhaps because our knowledge of what was happening is so frus-
tratingly incomplete. The establishment of the *Daily Courant* in March
1702 was to lead to daily play notices, but until 1705 Lincoln's Inn
Fields seldom advertised in the newspapers, and even Drury Lane did so
erratically. Incidental theatrical commentary is hard to come by: after
March 1702 we have nothing so helpful as *A Comparison between the Two
Stages*. The traditional picture of the period has it that by 1700 (if not
earlier), Betterton was at the end of his rope, Lincoln's Inn Fields was in
imminent danger of collapse, and Vanbrugh and Congreve out of pity
for the old man took over his license. This view derives from Cibber's
Apology,[1] and here again he exhibits his propensity for condensing time.
For his purposes, it made sense to move quickly from the stabilization of
Drury Lane in the late 1690s to the installation of the "Triumvirate"
management in 1710. Theatre historians have been too ready to follow
his summary, and they pause only long enough to mention the building
of the Haymarket, its initial "failure" as a playhouse, and the union of
1708, before plunging into the complexities of the Triumvirate.[2] Despite
the sparseness of evidence, a much sounder picture of the London theatre
world in the years just before the theatre in the Haymarket opened can
be constructed. It makes sense of fragments of information heretofore
ignored or presented in puzzlement by such scholars as Hotson and
Nicoll.

As we have seen, the New Theatre had survived its crisis and solidified
its position by the 1701–2 season. I do not mean to imply that either
company was in a flourishing condition. But though plaints about hard
times were frequent, prologues and epilogues at Lincoln's Inn Fields
ceased threatening the return of the playhouse to the use of tennis play-

ers. I am going to offer two hypotheses in this chapter: first, that by 1702 the two companies had arrived at a hitherto unrecognized *modus vivendi*; and second, that both companies were probably making more money than the managers admitted. Only with the advent of the new Haymarket theatre[3] does genuine competition resume.

I
Management, Profits, and the Signs of a *Modus Vivendi*

Two key pieces of evidence form the basis of my reassessment of the last years of the Lincoln's Inn Fields venture. The first is a lawsuit; the second is Verbruggen's Petition. The suit, summarized only briefly by Hotson, was initiated by Sir Edward Smith and three other minor share-holders against a long list of people connected with both theatres, in an attempt to collect undistributed profits. The suit dragged on until 1708 and was apparently settled out of court—or simply allowed to lapse when "one side of the Cause grew weary," in Cibber's phrase (1: 187). Any truth in Smith's lengthy allegations has been overlooked or dis-counted because some of the claims he makes are wildly exaggerated. (I will use Smith's name in reference to the bill of complaint, because the complainants are not related except in this lawsuit, and they have no convenient collective title.) The second piece of evidence, Verbruggen's Petition (1703?) complains that he and his fellow actors at Lincoln's Inn Fields were being systematically defrauded of their share of profits. Though brief, this document has not received the attention it should have. Nicoll printed a summary of it, but he misdated it by five years and left out crucial evidence which bears on that date.[4] In context, these documents greatly clarify the story of company management between 1702 and 1704.

Turning first to the lawsuit, we find that Bridget, the widow of Duke's Company counsel Richard Bayly, married Sir Edward Smith of Lincoln, bringing him half of one of the Adventurers' shares in Dorset Garden. Learning that this moiety had yielded no rent in nine years, Smith be-came suspicious. After much fruitless inquiry, in 1704 he and some other minor shareholders joined forces to try to collect the dividends they thought due them.[5] The charges they took to court and the demands they made sound absurd, though the allegations turn out to have some basis in fact. The complainants go furthest astray when they claim that the rebellion of 1695 was part of a long-standing conspiracy to defraud Dorset Garden shareholders of profits by pretending that no money was being made. Hotson reports some of the more astonishing fancies with amusement and says of the conspiracy notion, "it is quite impossible to believe in any such elaborate system of deceit as Sir Edward's complaint pictures."[6] Parts of the scheme as described are indeed ludicrous, but they reflect Smith's distance from the workings of the theatre world more than paranoia. A reexamination of his bill proves informative, and read with my reevaluation of the post-1695 competition, Smith does not sound nearly so hysterical as brief quotations can make him seem.

Either the complaining shareholders had a lawyer who did very thorough research, or perhaps Bridget Bayly Smith had also inherited some of her deceased husband's papers. Whatever the source, Smith lays a solid foundation for his claims by "reciting" the provisions of the Duke's Company patent and explaining as best he can the financial reorganization made after Sir William Davenant's death. Everyone involved seems to have had a different understanding of the arrangement, which Smith was shocked to find had been in force for many years, "although never reduced into writing." He covers the King's Company patent and then takes up the Union of 1682. This survey lays the groundwork for his principal points, which are as follows:

1) The indentures by which Davenant sold shares in his company carried no restrictions as to the "place" of acting: the shares continued in force even if Davenant's "heires Executors Administrators Assignes should remove or cause to be removed the said Company or their Successors to any other Theatre or Theatres." Thus the rights of the shareholders to profits should not be affected by which theatre was actually in use.

2) Betterton and William Smith are included in the patent power when they are made party with Charles Davenant to the union agreement. This interpretation and the point above allow Smith to extend his case from the Patent Company to include Lincoln's Inn Fields, still functioning under Betterton when this bill of complaint was exhibited (though his comanager was long since dead).

3) Smith recites a clause in the union indenture[7] which provides that "if any persons or Company should at any time thenafter act or shew any Playes or Interludes contrary to the said Covenant then all the Shares of

the said Charles Killigrew . . . should utterly cease" until such competition be broken up and dispersed. This clause, assuming it to be genuine, would make Killigrew responsible for suppressing any dissident
members of the King's Company who tried to set up a competing theatre. As Master of the Revels, he should not have found the job beyond
him. Smith is especially outraged by Killigrew's failure to suppress the
New Theatre because

the said Christopher Rich . . . hath often owned & acknowledged that his
late Majesty King William never granted the said New Company any Licince
or Authority to act . . . or if the Lord Chamberlaine did . . . yet that such
licence and Authority was invalid & illegall & could not have been supported
(if complained of & questioned) in prejudice of the said Letters patents. . . .
[But] the said Sir Thomas Skipwith Christopher Rich & Charles Killigrew
often pretended they would . . . apply to his Majesty in his privy Councell
for redress . . . but from time to time deferred the same. . . . [Upon Anne's
accession in 1702] they prevailed with your Orators to advance a Considerable
Sum of money to be lodged in a Sollictors Hand for that purpose And a
Petition was thereupon prepared to be presented to her Majesty in Councell
but the said Confederates the Managers of the said Letters Patents still frame
pretences to defer & put off the presenting. . . . And when they had thus
triffled with your Orators & delayed the said Affair for severall months by
very frivolous excuses and pretences they at last wholly refused to proceed any
farther in that matter.

This section of the bill outlines the most explicit challenge to the legality
of the New Theatre's license as compared to the patents, a challenge the
patentees never formally presented. We may speculate that the disagreements with them to which Killigrew refers in answering another bill
centered on this failure to assert himself as Master of the Revels.[8]

As Smith outlines the sharing agreement under the union indenture,
the profits (after bills and theatre rents have been paid) should be divided
into twenty shares, of which three go to Charles Killigrew, seven are to
be divided among the actor-sharers, and the other ten are divided
among the Adventurers in proportion to the shares each holds. Rich
contends that after Killigrew's three shares have been deducted, the seventeen parts are to be pooled and redivided into twenty parts for distribution to actors and Adventurers. This procedural question remained

academic, no profits having been declared, but it was one of the major points on which the patentees and the shareholders disagreed.

Smith believed the Patent Company had been making money, but since November 1694 no one had received any part of the £7 rent on Dorset Garden, which he considered (and Rich admitted) to be part of the "certain" charges. Repeated requests to examine company books had produced no useful results. Rich, Skipwith, and Zachary Baggs (the treasurer) claimed variously that there never were any accounts, or that they were kept upon "loose paper . . . and that the Same are lost or mislaid or that the Treasurers & receivers from time to time carried away the same."

Smith was particularly interested in examining the books because he was convinced that part of the "Artifices and Strategems to defraud your Orators" was the systematic falsification of accounts. He charged that the patentees had "made false & erroneous Books of Account charging therein lesse then they really received & more then they really and bona fide paid & took & had receipts & discharges from diverse persons trades-men & others for far Greater Sumes then they really have or ought to have paid or disbursed for or on Account of the Management of the said Theatres." He was also sure that the patentees had spent unreasonable amounts "to give and pay extraordinary Sallaries & Gratuities to foreign and other Singers Dancers & ffine Musicians [and] diverse other perfor-mances of the Stage. . . . [Although] whenever the Charges . . . [were incurred for] acting extraordinary Dancing Musick Vaulting or other per-formances . . . they received & had neare double prices of the Audience in respect thereof which did not only countenance the Extraordinary Charges thereof but . . . increased & added to the proffitts."

The patentees sometimes admitted "that the Receipts of the said theatres have notwithstanding such pretended Division [i.e., the actors' rebellion in 1695] been very considerable," but then they claimed that the necessity of paying rent on both theatres each acting day, regardless of which was used, had swallowed their income. Almost everyone who mentions the issue of theatre rent seems to have had a different idea of what it was supposed to be. In article 5 of the Reply of the Patentees, Rich acknowledged his obligation to pay £10 total rent, but appar-ently he paid nothing on either. As a "certain Charge," the rent should have been paid before any net profits were declared. On the other hand,

Smith calls £7 rent on a theatre in which "Plays have not been shewed or acted . . . above fifty times within these ten Yeares" both "extravagant and unreasonable," and he has the idea that a lesser rent had been agreed upon, to be paid only when Dorset Garden was actually used. Unless the investors' scheme was canceled, Smith is arguing against his own interests. Rent on the building was originally supposed to repay the investors and guarantee them a limited return for the use of their money. Profits paid after all charges had been deducted could not be guaranteed and were a bonus when they occurred.[9]

On another issue, the patentees claimed that benefits, now constituting as many as sixty performances a year, were necessary for both actors and house servants "to prevent their desertion & mutinying." Smith objected that no such number had ever occurred, the custom being "not above two in a Yeare [per recipient] . . . and then with the Generall Consent & Approbation of all the Sharers."

Smith charged that the patentees had tried actively to discourage him from pursuing his claims, in addition to obfuscating issues and stalling. They warned him that "in Case your Orators do proceed in this Suite," people the complainants do not know about who own shares would benefit, thereby diluting any profits they might be given out of the theatre. More threateningly, the patentees suggested that "the said Company are in debt for house rent & other things above ten thousand pounds and pretend your Orators must & are obliged to pay their proportions according to their respective Shares toward Payment of the said Debt." The patentees had made this argument in earlier cases, but had never managed to enforce it, as far as I can determine. Rich might have been able to make a case that shareholders were responsible for debts. On the other hand, he would have had to demonstrate that there were real debts, and he was trying very hard to minimize sharers' participation in the management of the theatre. His profound reluctance to show his books suggests that he was indeed hiding profits or misappropriations, not keeping the debts secret.

Since Hotson printed the principal sections of Smith's complaint that deal with Lincoln's Inn Fields, I will summarize rather than repeat them. Smith's claim to a share in the profits of Lincoln's Inn Fields is quite outlandish, and it is strictly secondary in the bill overall—indeed, from the number of careted references, I would guess that it was an afterthought—and it is not argued as forcefully as his primary case. He makes two basic points: that Betterton carried patent power with him to Lincoln's Inn Fields by virtue of having signed the 1682 union indenture; and that the apparently rival theatres were in fact cooperating with each other—by sharing actors, avoiding competition in slow seasons, and "shuffling, concealing and refusing to discover" their real income. He repeats Rich's refrain that the New Theatre, by its very existence, has prejudiced the Patent Company's business, a point Rich knew was good in law and could have been used had he sued Lincoln's Inn Fields in 1695.

The complainants charge that the patentees "refuse to account with & pay to your Orators what is & shall be due them . . . although they have received for & by their [acting] Plays in the said Theatre since any Dividend hath been made . . . the Sume of three hundred & fifty thousand pounds & upwards for which they ought to be answerable." Unfortunately Smith does not make clear whether he took the £350,000 to be gross income or the amount to be divided among shareholders; nor does he explain how he arrived at that figure. He was suing for ten years' worth of arrears. On Rich's own testimony we hear that the United Company was distributing roughly £800 in profits in good years, so the figure Smith claims is probably an estimate of box office receipts. It seems inflated, calling for an average receipt of £175 per acting night, which would have been far more than both theatres together could expect to gross.

Having made all their claims and supported them as well as they could, Smith and his friends conclude their bill with a long and probing set of questions that they want to see asked of the defendants. For example, they want to know "on how many days in particular since the Death of her late Majesty Queen Mary there has been any acting at the said Theatres in Dorset Garden and Drury Lane and Lincoln's Inn Fields." They want the defendants to "set forth whether they or any & which of them have & doe keep any & what Book or Books & papers of Account of the Receipts . . . & disbursements. . . . And [in] whose hands the Balance is."

The first round of answers has been lost. By the second round the defendants had sorted themselves into groups according to their allegiances, Skipwith and Rich answering together, actors in groups from their respective companies, adventurers singly or together. On some points the court settled for sworn testimony without documentation. The basic strategy of the Lincoln's Inn Fields actors was to assert that their records were not subject to audit on this claim because they operated by license, not under the patents, an argument the court accepted. Betterton in particular maintained that he should not be held liable for affairs of the Patent Company after December 1694 when he ceased to work for it, pointing to an agreement made in 1682. He admitted that—by oversight—it had not been written into the Articles of Union, but testified that Charles Davenant and Charles Killigrew had assured him that he would not be held accountable for company debts beyond the time of his employment in the company—an arrangement also made with William Smith. Rich very oddly insisted that because Betterton had been fired (a warped version of the story) he was still liable for Patent Company debts—but Charles Killigrew's testimony backs up Betterton's.[10] Obviously personal animosity between Rich and Betterton remained fierce.

The patentees determinedly gave as little useful information as possible in their answers, camouflaging this unhelpfulness in a flood of verbiage. When cornered, they gave the same list of the number of acting days they had recited in other cases since 1702. But the court pressed for documentation, ordering Skipwith to produce books held by the treasurer, Zachary Baggs. In February 1706 Skipwith reported that he had "applyed himselfe to the other Defendant Zachary Baggs and did severall times aske and Demanded of him the said Baggs the Bookes papers and accounts. . . . But he the said Zachary Baggs refused to deliver the said Bookes . . . telling him . . . that he the said Baggs was advised by his councell that he was and is intrusted as well for and on account of all other persons concerned and intrested in the said theatres . . . as for him this Defendant . . . and that the said Bookes papers and accounts were his Vouchers."[11] From written testimony it is difficult to prove attempts to conceal conspiracy, but this delaying tactic was one the Patentees used to great effect. Had they been willing to allow an audit of their books, why should the treasurer refuse to turn them over to a man who was, after all, one of the principal stockholders? Two more years had passed before on 21 December 1708 Baggs consented to leave the disputed books in the hands of a neutral overseer, so that Smith might consult them.[12] What damages Smith might hope to recover (if the books supported his claim) we can only speculate. He and other shareholders were still hounding Skipwith in the summer of 1709, when Henry Brett testified that "a considerable sume of money (but how much [he] knoweth not) is now demanded or claimed from [Skipwith] upon account of rent or arreares of rent or in some other manner."[13] By this time, of course, the new union had occurred and Rich had been permanently silenced by the Lord Chamberlain.

How many of Smith's angry charges have a basis in fact? The time referred to is a crucial factor, and one that misled Hotson. Many of the charges are patently fanciful in the context of 1695–96, but relatively close to circumstances eight years later. The idea that the Lincoln's Inn Fields breakaway was engineered to "shuffle and conceal profits" in a conspiracy plotted jointly by Rich and Betterton is belied by everything we know about the companies during the first seven years of the renewed competition. Rich had demanded notice from the authorities so he could try to block the formation of the company while the rebellion was still fomenting. And he tried to get the New Theatre closed on the ground that it was a public nuisance after it had begun operating.

On the issue of trading actors, we know Verbruggen and Doggett switched companies, but only after they had been "seduced" or caused a scandalous uproar—and the Lord Chamberlain promptly investigated the situation. But by the 1702–3 season, the charge that actors were shuttling back and forth comes nearer to the mark, as we will see. Speaking of a practice quite obvious by the time of his complaint (1704), Smith is accurate when he points out that it requires collusion—or at least an acquiescence which was lacking in the earlier stages of competition. A further contrast strengthens Smith's claim that competition had become a sham by 1703–4. When the situation changed, and actors began signing contracts with the Haymarket in the late fall of 1704, Rich flooded the Lord Chamberlain's office with furious complaints about illegal, unauthorized transfers.

Smith's lengthy and multitudinous particular charges can be reduced to two critical points. As of 1704, he claims 1) that there is no real animus between the two companies, and 2) that they are cooperating directly to avoid competition during Lent, vacation periods, and the off-seasons. This view contradicts the usual scholarly assumption that the companies maintained their animus unabated up to 1706. As I will try to show in due course, Smith's picture fits the facts as we have them for the rebel company's last seasons at Lincoln's Inn Fields. Some of Smith's charges and claims are preposterous, but his basic sense of an unofficial *modus vivendi* seems accurate.

My second major piece of evidence for this chapter, Verbruggen's Petition (Spring, 1703?), likewise has no known result, but it is a very sober and reasonable document—and one which by implication substantiates some of Smith's claims. Verbruggen begins by outlining his employment with the New Theatre[14] from 1697 to the present (unspecified), the terms of his contract, and the financial status of the company as it had been explained to him when he joined. He reports that he and several other actors have come to feel that their salaries do not accurately reflect the box office receipts, but that their requests for an audit (to use our term) have been repeatedly brushed off. Furthermore, the company debt has now grown from £200 to £800. As a result, the Lord Chamberlain recently agreed to a proposal that benefit profits should go to defray the debt. But although Betterton has consistently spoken against benefits of any kind, he is now ordering ads for "Othello to be acted on ffriday next with singing by the Italian Woman for his own benefit."

Twice the petition indicates that Verbruggen and the other shareholders feel that Betterton, Mrs Barry, and Mrs Bracegirdle have not been strictly honest in their record keeping, but the petition makes no direct accusations. Instead, Verbruggen asks the Lord Chamberlain to order a complete audit of the company's books and accounts of subscriptions,[15] so that the sharing actors may obtain their rights "without a suite at Law." He also requests that if some actors get paid directly from benefits, the rest of the company should be allowed profits from their own benefits too. In contrast to the speculations Sir Edward Smith hurled in all directions, Verbruggen's complaint is restrained in tone, sticks to specifics, and makes such reasonable requests that they could hardly be denied.

Unfortunately, the petition bears no date, but internal evidence allows us to narrow the time down.[16] Nicoll dates the piece "*c.* 1697/8 or later," and prints it in the first volume of his *History*, which is very misleading and has long prevented scholars from associating Verbruggen's statements with the practices described by Smith. Since, however, the petition is addressed to "the Earl of Jersey Lord Chamberlain of her Majesties Household" it must date from the spring of 1702 or later, and it cannot be later than 24 April 1704, when the *Daily Courant* announced that Jersey had left office. From references to an Italian female singer—evidently Margherita de l'Epine—I would put the date at spring 1703.

We have no conclusive evidence as to the results of this complaint.

Notes in the margin—"leave to examine ye books" and "a liberty to examine subscriptions"—indicate that the requests at least received careful attention. No scandal or lawsuit seems to have resulted. Certainly Betterton continued his management of the theatre, and Verbruggen and the other shareholders continued to act there. Two possibilities suggest themselves. Either the books passed the scrutiny of the actors' or the Lord Chamberlain's auditor; or Betterton settled the complaint with Verbruggen privately and avoided having to produce the books for official inspection. The second explanation seems the more plausible.

The petition implies that the cooperative design of the Lincoln's Inn Fields Company had eroded by 1703, if not earlier. Several of the sharing actors had retired, and we have no evidence as to who replaced them. The company, or at least the shareholders, were presumably still consulted on many issues—what entr'acte performers to hire, whether to risk investing in a mini-opera, when to end a season, whether to go to Oxford for the *Act*, and so forth. But in cases which required an immediate decision, or where outside authority was involved, someone had to be able to speak for the company. When the dancer L'Abbé complained that his contract was not being fulfilled, Betterton was evidently the person summoned to discuss the problem.[17] He seems to have reacquired many of his old responsibilities, if only because they could not be carried out efficiently by committee.

Verbruggen's petition asserts that receipts have been good "this last Winter" (1702–3, if my dating is correct), which is an interesting comment on the state of the New Theatre. He also expresses a strong suspicion that Betterton, Barry, and Bracegirdle were raking off large profits while crying poverty. This trio does seem in effect to have headed the Lincoln's Inn Fields group by this time. Thus the petition to the Queen asking for her protection from reformers is headed, "Thomas Betterton Elizabeth Barry Ann Bracegirdle & others Your Majesties Comedians."[18] Mrs Bracegirdle's name is often dropped; Betterton and Mrs Barry seem to have stuck in the minds of contemporaries as the two who really directed operations at Lincoln's Inn Fields. A letter to the Lord Chamberlain from Doggett (8 November 1703) on the subject of a temporary summer engagement at Oxford says the invitation came from Betterton and Mrs Barry.[19] Tom Brown had ridiculed them for their hauteur and conceit about 1700,[20] and some time after 1698 the embittered Robert

Gould rewrote passages in his satire "The Play-House" to libel them as managers (though the revisions are not known to have been printed until 1709).

When Betterton and the ladies began skimming profits is an important point, and difficult to determine. Partly this is a matter of definition. According to Rich, Betterton persuaded the company to reimburse him for the loss of his share of the Dorset Garden rent when the rebels set up at Lincoln's Inn Fields:

And he Urging that such their Acting there . . . [would] soe lessen the Receipts or Profitts thereof that the said £7 per diem could not be raised as formerly And that Consequently his said Rent of 20s per diem would be in danger of loosing. Thereupon the said Company in Lincoln's Inn Fields . . . came to some Agreement to Pay and give him, and accordingly have ever since the setting up of that Company (as these Defendants have been Informed) payd and given him the said Betterton 20s a Day . . . on publick Acting Days there.[21]

Such an arrangement might have seemed reasonable in 1695. Betterton was, after all, giving up his share of the Dorset Garden rent. But why should he continue to receive this lavish compensation once word got around that nobody else was getting rent from the Patent Company? Another ploy is hinted at in *A Comparison*, where Sullen prefaces his fancy about managers' prayers to Shakespeare and Jonson with the observation that "*Batterton*, being a cunning old Fox, bethought himself of a Project, whereby he might be rid of this beggarly Trade [i.e., the work of amateur playwrights], and 'twas a sure way to save the third Night *to himself*."[22] The only adaptation after 1695 for which Betterton usually receives credit is *Henry the Fourth*—but in the company's books he might, fairly or unfairly, have claimed others about which we know nothing.

The bitterest recriminations against the Lincoln's Inn Fields Managers appear in the dedication to an anonymous play called *The Lunatick*, published in 1705, but unacted.[23] "Franck Telltroth" gloats over the impending demotion of the "Three Ruling B——s," which he assumes will follow the opening of the Haymarket under a new license.

There will no no more Clandestine Sharing betwixt You without the rest; no more private Accounts, and Double Books; no more paying Debts half a score times over out of the Publick Stock, yet never paying them in reality at all.

There will be no more sinking Three Hundred and fifty Pounds at a time in the Money repaid on a famous Singer's Account, but never accounted for to the rest of the Sharers; no more stopping all the Pay of the Under Actors on Subscription-Nights, when you were allow'd forty or fifty Pound a Night for the House, besides the Benefit of the Galleries; no more sinking Court-Money into Your own Pockets, and letting the Sallary People and Under Sharers Starve without Pay; no more taking Benefit-Days in the best Season of the Year, and Dunning the Quality for Guinea-Tickets to help out the Defects of all the other above-named Perquisites; no fifty Shillings per Week for scowring Old Lace, nor burning it, and selling the Product for private Advantage; no Twenty Shillings a Day House-Rent; no sharing Profits with the Poetasters; nor Eating and Drinking out the other half before the Performance; no saving coals at Home, by Working, Eating and Drinking, &c. by the Stock-Fire; nor, in short, any Advantage to be made but by stated Sallaries, or the best Improvement of Natural Gifts, as far as Age, Ugliness and Gout will permit.[24]

This malicious and gleeful account contains some obvious distortions, but nonetheless adds to the weight of testimony against the senior actors.

Some of the complaints are just silly. Did Betterton and Barry spend their time in the theatre solely to avoid heating bills at home? The benefits of status in the profession cause unreasonable resentment in Franck Telltroth. For example, if "the Three Ruling B——s" did usurp "the best season" for their benefits (as later became customary), that would have been hard on the junior actors. But if they cared to dun "the Quality for Guinea-Tickets," that was surely their right. The fact that they could drum up more business that way than their juniors followed naturally from their years in the public eye. If the "Court-Money" referred to was payment for the command performances done jointly with Drury Lane in 1704, those fees might well have been considered income to be shared among the actors involved rather than payment to the company at large.

These snarls from a disgruntled hanger-on might be discounted, just as Sir Edward Smith's notion of conspiracies should be viewed skeptically. Cibber, when discussing Rich's habit of giving his actors only half their nominal salaries, goes on to say that after a prosperous beginning, the New Theatre was "reduced to the same Expedient."[25] Rich's practice is mentioned in an epilogue at the New Theatre in 1699, which makes the point that at Drury Lane "Drudging Players [are] bilk'd of half their Pay."[26] Presumably Lincoln's Inn Fields was forced to adopt this expedient during its hard times ca. 1700. But did Betterton and his friends perhaps conspire to conceal profits once the situation had improved? When a man of Verbruggen's undisputed status, a major actor potentially in line for Betterton's job, finds it necessary to demand access to the theatre's books on suspicion of fraud, the charge that Betterton, Barry, and Brace-girdle were skimming profits seems a real possibility. That there were any profits to be skimmed in the years 1702–5 is most significant, if true.

Verbruggen's complaint against Betterton is unavoidably reminiscent of Cibber's account of Rich's techniques for bilking his actors. Rich never allowed anyone to inspect his books, and his actors had no way to know what the financial circumstances of the company really were.[27] In this situation a junior actor had little recourse. If all except a handful of special members of both companies were getting shortchanged, neither complaining nor shifting companies would improve the situation. Disgruntled actors could tour in the provinces, or go to Ireland, which had a flourishing company at this time.[28] Or they could leave the theatre altogether. But if one company had been taking care of all its personnel noticeably better than the other after 1700, the members of the other would surely have complained vociferously.

A good deal of evidence suggests that after 1702 the theatres were by no means operating on the verge of collapse. Times were not good, especially for junior actors, but the managers seem to have done all right for themselves. With the theatrical climate indifferent or worse there was no point to costly theatrical warfare. Box office receipts would fluctuate less if a peace were arranged. The battles between new productions, and escalation of rival attractions, meant reinvesting profit at considerable risk. Both sides stood to gain from a period of truce.

Various pieces of information support the idea that the theatres had reached at least a tacit accommodation. Tying in with Smith's suit, the number of acting dates for Drury Lane plunged from an average of just above 200 performances a season (over six years) to 151 the year William died, when acting was suspended for six weeks. In 1702–3 they were back up to 185, but fell to 175 in 1703–4. We do not have comparable figures for Lincoln's Inn Fields, and the dates we can fill in on their calendar are far too few to allow even a guess as to whether the companies were systematically trading dark nights. But the drop in performances just at Drury Lane meant less opportunity to compete. To plan not to overlap is only a small step from there. And Cibber characterizes Rich as having given his actors "more Liberty, and fewer Days Pay, than any of his Predecessors."[29]

The heated competition we saw in the late nineties had become a thing of the past by 1702. By then each theatre was much more concerned with establishing a steady audience pool than with undermining the other's repertory. Both had to meet increasing competition from concerts. The next section of this chapter will show a definite change in attitude. Not only had head-on clashes like the *Iphigenias* ceased, but references to one another were fewer and much more tolerant. In fact these references seem to indicate, along with other evidence, that the two theatres were purposely trying to attract rather different sorts of audiences. Before we have regular newspaper ads a systematic survey is impossible. But insofar as we can judge from partial evidence, Rich was willing to cater to any taste, so long as customers paid. Lincoln's Inn Fields, in contrast, was more concerned with the artistic standard of its offerings. This division was by no means absolute, but by choice Rich took jugglers while the New Theatre imported expensive singers and dancers.

One clear sign of accommodation is the casual attitude taken by the managers toward actor transfers in these years. Few new actors were hired, since money for novelty was put into extra attractions.[30] But the number of uncontested transfers bears out Sir Edward Smith's contention that "a Very good Correspondence [is] kept up between their respective managers." In contrast to Rich's loud protests both before and after this period, neither manager appears to have complained while major actors like Powell, Doggett, and Bowen shuttled merrily back and forth from one company to the other.[31] Just how the Lord Chamberlain's approval was obtained in these cases—if it was—we do not know. Perhaps his office automatically approved a release and transfer if it was agreed to by the manager who was losing an actor. Routine transfers seem usually to have gone unrecorded by the Lord Chamberlain. P.R.O. LC 7/3 does contain a discharge for Powell from Rich dated 7 April 1705 ("This is to Certifie That Mr George Powell is at Libertie to dispose of him selfe as he thinks fitt"); perhaps it was collected when Powell was arrested in November of the same year. The most peculiar circumstance connected with Powell's repeated switching is an advertisement in the 17 June 1704 *Daily Courant* which says: "Note, That the Tickets given out for Tuesday in last Whitson-Week at the New Theatre in Lincolns-Inn-Fields, for the Benefit of Mr Powell, will be taken for this Play at the Theatre Royal." Theatres genuinely engaged in bitter competition do not accept one another's tickets for a benefit transferred because an actor has moved. Accommodation indicates a different climate.

One of Doggett's innumerable squabbles provides us an example of a grievance and a view of the casual way the New Theatre transacted some of its business. In the summer of 1703 the company had an invitation to perform during the *Act at Oxford* (which they had done at least one previous summer), and Betterton and Mrs Barry sent word to Doggett at Bath "to desire that [he] would goe and Play with the Company" for this limited engagement. The opportunity seems to have come up suddenly, if Doggett's dates are accurate. He had finished his contract for the season on 20 May and heard of this chance 23 May, just before leaving London for Bath. He accepted the invitation but asked for terms which Betterton was unwilling to meet. After an argument over terms and notice, Betterton gave the parts to someone else. However, Doggett neglected to complain about what he regarded as unfair treatment until much later. The petition is annotated on the cover, "8 November 1703. Upon examination ye complaint appeard groundless." Denied satisfaction, Doggett handed in his six months' notice of intention to quit on the twenty-ninth of the same month. He and Powell are both referred to by name in a July prologue at Lincoln's Inn Fields as having recently changed houses.[32]

An even more telling phenomenon than actor transfers appears at this time, one impossible to conceive at the height of the rivalry: mixed casts doing special performances. We do have record of a performance at Court by "both companies" on 4 November 1697 for King William's birthday.[33] On that occasion Motteux's *Europe's Revels for the Peace* was performed by personnel from Lincoln's Inn Fields. I would guess that Drury Lane mounted something of its own separately; we have no evidence. But abruptly in 1704 we find special performances at Court in which players from both companies cooperate in mounting a single play. Downes is our source: "From *Candlemas* 1704, . . . There were 4 Plays commanded to be *Acted* at Court at St. *Jame's*, by the *Actors* of both Houses."[34] Avery was able to match this report to known dates for *All for Love, Sir Salomon* and *The Merry Wives of Windsor*, all of them performed before Sir Edward Smith filed his suit. Little wonder Smith questioned the seriousness of the rivalry. Another instance of toleration is a private performance at the Grand Day festivities (1 November 1704) of the Inner Temple, when

Estcourt played Teague with a cast from Lincoln's Inn Fields in *The Committee*.

A number of actors from both houses cooperated to put together "subscription concerts," which from time to time were presented instead of plays at the theatres. We know almost nothing of how these programs were financed, put together, or scheduled. The purpose was apparently to compete with straight concerts of the sort presented at York Buildings and other places around town. Performers of all kinds seem to have been free to take part in these bills, without regard to which theatre they worked for. On 1 February 1704, for example, L'Abbé, Du Ruel, and Mrs Mayers, all of whom were under contract to Drury Lane that season, appeared in a concert at Lincoln's Inn Fields—in addition to their regular performance at Drury Lane, according to the ads for that day. Even more striking is a case in which exactly the same concert and masque appear to have been performed first at Drury Lane on 22 February 1704, and then again at Lincoln's Inn Fields on 7 March. A more complicated instance of such cooperation may have occurred at the premiere of the Congreve-Vanbrugh-Walsh afterpiece, *Squire Trelooby* at Lincoln's Inn Fields on 30 March 1704. If the cast printed in the 1704 pirate edition is correct,[35] it was made up of actors from both companies in equal proportions; the dancers named in the publicity are all Drury Lane performers. These unexpected combinations, advertised without comment, lead to the speculation that as of February and March 1704 the two companies were thinking about a union—which would help explain Rich's lack of hostility toward the Haymarket project.

Actors at both houses were evidently kept on short pay, and perhaps some of them would not have been averse to a union which promised better conditions. One compensation they did receive, however, was an increase in the number of benefits. Rich's excuse to Smith, that profits were nonexistent because sixty of two hundred acting days were devoted to benefits, does not seem borne out by the newspaper ads for his company. From the ads, I count about thirty-five benefits in all. And as with the "distress" benefits discussed earlier, actors' benefits had some attractions for management. Benefit clauses in most extant contracts specify that the actor had to pay house charges. Not by accident, benefits were generally held at the beginning or end of a season, when houses were apt to be thin. If the benefit drew enough audience to make the house charges, the management had covered overhead expenses it might otherwise not have made. The chance to add a significant lump sum to his income spurred the beneficiary to sell tickets and promote "his" show. Even if his profit were small, the opportunity made for good relations between actor and management.

Another result of the general loosening of control on actors was that some of them developed highly profitable side careers at the fairs—particularly Pinkethman, Doggett, Bullock, and Simpson. Other actors may have worked the fairs earlier, but we lack records to prove it. Pinkethman was particularly enterprising; Downes calls him "the darling of *Fortunatus*," adding that "he has gain'd more in Theatres and Fairs in Twelve Years, than those that have Tugg'd at the Oar of Acting these 50."[36] If the implied date (1696) is right, "Pinky" started early at this sideline. A postscript to the 26 October 1702 notice for *Love makes a Man* gives us a clue to his financial acumen as well as suggesting one way an actor might circumvent the management's double books: "All Persons that come behind the Scenes are desired to pay their Money to none but Mr Pinkeman." Presumably he collected this money because the night was his benefit, and he advertised because the date had been changed.[37]

Pinkethman was also allowed to set up a semiautonomous operation at Dorset Garden. The *Daily Courant* for 29 April 1703 carried the following ad:

Being the last time of Acting till after *May-Fair*.
    At the Theatre in *Dorset-Garden* to-morrow being *Friday* the 30th of *April*, will be presented *A Farce*, call'd, *The Cheats of* Scapin. And a Comedy of two Acts only, call'd, *The Comical Rivals*, or, *The School-Boy*. With several Italian Sonatas by Signior *Gasperini* and others. And the *Devonshire Girl*, being now upon her Return to the City of *Exeter*, will perform three several Dances, particularly her last New Entry in Imitation of *Madamoiselle Subligni*; and the *Whip of* Dunboyn *by Mr* Claxton *Her Master*, being the last time of their Performance till Winter. And at the desire of several Persons of Quality (hearing that Mr *Pinkeman* hath hired the two famous French Girls lately arriv'd from the Emperor's Court) They will perform several Dances on the Rope upon the Stage, being improv'd to that Degree, far exceeding all others in that Art. And their *Father* presents you with the *Newest Humours of Harlequin*, as perform'd by him before the Grand Signior at *Constantinople*. Also the Famous Mr *Evans* lately arriv'd from *Vienna*, will shew you Wonders of another

kind, vaulting on the Manag'd Horse, being the greatest Master of that kind in the World. To begin at Five so that all may be done by Nine a Clock.

This is a good example of a very mixed bill of the sort I will discuss in more detail in section II. Here the important thing to notice is that Pinkethman hired several of the attractions (presumably to appear at his Fair booth also, where they were later advertised). The program is much more a Fair presentation than a theatre bill—yet without claiming Patent Company sponsorship, the ad says "the last time of Acting," so the promoters seem to have thought of it as a kind of theatre performance.

All these elements add up to a pattern of jollying actors along and keeping them occupied with benefits and outside commitments—thus giving them less opportunity to brood over reports of shrinking profits and increasing debts. The people who branched out to the fairs came almost entirely from Drury Lane. This probably reflects both inclination and necessity. Cibber tells us that actors who were "too poor or too wise to go to Law with a Lawyer" often took "the Chance of having them [salary arrears] made up by the Profits of a Benefit-Play. This Expedient had this Consequence; that the Patentees . . . still kept the short Subsistance of their Actors at a stand, and grew more steady in their Resolution so to keep them, as they found them less apt to mutiny while their Hopes of being clear'd off by a Benefit were depending."[38] For the New Theatre records are too scanty to let us guess who got benefit days and how many of them were allowed. But both Verbruggen and Franck Telltroth suggest that the "Three Ruling B——s" were feathering their own nests.

The relatively peaceful coexistence between the two companies came to an abrupt end after the summer of 1704. The construction of Vanbrugh's Haymarket theatre introduced an entirely new element into the competitive situation—and one whose immediate effects have gone largely unconsidered. As a playhouse, the Haymarket proved unsatisfactory, and consequently its influence on the London theatre world is usually treated as a part of the Italian opera boom. But when Vanbrugh started buying land and signing up backers in the late spring of 1703, no one could have known this: to the theatre managers the advent of a new theatre must have seemed like a major complication, at best. Here we strike a major question: for what purpose was Vanbrugh building his theatre?

Following Cibber, theatre historians have usually said that Vanbrugh built the Haymarket "for Betterton's company," but there is in fact no contemporary evidence of this purpose.[39] Neither Vanbrugh nor Congreve mentions Betterton or the Lincoln's Inn Fields Company in extant letters and contracts connected with the Haymarket during the first year of the project.

We can scarcely imagine that Vanbrugh constructed an expensive theatre without having some idea who would occupy it. But if the assumption was that Betterton and the Lincoln's Inn Fields company would become his tenants, why should Rich continue the "very close correspondence" with the rival company described by Sir Edward Smith? Would Rich have played the game of mutual accommodation until the fall of 1704 with complacency if he had reason to believe that Betterton's company was on the verge of moving into a posh new theatre and gaining the outside capital it so badly needed?

Rich may have believed, as some historians have, that Vanbrugh was principally concerned with opera. The theatre seems to have been designed with an orchestra pit, in contrast to the older London theatres, which had experimented with the placement of musicians.[40] Vanbrugh's agreement with his subscribers refers to both "plays and operas," so he planned on both from the start. "Operas" in 1703 could mean the English "dialogue" form, the one familiar at the time; but at least two of Vanbrugh's contributors grew increasingly insistent that Italian opera be produced in London.[41] If the 1703 plan for a united theatre company in P.R.O. LC 7/3 represents Vanbrugh's tentative thoughts, he was not budgeting for the cost of imported star singers.[42] Whatever the details and changes in Vanbrugh's planning, Rich does not seem to have looked on the Haymarket venture as a threat until the fall of 1704, a subject to be taken up in the next chapter. He was probably convinced that a new union was in the offing and hoped to come out of the necessary bargaining in a dominant position. He did, after all, control the patent rights.

From the fall of 1703 on, Lincoln's Inn Fields marked time. The acting company remained virtually unchanged, though adjunct employees came and went; the company mounted no expensive shows; and although prologues and epilogues complained of hard times, the theatre continued to function. When genuine competition resumed in the fall of 1704, Rich was the one to revive it, and his animosity was directed not against Lincoln's Inn Fields, but against the Haymarket.

II
Advertising and the
Search for an Audience

During the period of truce from 1702 to 1705 the theatres acknowledged each other perfunctorily, not with the malice they had once shown.
They seem almost to have agreed to split the audience, Drury Lane ca-
tering to the less sophisticated, Lincoln's Inn Fields seeking an audience
satisfied with less flashy additions or even just unadorned plays. The
impulses had been at work all along, but at this point they are no longer
obscured by competitive furor. No clear pattern of success with new plays
emerged in these years, and consequently neither house spent much
money on productions, finding extras a better investment.

The difference in the audience sought by the two companies in the
quiescent years is easy to illustrate, at least in its extremes. The members
of the Kit-Cat Club, an informal organization of "gallants, statesmen,
warriors, and poets," had long been in the habit of attending the theatre,
and though we lack extensive records about them, they seem definitely
to have favored Lincoln's Inn Fields.[43] They are often said to have been
Vanbrugh's backers in the building of the Haymarket, but as the list of
subscribers proves, the Haymarket was not exclusively a Kit-Cat project.
However, several of the men who supported and encouraged Vanbrugh
belonged to the group, which became associated in the popular imagination with the Haymarket in part through Defoe's polemics.[44] The Kit-
Cats typically favored the refined, the cultured, the exclusive—in short,
the snobbish. In his account of the situation in the London theatre at the
time the Haymarket was begun, Cibber compares the audience at the
two existing houses this way: "These elder Actors [at Lincoln's Inn Fields]
. . . having only the fewer true Judges to admire them, naturally wanted
the Support of the Crowd whose Taste was to be pleased at a cheaper
Rate and with coarser Fare" (*Apology*, 1: 319). The other extreme in
tastes and behavior, according to one observer, came from the high proportion of military men wintering at home during the War of the Spanish Succession. Gildon put this opinion into the mouth of his own
persona in his *Life of Betterton*. Speaking of the decline of tragedy, he
says,

But I attribute this Disregard to *Tragedy* chiefly to a Defect in the *Action* [now
that Betterton had retired], to which we may add the Sowerness of our Tem-

pers under the Pressures of so long and heavy a War, and lastly to an Abundance of odd Spectators, whom the Chance of War have enabled to crowd the
Pit and Stage-Boxes, and sway too much by their Thoughtless and Arbitrary
Censure, either to the Advantage or Prejudice of the *Author* and *Player*. (Pp.
12–13)

Betterton agrees with this analysis. Loftis points out that "The theatres
were after all places of recreation alike for high government officials and
officers of the army and the navy,"[45] and the military men did not hesitate
to express their feelings. Prologues and epilogues in these years make
very clear the presence and proclivities of the majority of soldiers. The
prologue to *The Different Widows* (Lincoln's Inn Fields, ca. November
1703) puts their feelings about tragedy this way:

> Since *Flanders*, and the Fighting Trade came up,
> 'Tis thought Effeminate one Tear to drop.
> Damn *Tragedys* says one, I hate the strain,
> I got a Surfeit of 'em last *Campaign*;
> Come, prithee let's be gon to *Drury-Lane*.
> Thither in Crouds ye flock'd to see, Sir *Harry*,
> Or any Fop dress'd *All-A-Mode de Paris*;
> So 'twas but *Droll*, it never could Miscarry.

The epilogue to *Marry, or Do Worse* (Lincoln's Inn Fields, October 1703)
says casually that the prostitutes' business will pick up now that the
troops are coming back. The prologues for *Tunbridge Walks* (Drury Lane,
January 1703) and *All for the Better* (Lincoln's Inn Fields, ca. November
1702) also mention the influence of soldiers in the audience.

Naturally each theatre designed advertisements to attract its preferred
clientele. Two forms were available: "bills," which we would call posters,
and newspaper ads. Avery prints the text of one of the few surviving bills
in his introduction to part 2 of *The London Stage* (p. xc). He also observes
a practical advantage bills had over newspaper ads: copy could be made
up later than that for newspapers. Indeed, it was not uncommon for a
newspaper ad placed several days in advance to temporize "with a variety
of entertainments which will be express'd in the Bills"—an indication
that these bills remained the primary means of communicating with the
public. By tradition from the 1670s, bills used red letters to highlight
special features. The prologue to *The Governour of Cyprus* (Lincoln's

Inn Fields, ca. January 1703) refers to efforts to attract attention: *"Wide Folio* Bills on ev'ry Post we place / And huge RED LETTERS stare you in the Face." Newspaper ads were, of course, much smaller and shorter. They had the advantage of possibly reaching customers who did not see the "Great Bills."[46] For theatre historians, these ads are a relatively accessible goldmine, whereas few bills from the first two decades of the eighteenth century are still extant. A glance at the first five years of part 2 of *The London Stage* inclines one to lament Betterton's restraint in the use of the new medium. However, the information lost does not preclude our deducing some things about the advertising policies of the two theatres. Emmett L. Avery says in puzzlement that Lincoln's Inn Fields "for no apparent reason, used newspaper advertisements very irregularly."[47] The practical fact is that newspaper ads were at first a supplement to the bills posted around town; they were never an exclusive means of announcing performances for either company—and in these years, not even the principal one.

That Lincoln's Inn Fields did not buy newspaper space does not mean that it did not advertise. Between 1703 and 1705 the two theatres used newspaper ads in very different ways, for quite different purposes. As a rule Drury Lane advertised everything daily, usually pushing extras. Presumably they also posted bills daily. Their object was to reach the largest possible number of readers. Lincoln's Inn Fields, by contrast, bought newspaper ads only in rather specific circumstances, each of which marked some departure from routine. They often advertised new plays, or very old plays being revived, especially if the author's name was considered good box office. They advertised special occasions like benefits, new or particularly popular singers, or Betterton's first appearance of a season (e.g., 9 November 1704). They also called attention to performances at unusual times. Lincoln's Inn Fields reopened in September 1703, about two weeks before Drury Lane's people returned from Bath.[48] To reach as large a public as possible, Lincoln's Inn Fields ran four newspaper ads in that period. The next year they acted on 1 May, the beginning of May Fair, which was usually a dark period—so they advertised the performance, with the assurance that they would not cancel, even "tho' the Audience should be small."

These patterns suggest why Lincoln's Inn Fields advertised in the newspapers relatively seldom. Betterton, accustomed to the Great Bills, may have refused to see the utility of the new medium. Announcements at the end of each performance had always reached his core audience. We may guess that a smaller theatre depending on an established clientele (to whom the bills were also accessible) needed less advertising than a company in a larger house which needed to attract casual customers. This difference in advertising policy also makes sense in that Lincoln's Inn Fields seems to have hired fewer adjunct performers than Drury Lane, used such attractions less frequently, and required shorter ads even to outline special programs.

Competition in plays diminished almost to the vanishing point in these years. There were no head-on clashes and few instances of "topping" a rival's hit. We have records of a few duplicate productions, but the practice had probably been more extensive all along than we can document, and we have no comments to the effect that a show was driven off the boards by another version at the rival theatre. For example, on 21 September 1703 Powell did the title character in *Sir Courtly Nice* at Lincoln's Inn Fields. Cibber, for whom it should have been an ideal role, played it at Drury Lane on 30 October; the next recorded performance is back at the New Theatre, 4 February 1704. *The Committee* was in both repertories, and doubtless there were many other cases.

Neither house ever, so far as we can determine, took over a new play from the other. Perhaps the closest approximation of this kind of pirating was a 25 November 1704 Drury Lane performance of "Shakespeare's" *Henry the Fourth* with Estcourt as Falstaff. Cibber tells us that Estcourt made elaborate interpretive notes in the margin of his script, and we may guess that he used his talent for mimickry to copy Betterton. The date is significant: this production opened the same week that the Haymarket presented its inaugural concert. Drury Lane had not done the play since Betterton had had a personal triumph in it in 1700—their own ad says "Not Acted these Five years [at Drury Lane]"—nor had Estcourt played Falstaff in Dublin, so far as we know.[49] Powell had moved back to the Patent Company that fall. Did he suggest the old burlesque approach? Whoever had the idea, it is a sign of resumed competition.

"English" operas lost ground to concerts during this period, and there is a noticeable decline in the publication of playhouse music.[50] Neither company was willing to risk the expense of a new extravaganza, but they compromised with music lovers by renting the theatres out for concerts. Drury Lane did not even run its stock operas very often. The most popular vehicle for the display of their scenery was Mrs Behn's old farce, *The*

Emperor of the Moon (1687), into which they plugged machinery from other fancy shows. On 27 December 1703 they advertised it "With additional Scenes, being the Changes in the Dome, which were Originally us'd in the Opera of *The Virgin Prophetess*"; and on 31 December they expanded it "For the Entertainment of several Foreigners. . . . With an Additional Grotesque Scene,[51] and the Grand Machine, both taken out of the Opera of *Dioclesian*." The patentees seem to have moved a lot of scenery out of Dorset Garden in the summer of 1704. In the Great Storm of 1703 the little-used theatre may have suffered enough damage to make prudent the removal of anything that could be salvaged. At any rate, Drury Lane made a big selling point of having the original scenery in several revivals of old plays in the summer of 1704. On 9 June they presented *Psyche*, "Not Acted these Six Years. This being the first Performance of an Opera this Year. All the Scenes and Flyings as they were formerly presented." In August they advertised *The Empress of Morocco* (1673) with the original sets. Aside from such recycling, Drury Lane did not put much effort into spectacle.

The trend in these years was unquestionably toward more and more additions to an evening's entertainment. The off-season bills show this tendency most clearly, since at those times of the year the theatres had a smaller audience pool to draw on and needed to lure in every available patron. Drury Lane's ad for 5 June 1704 is a distillation of most of the attractions touted in summer ads. Surrounding—and smothering—a performance of Shadwell's *The Miser*, we find

Entertainments of Danceing by Monsieur du Ruell. And Mr Clinch of Barnet will perform these several Performances, first an Organ with three Voices, then the Double Curtel, the Flute, the Bells, the Huntsman, the Horn, and Pack of Dogs, all with his Mouth; and an old Woman of Fourscore Years of Age nursing her Grand-Child; all which he does open on the Stage. Next a Gentleman will perform several Mimick Entertainments on the Ladder, first he stands on the top-round with a Bottle in one hand and a Glass in the other, and drinks a Health; then plays several tunes on the Violin, with fifteen other surprizing Performances which no man but himself can do.

The lead headline announces that the occasion is to benefit Will. Bullock, and the Play is described as "A Diverting Comedy. . . Written by the Author of the Squire of Alsatia." The Bill concludes with Pinkethman dancing the Miller's Dance and speaking "a comical joking Epilogue on an Ass." The time was to be "exactly at five a Clock by reason of the length of the Entertainments," and the whole evening could be had "At Common Prices."

Both houses claimed to be disgusted with audience taste, though both catered to it. Lincoln's Inn Fields continued to criticize theatregoers in a steady stream of harangues, often delivered by Betterton. A particularly sarcastic example is the prologue to *As You Find It* (28 April 1703):

> And we shou'd be undone if you shou'd find
> Our Plays ingenious, or our Players unkind:
> For since elsewhere your Favour we observe,
> Hard Lines and easie Actresses deserve,
> Sure, Wit and Vertue too our House wou'd Starve.
> When to our Neighbours Joy th'exactest Play
> Must to a long and well writ Bill give Way,
> Or to th' Immortal *Trip* must yield the Day.
> Tho' our *French* Heels, and our *Italian* Voice,
> Show the Judicious Niceness of our Choice;
> Show, when put to't, that We on [=can?] play our Parts,
> And know the Way to win true *British* Hearts.
> But still we hope your Judgments soon may mend.

The conciliatory tone of the last line might make the lecture tolerable, but who wants a lecture every time he goes to a play? Drury Lane seems to have felt some pressure to maintain minimal artistic standards in its adjunct performers. The prologue to *The Old Mode and the New* (March 1703) tried a patriotic appeal to discourage the public's interest in expensive foreign stars:

> If Comick Scenes cou'd please like capring Tricks,
> Or could be sounded with Italian Squeaks,
> We might suppose this Play would last six Weeks.
> But since that only can your Mirth provoke,
> And you grow weary of Grimace and Joke,
> We too must try to traffick cross the Water,
> Five hundred raise for some rare foreign Matter.
> . . . .
> But then You'll say, that we must all confess
> 'Tis for the Nation's Fame, why truly yes:
> In time of War, when Gold's of use to some,

1000*l*. given tunefully from home,
Shews us the richest Fools in *Christendom*.

But no prologue, however scathing, was going to change the tastes of
the town, and Drury Lane's roster continued to include a large number
of French, Italian, and German artistes.

Meanwhile Bartholomew Fair felt the pressure of theatrical incursion
into its territory, and its bills begin to show more variety. Increasingly
elaborate dramatic representations were staged there, especially by Drury
Lane comedians. When vaulting proved very popular in theatre entr'actes,
the Great Booth at the 1703 Fair featured various tightrope walkers of
Continental fame, "To which is added, Vaulting on the High-Rope, and
Tumbling on the Stage. As also Vaulting on two Horses, on the great
Stage, at once."

The use of animal acts appears to have decreased in these years,
though we have no indication that the audience lost its taste for them.
Rather, the problem seems to have been one of maintaining novelty.
Cibber reports that Rich even negotiated for an elephant he hoped to
display at Dorset Garden:

His Point was to please the Majority, who could more easily comprehend any
thing they *saw* than the daintiest things that could be said to them. But in
this Notion he kept no medium; for in my Memory he carry'd it so far, that
he was . . . actually dealing for an extraordinary large Elephant at a certain
Sum for every Day he might think fit to shew the tractable Genius of that
vast quiet Creature in any Play or Farce in the Theatre (then standing) in
Dorset-Garden. But from the Jealousy which so formidable a Rival had rais'd
in his Dancers, and by his Bricklayer's assuring him that if the Walls were to
be open'd wide enough for its Entrance, it might endanger the fall of the
House, he gave up his Project. (*Apology*, 2: 6)

Indeed in 1704 Pinkethman had an elephant "Between Nine and Ten
Foot high, arriv'd from Guinea, led upon the Stage by six Blacks," from
whose back he spoke an epilogue in the best Haynes tradition. This
attraction would grace Pinky's May Fair booth for sixteen days, according
to his advance advertisements, and he may have wanted to use it in a
program like the one he had mounted at Dorset Garden in May 1703.

Winter bills were not usually so elaborate as summer programs. Lincoln's Inn Fields could work up ads with multiple attractions—most

performances had some additions—but they usually had more connection with some conventional element of theatre than Mr Clinch. A typical New Theatre ad in this period announces *The Country-Wife*, describes it as "Written by the Famous Mr *Whicherly*," and lists

several Entertainments of Singing and Dancing, *viz.* 1. The Chimney-Sweeper's Dialogue. 2. The Mad-Man's Dance. 3. The Turkey-cock Musick. 4. A new Dance perform'd by 16 Persons in Grotesq; Habits, in which a Black will perform Variety of Postures to Admiration. 5. Singing by Mrs. *Hodgson*, Mrs. *Willis*, and a Trumpet-Song never sung but twice on the Stage. Also an Entertainment of Musick which was perform'd before the Doge and Senate of *Venice* the last Carnival. And Mr. *Weaver* will perform *Roger a Coverly* as it was done Originally after the Yorkshire manner. (*Daily Courant*, 28 December 1702)

Drury Lane could also muster "artistic" bills. On 1 February 1703 they presented a subscription concert which combined singing in French and Italian, one act of *The Fairy-Queen*, dancing by Du Ruel, "lately arriv'd from the Opera at *Paris*," and a condensed, two-act version ("the best Scenes") of *Marriage A-la-Mode*. It lacked unity, but at least the evening did not feature monkeys.

Both newspaper ads and the Great Bills usually carried essential information such as curtain time and the scale of ticket prices. They also indulged in bits of puffery—usually to build up entr'acte performers rather than the regular actors. Any new dance or pantomime got extensive publicity, and if it could be connected with some foreign court, so much the better. New performers—even actors—got touted, whether they were merely new to London or had never been on stage before. But the theatres did not think in terms of advertising something like "The Famous Mr Betterton as Falstaff": Avery concluded that even much farther into the century there is no such thing as star billing, nor were names singled out in bigger or fancier type.[52] Copywriters were much more apt to feature authors by this time—"The Late Great Mr Dryden" was a particular favorite.

The phrase "At the Desire of several Persons of Quality" had become almost as predictable as the obligatory "Vivat Regina"—and may occasionally have been true. Both theatres regularly advertised performances for visiting dignitaries: snob appeal continued to be good box office. Ads do seem now and then to have promised more than was delivered: a postscript on the Lincoln's Inn Fields listing for 28 April 1704 says "particular Care is taken, that every thing mention'd in the Bill shall exactly be perform'd." Both theatres probably slipped up, sometimes because of cramming their bills. That same ad continues, "We shall begin exactly at 6 a Clock, by reason of the length of the Entertainment." In slack seasons ads carried the reassurance that the show would go on, a suggestion that it had not always done so. When the New Theatre announced an unusual May Day performance in 1704, and also during the slow season that year, their notices ended, "We shall not dismiss, let the Audience be what it will" (9 August 1704). Compared with the 1681 death agonies of the King's Company when it dismissed audiences, the phrase sounds jaunty rather than desperate.

Surveying the pattern of noncompetition in plays as it was established after 1701, we see that both companies put their energies and financial resources into cheaper extras on a rotating but permanent basis. The genuine double bill is still a rarity. One finds *The Spanish Fryar* and *The Wit of a Woman* together at Lincoln's Inn Fields on 24 June 1704, or *Sir Martin Mar-all* with *The School-Boy* at Drury Lane the following 4 October, but afterpieces do not become really frequent until a decade later. In these years the theatres promoted mixed entertainments, especially those featuring music. The consistency with which the nondramatic elements were advertised suggests that they believed those elements drew newspaper readers to the theatre.

III
PLAYS AND REPERTORY

By the season of 1703–4 Drury Lane was advertising in the *Daily Courant* so frequently that our record of its activities is nearly complete. We know a great deal less about the New Theatre's activities: competition had quieted down before daily newspaper advertising became possible.

One obvious change in new plays since the turn of the century is that the theatres had adjusted to government censorship, both moral and political. Whatever self-restraint this may have imposed on writers, they seldom complained about it. Other outlets could be found for occasional verse: the *Post Boy* of 9–11 March 1703 notes publication of a "Prologue sent to Mr. Row to his new Play, called *The Fair Penitent*," refused by the

theatre for being "too Satyrical." Only rarely did a theatre fall foul of the
Master of the Revels, and then the issues seem ponderous in comparison
to earlier censorship. For example, when Gildon revised Nathaniel Lee's
Lucius Junius Brutus, which had been banned as Whig propaganda after
a few showings in 1680, he had to try twice before the censor would
pass the new version. The title got changed to *The Patriot* and the scene
shifted to Renaissance Florence before Drury Lane was allowed to perform the play in 1702. Anything with political overtones was chancy,
but doubly so in the winter of 1703–4 when Whigs and Tories fought
bitterly over control of the government. Drury Lane had a fair success
with *The Albion Queens* (March 1704), a revamping of Banks's *The Island
Queens*, which had been banned twenty years earlier. The theatre took
the unusual step of advertising the coming attraction well in advance:
"Wheras the Play of *Mary Queen of Scotland* (till now wholly incorrect,
and imperfect, and long since Printed, though not suffer'd to be Acted)
hath been revis'd and amended, with most material and considerable
Alterations both in Title and Substance, and will be suddenly acted, by
Her Majesty's Permission, at the Theatre Royal in Drury-Lane" (*Daily
Courant*, 22 February 1704). Despite its tangential relevance to the question of Queen Anne's successor, the play made no direct comment on the
political issue being discussed, and the censor could let it pass. But
Drury Lane took care to get permission and publish the fact.

In July 1703 the Grand Jury of the City of London once again urged
the city aldermen to take "some effectual course . . . to prevent the
Youth of this City from resorting to the Play-Houses, which we rather
mention, because the Play-House Bills are again Posted up throughout
the City."[53] The next January we find the Lord Chamberlain reiterating
that no prologue, epilogue, song, or play (old or new) might be presented without a license from the Master of the Revels, and two days
after that order he sent a reprimand to the inattentive and unmethodical
Charles Killigrew to be more careful in his licensing of material for the
stage.[54] Thus galvanized, Killigrew seems to have seized on one of the first
scripts that came to hand and slashed it up. The preface to the anonymous *Love the Leveller* (January 1704) reports that the play was heavily
cut by "the last Correcting hand," a standard euphemism for the censor;
"nor could I ever conceive that representing the Cheats of the Priests of
Isis, could be a reflection on the Christian Priesthood." Such ostentatious
interference was rare.

Unofficial busybodies were another matter. No reform short of abolition would satisfy them, and even a spontaneous reaction by the audience could infuriate them. The Great Storm of November 1703 frightened everyone, and a Drury Lane audience's response to a momentarily topical passage in *Macbeth* was misinterpreted by the outraged Jeremy Collier:

We have lately felt a sad Instance of God's Judgments in the terrible Tempest. . . . Did not Nature seem to be in her last Agony . . . ? And if we go on still in such Sins of Defyance, may we not be afraid of the Punishment of *Sodom* . . .? What Impression this late Calamity has made upn the Play-House, we may guess by their Acting *Macbeth* with all its Thunder and Tempest, the same Day: Where at the mention of the *Chimnies being blown down*, . . . the Audience were pleas'd to Clap, at an unusual Length of Pleasure and Approbation. . . . Does it not look as if they had a Mind to out-brave the Judgment? . . . The throwing Providence out of the Scheme, is an admirable *Opiate* for the Conscience![55]

Spontaneous applause on that occasion might just as well have been a recognition of an ominous parallel, but Collier did not believe a Christian would attend the theatre, so he could not see it that way. He was not alone: the choice of "acting the 'Tempest' upon the next Wednesday after the late dreadful storm, at the new play-house in Little Lincoln's Inn Fields" was considered neither "proper" nor "reasonable" by the zealots who attended a meeting of the Society for the Promotion of Christian Knowledge.[56] By 1704, however, the reformers—one might even say "abolitionists"—must have been coming to see that although Queen Anne was willing to regulate the theatres more strictly, she would not close them.[57]

The brief survey which follows covers a depressing repertory. Neither theatre put much of its resources into new plays, and few of them did well. Contrary to the impression conveyed by Cibber, however, we will find that Lincoln's Inn Fields was certainly doing as well as Drury Lane.

1702–1703

Drury Lane mounted ten new plays, spreading them out from November to the end of June. Two succeeded, though one of those was only an afterpiece. Lincoln's Inn Fields concentrated its new offerings at the height of the season, opening a new play once each month from roughly December to May. One or perhaps two of them held the boards.

Lincoln's Inn Fields tried four comedies, all of them unsuccessful. Mrs Centlivre's *The Stolen Heiress* (December) is an attempt at split-plot tragicomedy in the Spanish mode, which deserved oblivion. Burnaby's *Love Betray'd* (ca. February), an unrecognizable adaptation of *Twelfth Night*, is a bad piece of playwriting which evidently suffered further in production. Casting problems arose,[58] and Burnaby complains in his preface that the "lesser people" were neglected. He also grouses that he had intended to have a masque in the fourth act, but "the House neglecting to have it Set to Musick," the effect was lost. In March Betterton's company tried an old gimmick and dressed up an anonymous pastoral, *The Fickle Shepherdess* with an all-female cast. A Lenten play, it was not really expected to enter the repertory. The last comedy of the season, Charles Boyle's *As You Find It* (April), was a reform play with a marital-discord theme. This piece probably ran fairly well, since we find apparent references to it in Drury Lane prologues and epilogues in June 1703 and January 1704.[59]

Lincoln's Inn Fields tried two tragedies, both in the pathetic vein. Oldmixon's *The Governour of Cyprus* (January) seems to have failed, to judge from the defensive tone of the preface. Rowe's *The Fair Penitent* (March)[60] ultimately became a stock play after it was revived by the Triumvirate in 1715, but initially it had mediocre success. Downes's analysis was that it was "a very good Play for three *Acts*; but failing in the two last answer'd not their Expectation."[61] The last performance of which we have any record in this period was on 8 June 1703.

No pattern is discernible in the series of comedies that failed at Drury Lane. The company delayed Manning's *All for the Better*, a reform-style Spanish romance, until the troops came back to winter quarters, but it did not amuse them. Cibber's preface to the quarto of his Spanish romance, *She Wou'd and She Wou'd Not* (November) says it rode a wave of enthusiasm following "Our Late happy News from *Vigo*," the decisive naval victory celebrated in London 12 November 1702. But in 1719 he admitted that it "did not pay the Charges on the Sixth Day."[62] Farquhar overturned the convention of favoring the younger brother in *The Twin-Rivals* (December). His introduction says that gossip had caused difficulties: "There was an Odium cast upon this Play, before it appear'd, by some Persons who thought it their Interest to have it suppress'd." His satire was apparently harsher than the audience was then prepared to tolerate, though the play became popular after 1716. Thomas Baker produced Drury Lane's only full-length hit of the season, *Tunbridge Walks*

(January). A humane comedy with a strong romance element, it was enormously popular. But Durfey's *The Old Mode and the New* (March), also a humane comedy with emphasis on farce and intrigue, failed. The mimic Richard Estcourt, acting in Dublin, sent Rich a humane comedy, *The Fair Example* (April), adapted from Dancourt. He did not publish it until 1706, after he had moved to London, when the dedication records that it was "acted sometimes, and put by ever since." Cibber retrieved the "Mass Johnny" parts from *Woman's Wit* and strung them together as a farce called *The School-Boy* (October). Played also under the title *The Comical Rivals*, it made a serviceable afterpiece for thirty years. Mrs Centlivre puts together a farce called *Love's Contrivance* (June) from snippets of Molière. It ran about six nights initially—according to the dedication, a "Reception beyond my Expectation"—but the play did not really catch on until it was shortened to an afterpiece. Richard Wilkinson's didactic reform comedy, *Vice Reclaim'd* (June) did not survive, in spite of the actors' general "Care and civil Usage." Not even Wilks's diligence could save it: late June premieres were seldom auspicious. Drury Lane's only tragedy this year was Gildon's revision of *Lucius Junius Brutus* as *The Patriot* (December). He professed himself satisfied with its reception, and said that the "Representation was extremely just in all the chief Parts"— but the play was not revived.

During the spring, rumors about Vanbrugh's plans for a new theatre must have started circulating as he worked to line up "Undertakers." On 15 June he started buying the land he needed. We cannot document a certain connection, but it seems more than coincidental that at just this time someone should think of refurbishing Dorset Garden. Pinkethman had mounted a pre-May Fair variety show there on 30 April 1703. Two weeks later the *Daily Courant* reported that "The Queen's Theatre in *Dorset-Garden* is now fitting up for a new *Opera*; and the great Preparations that are made to forward it and bring it upon the Stage by the beginning of *June*, adds to every body's Expectation, who promise themselves mighty Satisfaction from so well order'd and regular an Undertaking as this is said to be" (13 May). Was Vanbrugh thinking of using the old theatre for opera until he could build his new one? Was Rich reacting quickly to anticipated competition? We do not know. The plans did not materialize, although at the beginning of July the Grand Jury of London was still petitioning the Queen to put a stop to the effort: "we are informed that a Play-House within the Liberties of this City, which has been of late disused and neglected, is at this time refitting in order to be used as formerly. We do not presume to prescribe to this Honourable Court [of Aldermen], but we cannot question, but that if they shall think fit, Humbly to Address Her Majesty in this Case, she will be Graciously pleased to prevent it" (*Post Man*, 10–13 July 1703). No opera was performed—the building was really beyond repair, though three years later one more attempt was made to use it. But Vanbrugh was proceeding with plans which would radically alter the whole competitive situation.

1703–1704

Reversing what had seemed a trend, neither company had any luck with new comedies this season, except that Lincoln's Inn Fields added one long-popular afterpiece to its repertory. Betterton's company began work early. William Walker's humane comedy *Marry, or Do Worse* (early October) was scheduled before term time,[63] and Walker reported that "it was so hem'd in between the *Benefits*, that it seem'd meerly Confin'd to the Limits of a Single *Night* before hand; not that I have any reason to complain of the Civility of the House, as to the Performing, only the want of Time and Rehearsals." The whole experience left him vowing "I shall take great care how I Embark again in such an Affair, to be Toss'd and Buffeted by the rough Tempests of the *Town*." Mrs Pix offered a lively exercise in the reform mode, *The Different Widows* (November), but it left no trace except publication. Despite David Craufurd's debacle at Lincoln's Inn Fields in 1700, he brought them his only other play, a humane comedy called *Love at First Sight* (March). It ran exactly one night. He complained bitterly in his preface that this "distressed Play" was "mangl'd on the Stage," and it may well have been. In the opinion of the management, his weak script deserved only a Lenten showing, and probably had few rehearsals. The New Theatre had somewhat better luck with its afterpieces. Farquhar unexpectedly presented them with *The Stage-Coach* (January), a gem of a farce, which entered the repertory immediately. Thomas Walker contributed *The Wit of a Woman* (June), for which his dedication claimed a good first night, but if the piece was ever performed after August, we have no record of it. The summer premiere may have hurt its chances.

Lincoln's Inn Fields did manage to sell a tragedy this year. Although Hume finds Trapp's *Abra-Mule* (January) a "slack and slushy" example of "pathetic sensibility with a happy ending," the title role, a harem slave, provided Mrs Bracegirdle with an ideal vehicle. The play remained in the repertory for the next few years. Dennis was responsible for their other tragedy, a love and honor play set in French Canadian Indian territory in the midst of a war. *Liberty Asserted* (February), with Mrs Barry as an Indian Princess, took advantage of anti-French sentiment, and Dennis professed himself satisfied with eleven nights in five weeks. But we know of only one later performance, 2 May 1707.

Drury Lane tried two comedies in the winter. Steele wrote *The Lying Lover* (December), a play against dueling, as "suitable entertainment for a Christian Commonwealth"; but the audience was not ready for this sort of entertainment. The play eked out six nights and died. The anonymous author of *Love the Leveller* (January) bragged that it had "found so favourable a Reception, that I dare boldly say, the best Plays have hardly ever met with a fuller Audience, or the best Poets more Generous Friends." This claim seems quite misleading, since the calendar shows only two performances, and it is quite full for Drury Lane at this time. Contrary to usual practice, the second night was advertised as the author's benefit: was the theatre anxious to be rid of the piece quickly? The epilogue says glumly "We strive in vain to please a factious Age," and goes on to suggest that "The Rats, for want of Bread, devour our Scenes," while the "half starv'd" actors may have to "turn the Pit into a House of Prayer" in the hopes of drawing an audience. The plea is a comic exaggeration, but one which indicates no generosity on Rich's part. Drury Lane's only tragedy this year was Taverner's *The Faithful Bride of Granada* (January), a happy-ending heroic play which vanished without a trace except for its publication.

Once again, neither company had much reason to be pleased with its season. Drury Lane ran almost entirely on stock plays. Lincoln's Inn Fields did have one solid success (*Abra-Mule*), one highly successful afterpiece (*The Stage-Coach*), and one new show which probably made more than its expenses (*Liberty Asserted*). But *The London Stage* rosters for both show more singers and dancers than ever before.

1704–1705

This season is split between two chapters by the mid-season advent of the Haymarket. Most of the year's new plays are properly considered as part of the new competition fired by Vanbrugh. In July 1704 a special

Lincoln's Inn Fields prologue recapped the history of the competition we have been surveying and predicted the change which was coming. Making fun of the Haynes-Pinkethman gimmick of delivering prologues mounted on an ass, Francis Lee rode a dray horse onstage and made this comparison:

> Not that this House can boast a merry Strain,
> Equal to the Produce of *Drury-Lane.*
> *Whose fructifying Fancy forward shoots,*
> And *Porus*-like engages you with Brutes,
> But amidst our Discouragements we'd strive,
> To keep the Genius of this Stage alive,
> That droops with Grief, and with declining Head,
> Laments its Heroes from its Ensigns fled:
> While our Foes gain Addition from our loss,
> And no Deserters come from them to us.
> But why grieve I for Accidents of chance,
> Thus fares it with the Allies, and thus with *France*,
> Each in their turns their several Parties leave,
> And their Antagonists for Friends receive,
> Tho' for a time our Numbers do decay,
> If this *House will not do, another may.*
>
> *Hay-Market.*[64]

Neither company risked major new productions until after the first of the year. Lincoln's Inn Fields did mount Corye's farce, *The Metamorphosis*, as a main piece early in October, before the start of the term, and they tried to follow up the success of *Abra-Mule* with an imitation, *Zelmane*, the following month—but neither proved popular.

The Lincoln's Inn Fields Company was marking time until it could enter its new quarters. Meanwhile Rich was competing by preparing an opera for·production later and by beefing up his troupe a bit. He had recovered Powell and Doggett, and when the Irish comedian Richard Estcourt came to London in the summer of 1704, he found Rich anxious to do business. Estcourt seems to have handled himself very cleverly, playing the two companies off against one another. He spoke an epilogue for Lincoln's Inn Fields on 17 August, but we find him playing in *The Spanish Fryar* at Drury Lane on 18 October, and the *Diverting-Post* reported ten days later that "Mr. Estcourt the famous Comedian of Ireland" had "entered into Articles, with Christopher Rich Esq. to Play ten Times." He did a single special appearance with Lincoln's Inn Fields for the Inner Temple on 1 November, before settling down to become a major farceur at Drury Lane. In December the popular Letitia Cross returned from adventures abroad and a stint in Dublin, and Rich promptly signed her up again (*Diverting-Post*, 16 December).

Just when Rich found out that Betterton's company was going to move to the Haymarket we do not know, and that date is of some importance. If he attempted collusion with Vanbrugh, his offers were rejected and went unreported. Rich later had occasion to point out that he had tried to buy off the rebel company before the Haymarket opened. In a letter printed in *The Post-Boy Robb'd of his Mail*, he says that he "did humbly offer to his Lordship [the Lord Chamberlain] . . . that I wou'd receive them all [the Lincoln's Inn Fields actors] at such Salaries as his Lordship shou'd think reasonable; but his Lordship was pleas'd to declare, That Her Majesty intended to have two Companies, and he wou'd not permit me to entertain them."[65] The time of this offer was "before Mr. *Vanbrugh* and Mr. *Congreve* had obtain'd Her Majesty's License" on 14 December 1704, and was probably some three to six months earlier. Already in October Lincoln's Inn Fields was publicly asserting in the epilogue to *The Metamorphosis* that "better times shall come"; the *Diverting-Post* reported the imminent completion of the theatre in the Haymarket and the preparation of two Italianate operas for it; and Vanbrugh was setting out to steal Rich's best actors. The period of quiescence was over.

Since the period under consideration here is interrupted by the opening of the Haymarket, which is the subject of the next chapter, conclusions here can be kept brief. One fact stands out: rivalry aside, the clear direction of the theatre in these years was toward the circus. The trend around the turn of the century continued, as plays increasingly became just one element in a variety show.

From the repertory survey, however, we can draw some distinctly surprising conclusions about the popularity of various sorts of plays. Long-standard accounts such as Nicoll's *History* and John Harold Wilson's *A Preface to Restoration Drama* (1965) give the impression that the old Restoration play types were driven off the boards by audience preference for the new "sentimental" comedy and pathetic tragedy. This is, at least, the standard explanation of the failure of *The Way of the World* to achieve the success expected. But as Hume points out, we have found remarkably few sentimental comedies. The clearest example, Steele's *The Lying Lover*, was a failure. Audiences were, however, receptive to humane comedies, and to plays demonstrating a reform, like Cibber's *The Careless Husband* (1704) and Mrs Centlivre's *The Gamester* (1705). The pattern in tragedy is even clearer—basically, the genre was not popular. Pathetic plays were few and mostly unsuccessful, including even *The Fair Penitent*, which later became a stock play. The most successful tragedy of these years, *Abra-Mule*, was a late heroic carry-over, reminding one of nothing so much as 1670s-style Elkanah Settle, sans rhyme but plus happy ending. By Nicoll's outline, we ought also to be finding a boom in pseudoclassical tragedy (*Cato* is the sort of piece he has in mind), but there are no signs of popular support for attempts at it.

Having looked at the state of the theatre companies just before the Haymarket opened, we can reevaluate two memories in Cibber's *Apology*. First, the intense competition he described in the late 1690s should not be generalized: by 1702 the theatres had learned to live and let live. Second, the notion Cibber fostered of bare subsistence or imminent collapse (especially at Lincoln's Inn Fields) is not borne out by the apparent condition of the companies. Both appear to have been at least marginally profitable, though most of the money seems to have been disappearing into the pockets of the managers while actors struggled along on half pay. The Lincoln's Inn Fields Company was not at its last gasp. It had some elderly personnel (Betterton, Bright, Underhill); but it had been rebuilt into a solid operation, and Vanbrugh had reason to think that profitable operation with that company would be possible in better quarters.

Theatre historians are now repairing the neglect to which their predecessors relegated the 1702–5 period. These years saw the appearance of the multiple bill; the afterpiece tradition began to get established; and extraneous entertainments got a real stranglehold on the theatre. In short, these years saw the acceptance of some of the major features of the eighteenth-century theatre. Competition resumed with the advent of the Haymarket, but on a different basis. The question became not which theatre would dominate but whether the London audience would support straight plays. The rocky years before the new union of 1708 were to yield inconclusive but discouraging answers to that question.

Chapter 7

The Haymarket Years
and the Union of 1708

STRICTLY speaking, when Vanbrugh and Congreve gained a new license and moved Betterton's former company into the new Haymarket theatre, the Lincoln's Inn Fields experiment might be considered at
an end. Alternatively the reorganization of September 1706—termed a
"Union" by Downes—could be viewed as the point at which the company lost its distinctive character. By then Betterton had, in effect, been
replaced. For a variety of reasons, however, I have chosen the Union of
1708 as the terminal point for this study. Only then did the theatrical
competition fired by the rebellion of 1695 come to an end, and only then
did Christopher Rich regain his hold on actors and a monopoly in plays.

The Haymarket years are confusing ones. Although Cibber remains
our fullest narrative source, other evidence is now expanding our view of
this decade. After piecing together fragments of fact, opinion, and gossip
in the context of increasingly full performance records, we can reassess
Vanbrugh's ventures in theatre and opera. We will find that the Haymarket basically carried on the policies of Lincoln's Inn Fields, rather
than relying heavily on Italian opera—and under Owen Swiney's management in 1706–7 the company proved that it could operate profitably
with straight plays. At the same time, however, Rich was finding at
Drury Lane that a new form of opera could indeed hold a potent appeal
for the London audience. Vanbrugh thereupon very unwisely used his
influence and his friendships in the Lord Chamberlain's office to engineer
the Union of 1708, giving him exclusive rights to perform opera at the
Haymarket, at the cost of returning all actors and straight plays to Drury
Lane. With competition in plays eliminated, this investigation comes to
a close.

I

RENEWED COMPETITION, 1704–1706

Vanbrugh laid plans and obtained backing for a new theatre in the spring of 1703, and after many delays he was finally able to hold an official inaugural concert in a semicompleted building in late November 1704. The *Diverting-Post* for 25 November–2 December 1704 tells us that "*Segniora Sconiance*, a Famous *Italian* Singer, who lately came from those Parts, had a few Days since the Honour to Sing before Her Majesty with great Applause, upon the First Opening of the *THEATRE* in the *Hay-Market*, erected by the Contribution of the Nobility. She is to Sing several *Italian* Songs, never Sung in this Kingdom before, Compos'd by the most Celebrated of the Modern *Italian* Masters." Signora Sconiance is otherwise unknown to scholars, at least by this name, though Curtis A. Price suggests she may have been one of the imported singers in *The Loves of Ergasto* in April.[1] The theatre was far from ready for occupancy, but Vanbrugh must have been getting anxious to open his building and show his subscribers something for their money. Unlike Dorset Garden and Drury Lane, which were built to make a profit for investors, the Haymarket was privately owned by Vanbrugh. He raised about £3000 of the cost from "thirty Persons of Quality" (as Cibber terms them) who were promised free admission to all "Plays and Opera's" performed in the building.[2] Since this privilege was designed to expire upon the death of the subscriber, Vanbrugh arranged a rather good deal for himself. As proprietor of a resident theatre company he would be entitled to the profits, and he would have no rent to pay.

The inaugural concert in late November may well have been a hurried response to Rich's preparations to mount an Italian opera at Drury Lane—*Arsinoe*, which opened in January. With competition again heating up, Vanbrugh was ready to take responsibility for the company he and Congreve were to operate, and on 14 December the Lord Chamberlain granted a license:

Anne R

Whereas we have thought fit for the better Reforming the Abuses and Immorality of the Stage, That a New Company of Comedians should be Establish'd for Our Service, under stricter Government, and Regulations, than have been formerly.

We therefore, reposing especial Trust and Confidence in Our Trusty and Well beloved *John Vanbrugh* and *William Congreve* Esqs; for the due Execution and Performance of this Our Will and Pleasure, do Give and Grant unto them the said *John Vanbrugh* and *William Congreve*, full Power and Authority, to Form, Constitute, and Establish for Us, a Company of Comedians, with Full and Free License to Act, and Represent, in any convenient Place, during Our Pleasure, all Comedies, Tragedies, Plays, Interludes, Opera's, and to perform all other Theatrical and Musical Entertainments whatsoever; and to Settle such Rules and Orders for the good Governmene [sic] of the said Company, as the Chamberlain of Our Houshold shall from time to time Direct and Approve of.

. . . By Her Majesty's Command,

Kent

(*London Gazette*, 21–25 December 1704)

Nothing whatever is said about the relation of this company to existing companies. In appearance, this is simply a fresh grant. We possess no revocation of the 1695 Lincoln's Inn Fields license. Downes's version is that Betterton "Assign'd his License, and his whole Company over to Captain *Vantbrugg* to *Act* under HIS." In fact the Lincoln's Inn Fields license was not Betterton's alone, but lacking definite evidence, we may guess that Vanbrugh offered satisfactory terms to the Lincoln's Inn Fields performers, who then signed away the rights conferred on them by the 1695 license. At all events, the actors' new agreements appear to have been for straight salaries. That may have been a great inducement: a share in nonexistent profits is hard to live on, and Vanbrugh seems always to have tried to pay his performers the salary that was due to them.

Vanbrugh apparently meant to oversee the daily operation of the company. From December 1704 to the end of the 1705–6 season, he maintained control over it, and during that time I will refer to the company as Vanbrugh's. He was spreading himself thin: while running the theatre, he was trying to supervise the building of Blenheim, a project which, after June 1705, often took him out of town; he was serving as comptroller of the Board of Works; and his appointment to the College of Heralds brought with it prestige but also nuisances.[3] He had no managerial experience, and even had he been devoting his full attention to the Haymarket, he would have needed advice and some expert assistants.

Initially, at least, much of his help must have come from his partner Congreve and from Betterton.

Congreve's share in the Haymarket was evidently based on his prestige as a writer, his new-found interest in libretto writing, and his membership in the Kit-Cat Club. Perhaps Vanbrugh originally hoped that Congreve would take part in the daily management of the company. For example, Congreve seems to have proposed a contract settlement to Haym's pupil "the Baroness" at the end of the 1704–5 season. However, the division of responsibility between the partners was not clear, or they misunderstood one another, and Vanbrugh disregarded Congreve's offer.[4] Whatever his financial and managerial agreement, Congreve soon grew disenchanted and withdrew—apparently because he could not afford to lose money as he was doing. Genest asserts that he retired at the end of the 1704–5 season, but without citing any evidence. Cibber's recollection was that "the Prospect of Profits from this Theatre was so very barren, that Mr. *Congreve* in a few Months gave up his Share and Interest in the Government of it wholly to Sir *John Vanbrugh*."[5] But as late as 9 December 1705 we find Rich accusing Congreve along with Vanbrugh of plotting to "seduce" the singer Mrs Hooke (alias Harcourt) away from Drury Lane. On 15 December 1705 Congreve writes to his friend Keally, "I have quitted the affair of the Hay-market. You may imagine I got nothing by it."[6] He goes on to say that he "was dipt," that is, involved in pecuniary liabilities (OED); and he quotes Terence to the effect that he has had to redeem himself from captivity as cheaply as possible. Since he had written to Keally in October or November but considered his withdrawal news in December, we may infer that Congreve dropped out early in the 1705–6 season.

Betterton's place in the hierarchy is not easy to determine. He had vast prestige and was still a leading actor, but he was seventy years old in 1705, and he was starting to cut back on the number of his appearances.[7] There are indications that he was consulted on some points of management and that he continued to supervise some new productions. Thus, for example, in the preface to *Almyna* (staged in December 1706) Mrs Manley says that her play was "admirably Acted . . . owing to Mr. *Betterton's* unwearied care, (who is desired to accept the Author's acknowledgements for so faithfully discharging the Trust that was repos'd in him)." We can scarcely doubt that Betterton took an active part in mounting this play. Since Vanbrugh would have had little time to oversee new productions, some of the responsibility logically remained with Betterton, at least until the fall of 1707 when he drastically curtailed his activities.

One strong indication of Betterton's influence on Vanbrugh is the style of two of the Haymarket's three operas in the spring of 1706. *The British Enchanters* and *Wonders in the Sun* are both "English operas," interspersing song and dance and fancy scenic effects in a spoken text. Betterton had been staging shows like this for more than thirty years. Estcourt's epilogue to the Drury Lane production of *Camilla* (March 1706) confirms the idea that initially, at least, the Haymarket style was that of Betterton. Referring scornfully to the rejected union proposal of 1705, Estcourt had Mrs Oldfield say,

> Our Neighbors lately, with an Ill Design,
> Strove the Contending *Play-Houses* to Join;
>
> . . . .
>
> Our *Prince*, not envious of his Rival's Throne,
> Lives like First Monarchs, happy with his own.
> Too kind to wish his Enemies shou'd yeild,
> He left 'em free,—New *Theatres* to Build.
> And see what Fruits from Our Divisions spring,
> Both Houses now Italian *Musick* Sing.
> The Fair can only tell, which pleases best
>
> . . . .
>
> But this We know, had that dire Union been,
> You ne'er in *England* had *Camilla* seen.
> They wou'd some *Masque* have shewn, or *Country Farce*;
> *Paris's Judgment*, or the *Loves of Mars*
>
> . . . .
>
> To please this Audience, we'll no Charges spare,
> But chearfully maintain a Vigrous War.
> New Funds we'll raise, and heavy Taxes lay,
> Dancers and Singers (Dear Allies) to pay.
> Acting shall Shine, and Poetry Revive,
> And Emulation make our Empire Thrive.

The Haymarket had produced one opera much closer to the Italianate form that spring, *The Temple of Love*, "consisting all of Singing and Dancing," Downes tells us, and this was probably what Estcourt had in mind when he says that because of the competition, "Both Houses now Italian *Musick* Sing."

After the rather dismal 1705–6 season Vanbrugh realized the necessity of proper supervision for his company, and imported the talented Owen Swiney as manager—a subject to be taken up in detail when we get to the protounion of 1706. Swiney could devote full attention to the theatre in a way that the harried Vanbrugh could not. To see what Vanbrugh thought he was doing in the first two seasons of the Haymarket's operation is hard. He seems to have had no clear sense of direction for the company, nor did he understand the realities of theatre as a paying business. The first partial season shows numerous signs of confusion, inefficiency, missed opportunities, and bad judgment.

1704–1705

While the Lincoln's Inn Fields Company marked time, awaiting the completion of its new quarters, Rich set aggressively to work. Vanbrugh was planning to make a great splash with opera: very well, Rich could play that game too. The first issue of the *Diverting-Post* (28 October 1704) reported that "The Play-House in the Hay-Market . . . is almost finish'd, in the mean time, two Opera's translated from the Italian by good Hands, are setting to Musick, one by Mr. Daniel Purcell, . . . the other by Mr. Clayton, both Opera's . . . are to be performed at the Opening of the House." *Arsinoe* was Clayton's only opera before *Rosamond* (1707) and is surely the piece referred to. Yet six weeks after the announcement above, the paper reported that Clayton's opera "after the *Italian* manner" would be produced at Drury Lane, as it was in January. The Patent Company had other ploys in mind also. A series of notices in the *Daily Courant* in November and December report that Dorset Garden had been repaired and would again be available for music, dancing, and theatre performances. Rich did not, so far as we know, actually make use of the ramshackle old theatre, but he was aware he needed to fight spectacle with spectacle. He also made some effort to steal useful performers from the rival company: among the papers in LC 7/3 is a copy of a letter from Sir John Stanley, dated 27 November 1704, specifically enjoining Rich not to engage Lincoln's Inn Fields performers.

In *Arsinoe* Rich acquired a valuable property. The opera received its premiere 16 January 1705 and enjoyed fourteen public performances its first season. Roger Fiske comments glumly of this piece, "It is tragic that playhouse audiences were taken in by this nonsense. *Arsinoe* was monstrously successful, the silliness of both words and music passing unnoticed."[8] Silly it may have been; but in mounting it at Drury Lane, Rich both enjoyed its success and deprived Vanbrugh of an impressive entree for his new theatre. And since the other piece on which Vanbrugh was counting, Daniel Purcell's *Orlando Furioso*, remained unwritten, he was left without any good opera with which to open his new theatre.

Rich seems to have mounted *Arsinoe* with exceptional speed and presented it with skill. With music by Clayton and libretto translated by Motteux, the show opened nearly three months before the Haymarket could stage its first production. The advertisements for *Arsinoe*, taken together, make up a pattern which proved typical of the early Italianate operas. The costs were underwritten by subscription, as the more elaborate concerts had been in the past.[9] Subscribers were rewarded with special seats in the boxes and the pit. As a further enticement to fans of the various performers, "The Boxes on the Stage and the Galleries" were "for the Benefit of the Actors," according to the *Daily Courant*. The innovation *Arsinoe* represented to the London theatre audience was also advertised: it would be "all sung"—in this case in English. Rich was not, however, risking a performance of opera by itself: because *Arsinoe* was short, the program also included dancing by L'Abbé, du Ruel, and at least four others, as well as singing "In Italian and English before and after the opera." Thus Rich contrived an experiment both cautious and daring: he minimized his outlay as much as possible, and buttressed the innovation with familiar adjuncts, but he also stole Vanbrugh's thunder by introducing Italianate opera to London.

Drury Lane happens to have advertised every acting day just at this time, so we may also note from *Arsinoe* another pattern. The opera premiered on Tuesday 16 January, but did not reappear until Thursday the twenty-fifth. Performances, even a special command performance at St. James's Palace, came at intervals, not day after day. Thomas Clayton, the composer and musical director, wanted to insure that the voices of his singers would not be strained. Himself an enthusiastic promoter of Italian opera in England, Clayton admits in his preface that the London audience would take some educating.

The Design of this Entertainment being to introduce the *Italian* manner of Musick on the *English* Stage, which has not been before attempted; I was oblig'd to have an *Italian* Opera translated: In which the Words, however mean in several Places, suited much better with that manner of Musick, than others more Poetical would do.

The Stile of this Musick is to express the Passions . . . And though the Voices are not equal to the *Italian*, yet I have engag'd the Best that were to be found in *England*; and I have not been wanting, to the utmost of my Diligence, in the instructing of them.

The Musick being Recitative, may not, at first, meet with that general Acceptation, as is to be hop'd for from the Audience's being better acquainted with it.[10]

Various contract disputes in P.R.O. LC 7/3 tell us that opera singers were often paid by the performance rather than on a salary basis; and because of higher fees and orchestra salaries, operas were more expensive to run than plays, even after the initial investment. The Patent Company wisely opened a new comedy, *Farewel Folly*, close to the premiere of the opera, offering novelty in both fields while giving singers the rest they required.

Rich had been doing well with plays. Cibber's very successful *The Careless Husband* premiered early in December, and the popularity of this easygoing reform comedy helped bring about the early demise of Rowe's one comedy, *The Biter*, at Lincoln's Inn Fields. Motteux's mediocre *Farewel Folly* ran half a dozen nights in January in tandem with *Arsinoe*. Lincoln's Inn Fields made no effort to answer the opera directly. The company advertised only three plays in January, one of them a benefit. In February Vanbrugh's company did score a success with Mrs Centlivre's *The Gamester*, an antigambling tract which ran at least a dozen times in the first three weeks of the month. Drury Lane tried to counter hastily with John Dennis's *Gibraltar*, a "Spanish romance" which attempted to capitalize on the topicality of the recent British victory at Gibraltar. Probably the company was a bit overextended: the play was advertised for 13 February but postponed to the sixteenth. Dennis—a cantankerous author and not the most impartial witness—complained bitterly about the acting and said that problems in rehearsals were "so numerous as never had befaln any Play in my Memory." The February round belongs to Lincoln's Inn Fields—but *Arsinoe* was prospering, and as other plans fell through, Vanbrugh and Congreve still had no opera with which to open the Haymarket.

The renewed sense of genuine hostility between the two companies is evident in a squabble which occurred in March. Both were working up farces based on Molière's *L'Amour Médecin*. Owen Swiney was responsible for Drury Lane's version, *The Quacks*. Lincoln's Inn Fields's adaptation, called *The Consultation*, was never printed, and we know neither who wrote it nor how similar it may have been to Drury Lane's play. According to the title page of *The Quacks*, the play was "Acted after being twice forbid," and Swiney's preface says that it "was to be stiffled, because the other House were to Act one upon the same Subject." Rich complained to the Lord Chamberlain later that year, "Mr Swynys Play stopt . . . & no Just reason for Stopping it but kindness to Mr Vanbrugh."[11] These plaints turn out to be disingenuous. By careful reconstruction from broadsides and gossip in the papers, Albert Rosenberg has demonstrated that *The Quacks* contains sharp personal satire on the Kit-Cat Club, and especially on its secretary, Jacob Tonson.[12] Swiney was forced to delete most of the satire before the play was allowed on the stage. *The Consultation* did not make its appearance until 24 April, after the opening of the Haymarket. Neither play seems to have survived the season. Swiney's prologue is interesting, however, for its comments on the revival of theatrical hostilities.

> Of what importance is our Muses breath,
> Twice has the Bantling been expos'd to Death!
> 'Twas born with Teeth, but those in fearful doubt
> Wisely the first Inquisitor struck out.
> Let every Quack be Comforted to Night,
> Care has been taken that he shall not Bite;
> Maim'd as he is, he Trembles to Engage,
> The slow Productions of yon Rival Stage.
> On deep Designs the coupled Bards have hit,
> And wisely wou'd Engross, all Foreign Wit.
> And think the surest way to gain the Town
> wou'd be to shew, but little of their own.
> Like Kings of *Brentford* they'd our realms surprise,
> Supported by great Armies in Disguise:
> But fear we can't from their united Trouble,
> When jaded *Pegasus* must carry Double!
> Safe in your Favour, we their Threats dispise,
> Our Watchful Parties cut off their Supplies.

> As this Nights treat (which to their Care we owe)
> Was French Provision going to the Foe!
> In Art's of War we've still Superiour been,
> And starv'd the Garrison of *Lincolns-Inn*.
> The new made Fort, from the thin Remnant gleans,
> Their Tatter'd Monarchs, and their Aged Queens!
> With Force and Fraud they threaten from afar,
> And big with Promis'd Aid, renew the War.

By this time—29 March, when *The Quacks* was finally allowed—Drury Lane knew that the Haymarket was about to open with an imported Italian opera. The cocky sneers in this prologue undoubtedly reflect some alarm. In the event, however, Drury Lane need not have worried.

Arsinoe had given the Haymarket managers pause on several bases. Two months before the theatre commenced regular operation, its proprietors had no idea what they would mount first, save that they had lost their edge in Italianate opera. Congreve, writing the news to his friend Joseph Kéally in Ireland on 3 February 1705, commented unhappily, "I know not when the house will open, nor what we shall begin withal; but I believe with no opera. There is nothing settled yet."[13] English opera productions normally took several months to prepare; and the company lacked a full complement of singers trained in the new music. Vanbrugh was anxious to get his theatre going, in part to recoup his own investment.[14] All the signs point to a precipitate and ill-considered opening. A good deal of confusion has surrounded our impression of the whole affair. Downes, our most immediate source, says only this: "And upon the *9th* of *April* 1705. Captain *Vanthrugg* open'd his new Theatre in the *Hay-Market*, with a Foreign Opera, Perform'd by a new set of Singers, Arriv'd from *Italy*; (the worst that e're came from thence) for it lasted but 5 Days, and they being lik'd but indifferently by the Gentry; they in a little time marcht back to their own Country" (*Roscius Anglicanus*, p. 48). This opera, unnamed by Downes, has been convincingly identified as Greber's *Gli Amori d'Ergasto* (*The Loves of Ergasto*) by Alfred Loewenberg.[15] Cibber's muddled account says that the Haymarket "open'd . . . with a translated Opera to *Italian* Musick, called the *Triumph of Love*" which "had but a cold Reception, being perform'd but three Days, and those not crowded."[16] Nalbach compounds Cibber's mistakes by saying that "*The Triumph of Love* . . . was not produced until July 1705 at the theatre in

Lincoln's Inn Fields"—a mistake borrowed without acknowledgment from Summers's edition of Congreve. Actually, no such work was performed anywhere in 1705.[17] As Fiske observes, Cibber has simply confused and conflated the titles of two later operas (*The Temple of Love* and *Love's Triumph*). Fiske goes on to argue, however, relying on Cibber, that the work "almost certainly . . . was sung in English," and that it was done "with English singers as well as Italian."[18] This seems unlikely. Fiske may well be correct in hypothesizing that Vanbrugh approached Margherita de l'Epine ("Greber's Peg") for help in rustling up an opera in a hurry, and Haym's pupil, "the Baroness," sang in it. But Fiske does not mention Downes's account, and though Downes's slips and chronological errors are legion, I am inclined to think that he knew the difference between Lincoln's Inn Fields's house singers and strangers imported from Italy. As Nalbach observes, Congreve's epilogue for the occasion suggests that the audience has been hearing Italian ("In sweet *Italian* Strains our Shepherds sing"), and says that not only "our House and Scenes are new, / Our Song and Dance, but ev'n our Actors too."[19] The epilogue to Steele's *The Tender Husband*, spoken by Estcourt at Drury Lane on 23 April, protests against Italian singers, and implies the use of a castrato.

> No more th' *Italian* squaling Tribe admit,
> In Tongues unknown; 'tis Popery in Wit.
> . . . .
> Husbands take Care, the Danger may come nigher,
> The Women say their Eunuch is a Friar.

In his haste to get the Haymarket going with an opera, Vanbrugh suffered a humiliating misfire with his imported novelty—and then found that he had nothing to fall back on. Downes continues with an unusually detailed account, making his own opinion clear:

The first Play *Acted* there, was *The Gamester*. . . . After that, *She wou'd, if She Cou'd*; and half a Score of their old Plays, *Acted* in old Cloaths, the Company brought from *Lincoln's-Inn-Fields*. The Audiencies falling off extremly with entertaining the Gentry with such old Ware, whereas, had they Open'd the House at first, with a good new *English* Opera, or a new Play; they wou'd have preserv'd the Favour of Court and City, and gain'd Reputation and Profit to themselves. (P. 48)

The Lincoln's Inn Fields productions of *The Indian Emperour* and *The Merry Wives of Windsor* were used at the Haymarket in mid-April when *The Loves of Ergasto* quickly flagged. *The Consultation* was added to *Ergasto* and played as a double bill on 24 and 25 April. Mrs Pix's *The Conquest of Spain*, mounted in mid-May ("The first new Play *Acted* there"), proved a disappointment, expiring in six days. Clearly the Haymarket owners had no season planned beyond their hastily arranged opera. The company muddled on through the spring with old plays—*The Humorous Lieuten-ant*, *The Gamester*, *Venice Preserv'd*, *Don Quixote*, *Amphitryon* (mounted a week earlier at Drury Lane), *The Scornful Lady*, *The Adventures of Five Hours*, *Othello*, *The Man of Mode*, *Rule a Wife*, *The Virtuous Wife*. At least four of these plays had not been acted at Lincoln's Inn Fields so far as we know for several years: their reappearance at this time suggests a com-pany floundering around looking for ways to attract an audience, as does the performance of *Love for Love* "Acted all by Women" on 27 June. Vanbrugh and Congreve apparently had a bad spring. Drury Lane, meanwhile, had no great success with Steele's *The Tender Husband* in late April, and contented itself with stock plays and revivals of *Beggar's Bush* (altered by Henry Norris) and *The Loyal Subject*.

The temporary return of Vanbrugh's company to the Lincoln's Inn Fields theatre in July has occasioned a great deal of commentary from scholars. Nalbach and others have imagined that the move reflects the allegedly unsatisfactory acoustics and location of the Haymarket thea-tre—points on which Cibber harshly criticizes it.[20] In fact, we have solid evidence that the theatre was not fully completed when Vanbrugh rushed into it to "answer" *Arsinoe* in April 1705. In his *Review of the Affairs of France* for 3 May, Defoe reports gleefully that "the Founders of this Struc-ture . . . Complain of Deficient Funds for the Compleating the Build-ing." And in the *Daily Courant* for 19 July 1705 Vanbrugh's company advertised a performance of *Amphitryon* at Lincoln's Inn Fields, adding: "Note, That the Company will continue to Act there till Her Majesty's Theatre in the Hay-Market be intirely finish'd" This tells us in so many words what everything else about the bungled fragment of a season at the Haymarket would lead one to suspect: Vanbrugh moved the com-pany in before the theatre was fully rigged and operational.

Despite the revival of competition, we can see one clear sign of accom-modation on both sides at the end of this season: throughout the month of June the two companies acted on alternate nights. The war had been renewed, but without quite the animosity or the direct clashes which had characterized the start of hostilities ten years earlier. But would competition continue at all? As I suggested in the last chapter, Vanbrugh had evidently had some kind of union in mind from the beginning. In June 1705 he formally broached the idea to Rich through the Lord Chamberlain's office. Our principal source of information is Gildon's account in the 1706 edition of *The Post-Boy Robb'd of his Mail*, here rearranged to untangle the order of events.[21] On 7 June and again on 21 June 1705 Sir John Stanley, Kent's assistant, wrote to Rich "intimating my Lord *Chamberlain's* Pleasure" that Rich "shou'd bring in Proposals for uniting the two Companies." Those letters are lost, and we cannot determine what sort of union they proposed or hinted at. However, further negotiations are clearly documented.

Gildon introduces Rich's reply to Stanley with a long catalogue of derogatory comments about Vanbrugh. First, since he located his theatre "at the Fagg-End of the Town," getting to it is "an insupportable Expence." Second, he has built "a Theatre in nothing better than what we had before, except in the Front, or Case, which signifies little to the Business of the Place." Third, when he was preparing to open, Vanbrugh took "no Care to engage the Players of *Drury-lane*, who kept out of Articles a long time [after the 1703–4 season?] in expectation of being sent to; but he either through Pride, Negligence, or something worse, never minded till they were all engag'd." Fourth, Vanbrugh has taken the "Direction and Advice of those very People in the Government of this New Company, who had before ruin'd two Companies, and brought them from the Admiration, to the Contempt of the Town." Fifth, Vanbrugh has attempted, "contrary to all Reason or Justice in the World, to destroy the Patent, and unite the Companies." Given this preamble, we cannot expect the following correspondence to reflect much credit on Vanbrugh; in its essentials it seems an accurate but not disinterested documentation of one side of the story.

Rich made no immediate reply to Vanbrugh's offer, but sometime (probably in the middle of June) a majority of the Drury Lane actors sent a petition to the Lord Chamberlain begging him not to force them to join the Haymarket, since "a union of the two companies cannot be without great prejudice, if not utter ruin, to them and their numerous families."[22] On the other hand Vanbrugh was probably well aware that some of Rich's actors were ready to entertain the idea of union, petition or no petition. The *Diverting-Post* for 9–16 June printed "An Epilogue for the *Theatre Royal*" which takes up the subject.

> Why may not we (Combin'd) resume each *Grant*,
> Which we all know to be Exorbitant?
> Yes, this perhaps might do; had we one Heart,
> But we a House divided are; One Part
> R——h-Ridden are,—there's small pretentions,
> The other Part wou'd do't,—but they have Pensions;
> So that in vain, each way we seek Redress,
> In vain we strive t'avoid being Penny-less.

Of the fifty-two people listed in *The London Stage* 1704–5 roster for Drury Lane, thirty-two signed this petition.[23] Powell is on the roster but had left the company; Mrs Mountfort and Mrs Mills are not on the roster but signed the petition. Of the signers, twelve moved to the Haymarket a year later. The performers in both companies must have realized that a union would put a certain number of them out of work. Estcourt's flippant, ironic dedication to Rich of *The Fair Example* (published late in the fall of 1705) is a tricky document to interpret with confidence, but as I read it, Estcourt is thanking Rich for holding out "against an Union that might have crusht or sunk the Actors," while remaining aware of the irony of treating Christopher Rich as the champion of actors' rights.

To return to the letters in *The Post-Boy Robb'd*, on 19 July 1705 Vanbrugh produced in writing his "Proposals for the Reducing the two Companies of Players into one." As Gildon prints them, they were as follows:

1st. That the Patent Adventurers on .their ceasing to act by Vertue of their Patent, be admitted to a Moyety of the clear Profits, which shall arise from the Company now establish'd by the Queen in the *Hay-Market*.

2d. That there shall no Regard be had to each Companies past Debts, Engagements, or Stock, their Concern together being forward, not backwards.

3d. That the Persons to be intrusted for the Management, be Nam'd by the Queen, to be at any Time chang'd and remov'd, as she shall think fit.

4th. That if these three principal Heads be agreed to, the Settlement of the inferiour Matters, may be refer'd to my Lord *Chamberlain*.

J. Vanbrugh

These proposals are obviously outrageous, and "About the 25th of *July*, Mr. *Rich* sent the following Answer to Sir *John St——ley*":

To receive any Persons (others than Actors, Singers, Dancers, and Performers) into any Part, Interest or Share, with the Proprietors, under the Patents, is not in my Power, without a Breach of Trust, which I cannot answer to the rest of the Proprietors, who may tear me to pieces with Law-Suits, if they shou'd see me . . . prejudice their Rights and Properties. . . . Sir, I am a Purchaser under the Patents, . . . and am not only accountable to the rest of the Proprietors, and lyable to several New Debts, but also under Covenants with several Actors, Singers, and Dancers, for the whole Undertaking. And when after ten Years Employment, Expence, and Diligence, I have (notwithstanding many Difficulties) succeeded; so that the Company has the good Fortune to please the Town, and the Profits begin to reimburse, and pay the Monies and Debts contracted: If I shall now be depriv'd of reaping the Benefit of such my Labour and Charges, what must the Effect be, but the undoing of my self, and of the Interests of those engag'd with me . . . ?

And now, Sir, with Submission, I do not see upon the whole Matter, how such an Union, as seems to be intended, can have a good Effect, if one considers either the Inclination of the Quality, and Gentry, who have always declared for the keeping up of two Companies (and to that purpose, subscribed to the Building of a New Theatre) or the Management of the New Theatre, since it was open'd, which has not been such, with all the Advantages of setting forth, as wou'd invite others to put the whole under the same Govenment, in order to pay a very large Rent to Mr. *Vanbrugh*, for that which cost him little or nothing, beyond the Subscriptions received by him. And, with regard to the Players themselves, since they have already, in a Petition to his Lordship, declared themselves content with the Terms, under which they act here, and apprehensive of great Hardships, if not utter Ruin, which they conclude will be brought upon them by such a Union. . . .

These, Sir, are some of the Reasons, which I humbly offer against a Union in general; and having on Thursday last, receiv'd Mr. *Vanbrugh*'s Proposals in writing, I am the more confirm'd in my Opinion against it: For by the first, he wou'd have us cease to Act by Virtue of our Patents; and in the second, he declares, That no Regard shall be had to the Companies past Debts, Engagements, or Stock, and how an Union can be either practicable, or safe, with respect to the Interest of all Parties upon this foot, I cannot conceive.

Vanbrugh had much to gain from a union, and perhaps some of the actors would have benefited, but what inducement could Vanbrugh offer the wily Christopher Rich? Even had Vanbrugh's proposals been less extravagantly one-sided and full of loopholes, it is hard to see how he could have made a convincing case for his power grab. The Haymarket had enjoyed little success in its first partial season, and Rich was firmly convinced that he would do better by holding his ground than by letting Vanbrugh have a monopoly in return for a share of the proceeds.

1705–1706

Frustrated in his plans for a comfortable monopoly, Vanbrugh set out to wage a vigorous campaign in his first full season at the Haymarket. This renewal of competition is identifiable from the sudden increase in duplicate productions, simultaneous premieres, and the collision of operas in the spring. Among the stock plays mounted by both companies were *Amphitryon*, *The Committee*, *The Rover*, *Sir Salomon*, and Shadwell's *Timon*. Direct competition was the order of the day. When the Haymarket put on *The Merry Wives* (13 December), Drury Lane countered with *Henry the Fourth* (15 December). New productions regularly opened within days of one another, in a renewal of the acrimonious spirit of 1695.

We know little about details of the infighting between the two companies. One clear sign of significant competition from the Haymarket, however, is a protest by Rich to the Lord Chamberlain on December ninth, in which he objected to Vanbrugh and Congreve's having offered Mary Hooke (alias Harcourt) a contract, since she had previously signed articles for five years with the Patent Company.[24] He complained that since Christmas 1704, Powell, Bowen, Doggett, Mins, Husbands, Mrs Bicknell, and Mrs Baker had all been lured away to the Haymarket, and that Newman (a prompter) and Hood (a dresser) had also been tempted. We should note, however, that this situation was by no means new and surprising. At least three of these people had joined the Haymarket during the previous spring (Powell, Bowen, Mrs Baker), and two more were with Vanbrugh's company when the 1705–6 season opened. Vanbrugh was not suddenly starting to raid Rich's personnel: only after the Haymarket appeared to get off to a good start in its first full year did Rich feel threatened enough to complain.

The Haymarket reopened on 30 October 1705 with the premiere of Vanbrugh's own *The Confederacy*. Drury Lane chose the same night for its first premiere of the season, Baker's *Hampstead Heath* (a revision of *An Act at Oxford*, banned in 1704). Neither show flourished, though Vanbrugh's was occasionally revived. Drury Lane's next new play was Mrs Centlivre's *The Basset-Table* (20 November), an obvious imitation of her own play *The Gamester*, which had been well received in a production at Lincoln's Inn Fields the previous spring. This reprise lasted only four nights. The Haymarket countered with Rowe's *Ulysses* on 23 November ("all new Cloath'd, and Excellently well perform'd," Downes tells us), a production which ran ten nights in its first month.[25] Drury Lane replied, not very successfully, with Cibber's dreary tragedy, *Perolla and Izadora* (3 December). An exchange which demonstrates the prevailing hostility occurred in early January, when the Haymarket put on *The Faithful General*, an adaptation "by a young Lady" of *The Loyal Subject*. She implied that it was not well presented, but part of the reason for its three-night run was that Drury Lane hastened to offer the "Beaumont and Fletcher" original. Newspaper ads place them a day apart; the preface to the 1706 quarto of *The Loyal Subject* says it "appeared on the Stage the very same Day" as the adaptation, and observes smugly that the town "quitted the Imposter to embrace the Legitimate."

Among the rest of the new plays tried by the two companies during this season the advantage clearly rests with Drury Lane, though only on the basis of a single success—Farquhar's *The Recruiting Officer* (8 April), which enjoyed ten performances late in the year. Vanbrugh's *The Mistake*, a vigorous translation of Molière's *Le Dépit amoureux*, lasted only six nights (Lincoln's Inn Fields, 27 December). Mrs Trotter's *The Revolution of Sweden* (February) and Mrs Pix's *Adventures in Madrid* (June) both failed at the Haymarket. Drury Lane fared no better with an anonymous comedy, *The Fashionable Lover* (early May). The crucial factor in assessing the season for each house was its luck with operas. ˙

Round one of the musical battle had gone decisively to Rich. Vanbrugh was apparently now determined to strike back, and in the surprisingly brief span of six weeks he mounted three major operatic productions. He may have been trying to feel out public taste, or perhaps he wanted to hedge his bets: one was an "English opera," one was Italian, and one was sui generis. The first, *The British Enchanters* (21 February) was much the most successful. "Wrote by the Honourable Mr. *George Greenvil*; very Exquisitly done, especially the Singing Part; making Love the *Acme* of all Terrestrial Bliss: Which infinitely arrided both Sexes, and pleas'd the Town as well as any *English* Modern Opera," Downes reports.[26] And while Granville's claim of "an uninterrupted Run of at least Forty Days"[27] is an exaggeration made long after the fact, the opera did enjoy twelve advertised performances its first season. Drury Lane responded first with standard comedies, and then with increasing desperation offered *Arsinoe*, *King Arthur* ("Not perform'd these Five Years"), *The Tempest*, and *The Island Princess*. Thus far the advantage lay with Vanbrugh.

The Haymarket's second opera, the Italianate *The Temple of Love* (7 March) "lasted but Six Days, and answer'd not their Expectation," according to Downes. Rich riposted successfully at the end of the month with Bononcini's *Camilla* (30 March), adapted by Swiney and Haym. *Camilla* was to be the most popular of all the early Italianate operas in England, but its vogue started slowly. The singers managed ten performances spread out over four months.[28] Thus although *Camilla* was to prove a crucial prop for Drury Lane the following year, initially it gave the Haymarket no great cause for alarm. The Haymarket's own last new opera, however, was a fiasco. Durfey's *The Wonders in the Sun* (5 April) is a weird and wonderful piece, quite unique. It mingles low humor and machine staging tricks with *Erewhon*-like satire and political commentary. It has had some defenders among twentieth-century critics: Fiske admires it, and Hume concludes that "the baffling complexities of the fantastic allegories in this peculiar farrago . . . should not be allowed to deprive Durfey of credit for a truly brilliant production."[29] But in its own time, the experiment failed. "It lasted only Six Days, not answering half the Expences of it," Downes reports glumly.[30] Doubtless the fact that Drury Lane opened Farquhar's *Recruiting Officer* on the third night did not help. Downes implies that this loss wrecked the season. He goes on to say, "After this, Captain *Vantbrugg* gave leave to Mr *Verbruggen* and Mr *Booth*, and all the Young Company, to Act the remainder of the Summer, what Plays they cou'd by their Industry get up for their own Benefit." To sum up, we notice that Drury Lane had not done especially well until the success of *The Recruiting Officer*; but with *The Wonders in the Sun*, the Haymarket ruined an already mediocre season. By 30 April 1706 Congreve was writing to his friend Keally: "I believe the Play house cannot go on another Winter. Have heard there is to be a Union of the two houses as well as Kingdoms."[31] Vanbrugh's first full season had ended in demoralizing failure.

II
THE PROTOUNION OF 1706

In the summer of 1706 Vanbrugh appears to have assessed his commitments and realized that he needed a manager competent to run the theatre on an everyday basis while he devoted himself to other projects. He arranged to "farm" the business, "the Direction and Government of the Queens Company of Actors in Her Majestys Theatre in the Haymarket," to Owen Swiney at the rate of £5 per acting day over the next seven years.[32] In some ways the choice of Swiney is surprising. Vanbrugh might have promoted a member of his own company rather than hiring someone whose experience had been gained under Rich. At least two Haymarket actors were plausible candidates. John Verbruggen had assisted Betterton for a number of years, and he and Barton Booth (another possible manager) were running the summer company in 1706. Vanbrugh's choice was, however, a wise one. Swiney had worked for Rich at Drury Lane for a number of years before joining the army, and he knew the business. He had translated the book for *Camilla* and thus had some experience with opera. He appears to have handled his actors tactfully while running the company in a disciplined and profitable way. The *Muses Mercury* for January 1707 (published in February) lauds "those Gentlemen, who are the *Protectors* of the Stage" for the reorganization of the theatres, and praises Swiney's "Direction" of the Haymarket, saying that his "Experience in the Management of such Things [is] too well known to need a Comment."

Swiney's appointment at the Haymarket was either part of or the catalyst for important shifts in company personnel and organization. The reorganization of London theatre imposed by the Lord Chamberlain in January 1708 has distracted scholars' attention from these earlier changes—but Downes actually ends his chronicle with this "Union":

From *Bartholomew* day [23 August] 1706, to the 15*th*, of *Octob.* following, there was no more *Acting* there [i.e., at the Haymarket].

In this Interval Captain *Vantbrugg* by Agreement with Mr. *Swinny*, and by the Concurrence of my Lord Chamberlain, Transferr'd and Invested his License and Government of the Theatre to Mr. *Swinny*; who brought with him from Mr. *Rich*, Mr. *Wilks*, Mr. *Cyber*, Mr. *Mills*, Mr. *Johnson*, Mr. *Keene*, Mr. *Norris*, Mr. *Fairbank*, Mrs. *Oldfield* and others; United them to the Old Company; Mr. *Betterton* and Mr. *Underhill*, being the only remains of the Duke of *York's* Servants, from 1662, till the Union in *October* 1706. Now having given an Account of all the Principal Actors and Plays, down to 1706, I with the said Union, conclude my History. (*Roscius Anglicanus*, p. 50)

Downes saw the reorganization of 1706 as a union of the acting companies, in part because he was replaced as prompter in the course of it. But some of the motives behind the reorganization remain unclear.

As early as April 1706 Vanbrugh had been hard at work again promoting a union, or so I interpret a remark in a letter from the Duke of Montague to Lord Halifax on 26 April: "Mr Vanbrooke, who is to waite of you to Hannover . . . [was supposed to] be ready in foure dayes, but the Duchesse of Marlborough told me this morning, that he is now upon making an agreement betweene the two playhouses, and after that he will not go till he has settled matters at woodstock."[33] Upon his return from the Continent, on 14 August he signed the agreement with Swiney. The next day he signed contracts with Wilks (to be responsible for rehearsals), Norris, and Mrs Oldfield. He is named in contracts with Mr and Mrs Mills, Bullock, Theophilus Keene, and Thomas Newman, the new prompter, on 20 August, though he did not sign them. After 15 August Swiney apparently used his discretion and made contract arrangements himself, as their agreement permitted.

By 3 September the news was out: the Newdigate Newsletters reported (inaccurately) that "her Majestie has ordered all her Servants belonging to the severall Playhouses to act in conjunction with those at the Haymarket only otherwise they must expect not to act any where else."[34] Congreve, better informed, wrote Keally on the tenth:

The play-houses have undergone another revolution; and Swinny, with Wilks, Mrs Olfield, Pinkethman, Bullock, and Dicky [Norris?], are come over to the Hay-Market. Vanbrugh resigns his authority to Swinny, which occasioned the revolt. Mr Rich complains and rails like Volpone when counterplotted by Mosca. My Lord Chamberlain approves and ratifies the desertion; and the design is, to have plays only at the Hay-Market, and operas only at Covent Garden [i.e., Drury Lane]. I think the design right to restore acting; but the houses are misapplied, which time may change.[35]

Rich must have protested with his standard formula that such an arrangement would work to the detriment of "the Persons concerned in the Patent," but his claim was vehemently denied by some of his fellow patentees. Interestingly, these people felt that the opera would prove lucrative, and that Rich, if possessed of an operatic monopoly, would be forced to keep new books and declare the vast profits they supposed would accrue. They pointed out

That in 12 years Past that Mr Rich has had the Management in his hands, tho' 'tis notorious he has spent vast sums himself he has not divided with those Concerned with him one Single Shilling—

That he own'd Last year that he Lost by his Players what he got by the Opera & by consequence his Desire of keeping them on, Can be for nothing but to Confound and Embroyl ye account and give him Pretence to make no Dividend

That if he has the Opera Single & entire ye Profits must be so Certain and ye accounts will be in so short and Plain a Compass that 'twill be impossible for him to deceive the People any Longer who have Claims to a Share with him

Whereas if he goes on in this confused Jumble of a Double Company there is no manner of Reason to believe they will fair any better for 12 years to come than they have done for 12 years Past.[36]

However unrealistic this view of the profitability of opera or of Rich's ability to juggle his books, the document confirms the fact that Rich opposed the straight generic split. He won his point: along with the exclusive right to offer full musical productions, Drury Lane continued to hold the right to perform plays.

Cibber's account of the reorganization in 1706 sounds so convincingly like an inside story that we are apt to repeat it uncritically. But Cibber was not a witness to most of this affair—he had not yet come back to London after the summer—and his report of it was written much later. If we try to correct for his inclination to place himself centerstage, we see a rather different picture. Vanbrugh wanted a manager to run the Haymarket for him, and, following the success of Italian opera at Drury Lane, he was apparently looking for someone qualified to produce operas. Hence he passed over people like Verbruggen and Booth and approached Swiney. Swiney, indebted to Rich, informed him of Vanbrugh's offer. They may well, as Cibber claims, have made a verbal agreement to rig competition and split the profits. But once the Lord Chamberlain had allowed the transfer of Rich's leading actors, can we imagine that Swiney (Mosca) would tell the actors they must go back to Rich (Volpone) on the strength of private agreements between the managers? Congreve's analogy was more accurate than we knew.

We may still wonder why Rich agreed to the changes, as he soon did. He had few friends at Court, and he was probably the victim of a double-cross, as Cibber suggests. Yet when Cibber, trying to negotiate a higher salary for 1706–7, asked, *"But, Master, where are your Actors?"* he found Rich unconcerned. "His Notion was that Singing and Dancing, or any sort of Exotick Entertainments, would make an ordinary Company of Actors too hard for the best Set who had only plain Plays to subsist on."[37] When Swiney wrote Cibber 5 October 1706 inviting him to join the Haymarket company, most of the excitement had already died down.[38] Rich had been given a sop for the actors he lost: an agreement that the Haymarket would be enjoined from using entr'acte song and dance, while Drury Lane would be allowed to offer plays, operas, and musical entertainments. We possess no explicit statement to this effect, but ads for this season back up the deduction. A supplementary bit of evidence is Granville's angry demand that the Lord Chamberlain stop the Haymarket from performing *The British Enchanters* "without Singing & Dancing Mauger the necessity thereof," which the author could "deem no other than a design to murder the Child of my Brain."[39] Would Swiney's company have mounted an "opera" without singing if it had had any choice? Given what we now know of the financial disasters in store for Italian opera companies in London, Rich's satisfaction may appear unwise. But recollecting the opinion of his fellow stockholders about the profits to be made from operas, we must acknowledge the careful businessman's approach. Rich did not want to depend solely on opera, but he had apparently made a lot of money. on *Arsinoe*, and *Camilla* was proving a sturdy prop. The costs, especially in fees paid to singers, had not yet gotten out of hand. As Congreve said, the houses were "misapplied" if Drury Lane was to feature operas, but Rich cannot have wanted to yield a lucrative novelty to Vanbrugh or Swiney. Furthermore, Rich took the recourse he understood best and sued every individual he had a claim against.[40]

The immediate strategy of the *"deserted Company* of Comedians" at Drury Lane (as their ad for 24 October 1706 terms them) was to rely on music. The prologue for their first performance of the season says

Alas! we have little left t'invite ye,
But Musick—which you Swear shall not delight ye.
Yet all my Hopes are on this Notion bent,
'Twill please the Ladies; for 'tis Innocent.[41]

The Patent Company featured singers and dancers, and it depended heavily on *Camilla*, which was advertised seventeen times between late November and the end of February. The pattern of ads is such that I believe they record most performances. On 1 February Philip Perceval wrote Sir John Perceval: "The opera of Camilla has been one of the chief diversions of the town this long time, and business is forgot. Next week we expect a new one, and soon after another. . . . Great things are expected of them both."[42] Had these operas (*Rosamond* and *Thomyris*) done as well as his last pair, Rich might have been justified in feeling that he was well rid of his expensive and grumbling actors. The amazing thing about the 1706–7 season is that Rich contrived to mount any plays at all. His principal actors were at the Haymarket, performing plays which had been Drury Lane staples. Rich sometimes attempted to compete directly, a policy which can only have forced unflattering comparisons of his remnant with the other company. If we look at casts of *The Recruiting Officer*, which had premiered in the spring of 1706 at Drury Lane, we can get a clear sense of the difference the shift of personnel made to Rich's company. In the Haymarket production advertised for 14 November 1706, seven members of the original cast played the roles they had created. The other seven named characters had to be recast: three of the actors from the first production were apparently no longer working in the London theatre; the other four had stayed at Drury Lane. The Patent Company pulled together a new production to open their fall season, recasting a minimum of ten of the fourteen principal parts. The difference in time and energy needed by each house to make the show presentable is enormous. And when, on 30 October, the two productions played head to head, Rich could think of no better claim than to advertise that "The true Sergeant Kite [Estcourt] is perform'd in Drury Lane."

The actors who had transferred were delighted to get away from Rich. Their attitude is reflected in Farquhar's prologue for the opening of the Haymarket on 15 October 1706:

Great Revolutions Crown this Wond'rous Year,
And Scenes are strangely turn'd, abroad, and here;

A Year mark'd out by Fate's Supream Decree
To set the *Theatre*, and *Europe* free:
A Year, in which the Destinies Ordain
The Mighty Monarch *LEWIS* to Restrain,
And the Dramatick Prince of *Drury-Lane*.
Both boldly push'd, to make the World their Prey,
Beggar'd their Subjects to inlarge their Sway;
But here, we own, the Simile does break,
Our Prince ne'er hurt us for Religion's sake.
    To you the Asylum of the Refugee,
Like Poor Distressed *Camisars* we flee;
Who Starv'd beneath our Vines, like those in *France*,
To feed those Damn'd Dragoons of Song and Dance.
The Muses Cause we own, here stand our Ground,
With Sense to Combate all the Power of Sound:
They take the Foreign; we the *Brittish* Law,
The Poets ours, and theirs the Fa, la, la.
You—whose Subscriptions rais'd this fair Machine,
Whose timely Loan recover'd lost *Turin*,
Declare for Action in this Glorious Reign.[43]

Both Vanbrugh and Swiney seem to have had a good reputation for trying to pay actors what they were owed. In the midst of the financial disasters of the spring of 1708 Vanbrugh wrote to the Lord Chamberlain, "I must upon the whole, beg you to believe, That on any of these occasions 'tis my nature & my principle to overdo, rather than have the least pretence for Complaint."[44] He put a lot of his own money into the Haymarket company and never recovered it. To judge by the few Patent Company contracts extant, Rich offered important actors a guaranteed minimum plus a percentage of profits, the "actors' shares" plan. The fact that the shares paid nothing (by Rich's own admission), and that the "guaranteed" minimums were seldom actually paid in full, made the offer of higher, genuinely guaranteed salaries a potent lure to the Drury Lane actors. Cibber joined the Haymarket in November 1706 after Rich refused to increase his salary, and he recalled with some wonder that the actors "were all paid their full Sallaries, a Blessing they had not felt in some Years in either House before."[45]

During this one season the Haymarket mounted straight, unadorned plays against whatever Rich cared to offer. (I presume that the Haymarket used "Act music," but it did without the featured extra attractions which had become so popular in the preceding decade.) Neither company offered many new productions. The Haymarket mounted six—of which only Farquhar's *Beaux Stratagem* (March) enjoyed significant success, then or later. Centlivre's *The Platonick Lady* (November), Manley's *Almyna* (December), and Edmund Smith's frigid *Phaedra and Hippolitus* (April) had little to recommend them. Vanbrugh's *The Cuckold in Conceit* (March; lost) was simply an afterpiece translated from Molière, while Cibber's *Marriage A-la-Mode* (February) is merely a pair of comic subplots stitched together from Dryden tragicomedies. Drury Lane's new productions numbered precisely two—both operas. Addison's *Rosamond* (4 March) was a misfire, betrayed by Clayton's music. Heidegger's *Thomyris* (1 April), however, justified the advance of 1200 Guineas by subscribers, who held reserved seats for the first six nights[46] —and it sharpened Vanbrugh's appetite for exclusive rights to opera in London.

We find occasional signs of competition in this season—for example, simultaneous performances of *The Recruiting Officer* on 17 April—but the two companies were not really directly comparable. The Haymarket sported all the best actors in London except Powell, Estcourt, and Pinkethman. Swiney engineered a remarkably smooth transition in which the best elements of each group combined to make up new productions of the stock plays they had in common. For example, *The Committee*, an old play recently popular with both companies, was played 2 December 1706, basically with men from the Drury Lane contingent and women from the Haymarket. Not all the combinations were this schematic, of course, and casts apparently varied somewhat, especially in plays that included Betterton's great roles. When he played Hamlet 10 December the advertised cast was almost all "Haymarket" actors, but Wilks played the title role on 11 January supported by a combined cast.

The addition of several frontline performers to the Haymarket company naturally forced some others out. Downes probably ends *Roscius Anglicanus* with the 1706 union because he had been edged out in that reorganization: Swiney refers to a pension for him in correspondence with the Lord Chamberlain's office in January 1707,[47] and the former Drury Lane prompter, Newman, shared a Haymarket benefit with two actors the following 9 May. Some of the actors evidently found themselves in a worse position. Old George Bright, a member of the company and its predecessors for more than twenty-five years, wound up in debtors' prison. Indeed he complained that his salary had been long unpaid, and that the company offered him the money he needed only on the condition that he sign papers waiving his rights in the stock of scenery and costumes (which were being sold to Vanbrugh)—sending John Mills (who had just come over from Drury Lane) as their emissary.[48]

The squeeze affected important actors too. Anne Bracegirdle walked off the stage in February, after which (when we have cast information) Mrs Bradshaw and Mrs Oldfield replaced her. At just this time Congreve and Eccles thought they had reached agreement with Rich to do their *Semele* at Drury Lane, and Mrs Bracegirdle was presumably the singer for whom the piece was written.[49] The May issue of the *Muses Mercury* carried a poem begging Mrs Bracegirdle to ignore "the *Man* . . . / Who like a Tyrant rules *Apollo*'s Art" and return to the stage, but she did not. John Verbruggen left the London theatre at the end of this season and went to Dublin.[50] By the following fall so young a player as Mrs Porter was complaining about the way she was being treated.[51] Not even Swiney could keep everyone happy.

Mullin's account of the building and first years of the Haymarket leads one to suppose that the venture was a disastrous financial failure which soon fell into complete disarray and had to be rescued by the union order of 1707.[52] However, this picture overlooks the prosperous interlude of the 1706–7 season, when even Cibber admits that under Swiney's management "Plays . . . began to recover a good Share of their former Esteem and Favour; and the Profits of them in about a Month enabled our new Menager to discharge his Debt (of something more than Two hundred Pounds) to his old Friend the Patentee," and that "not only the Actors (several of which were handsomely advanc'd in their Sallaries) were duly Paid, but the Menager himself, too, at the Foot of his Account, stood a considerable Gainer."[53] Vanbrugh confirms Cibber. After selling out in the spring of 1708 he wrote the Earl of Manchester that Swiney had "a good deal of money in his Pocket; that he got before by the Acting Company." Vanbrugh also mentions that Swiney "has behav'd himself so as to get great Credit in his dealings with the Actors," advancing this as a reason for confidence in Swiney's ability to manage the opera.[54] In sum, the evidence suggests that by offering straight plays—and few new ones—the Haymarket Company enjoyed real prosperity this season, and as far as one can judge, Rich had a decent year following a very different repertory policy. The rearrangements of September 1706, however, were to prove tenuous and short-lived.

III
THE UNION OF 1708

The forces which brought about the Union of 1708 were at work long before the fall of 1707. One can fairly say that from the spring of 1701 pressure for a new union is frequently in evidence. The author of *A Comparison between the Two Stages* (published in March 1702) hoped to promote a union, and Vanbrugh seems to have envisioned several possible combinations while actively working on the Haymarket. At the time of the reorganization of September 1706, as we have seen, Congreve had predicted that a further adjustment would be necessary. The new-found popularity of Italian opera was a complicating factor—one finally seized upon by Vanbrugh for what he believed was his own advantage. As director of the Patent Company, Rich could block any attempt to combine the two managements and their companies. Very well then, Vanbrugh would achieve his "Union" by separating opera from straight plays and taking an opera monopoly for himself. The union actually upset a reasonably stable and profitable situation: it occurred only because of Vanbrugh's strongarm tactics. Ironically, what he won was the chance to go broke in a hurry in 1708.

The Drury Lane management underwent some change in 1707, though we cannot be certain how significant it was. Sir Thomas Skipwith, long Rich's closest sharing associate, got so disgusted with the situation that he made a gift of his shares to Col. Henry Brett. Later court testimony indicates that Skipwith had been making essentially nothing from the theatre.[55] Cibber tells us that "immediately after Mr. *Brett* was admitted as a joint Patentee, he made use of the Intimacy he had with the Vice-Chamberlain to assist his Scheme of this intended Union. . . . The Scheme was, to have but one Theatre for Plays and another for Operas, under separate Interests. And this the generality of Spectators, as well as the most approv'd Actors, had been for some time calling for as the only Expedient to recover the Credit of the Stage and the valuable Interests of its Menagers" (*Apology*, 2: 46). I doubt that Brett was more than a minor figure in the complexities of arranging an opera monopoly. Cibber always liked to put himself and his acquaintances in the center of events. Vanbrugh's summation, written to a friend soon after the union had been accomplished, goes this way: "at last I got the Duke of Marlborough to put an end to the Playhouse Factions, by engaging the Queen to exert her Authority."[56] This seems like a very plausible explanation of the heart of the matter.

A year earlier Rich had fought successfully to retain the right to mount both plays and operas. Now Vanbrugh was after the opera concession. Could Rich have held onto opera at the price of ceding plays to Vanbrugh? We cannot tell, but after two and a half seasons perhaps Rich had a more realistic idea of the costs of opera and could see the problems inherent in it. By the fall of 1707 he was squabbling fiercely with his opera performers, and we may wonder if he did not see some advantages in the prospect of being rid of them. Rich's singers were in open rebellion. The *Post Boy* for 13–15 November ran the following announcement: "Whereas the Names of Mrs Margarita de l'Epine and Mrs Tofts, are mention'd in the Bills for the Opera of Camilla, as if they were to perform the parts of Prenesto and Camilla . . . That the Public may not be impos'd upon, This is to give Notice, that the same is done without their Consent; and that they do not intend to perform; there being no Articles of Agreement between them and the Managers . . . who have of late declin'd coming to any with them."

The *Muses Mercury* for October (published after 25 November 1707) tells us that the performance was indeed prevented. Rich's troupe limped on for another month, torn by dissension. A letter of 18 December from Mrs Tofts (who performed with the company earlier that month) to the Lord Chamberlain's office vehemently protests Rich's failure to pay past bills and the lack of a contract. Indeed the lady says that unless a settlement is reached, "I am resolv'd never to sett my foot upon ye stage again."[57] On the thirty-first Dieupart entered a long protest with the Lord Chamberlain in behalf of several singers and dancers—Margherita de l'Epine, Mrs Tofts, Valentino, Ramondon, Cherrier, M and Mlle Desbarques.[58]

As Rich was well aware, Vanbrugh was actively working to subvert Drury Lane's operatic productions. On 9 December 1707 the Haymarket actually advertised *The Royal Amazon* (i.e., *Thomyris*), a Drury Lane opera, and listed singers who were scheduled to appear that day in *Camilla* at Drury Lane. Apparently the Haymarket had to remain dark that day: Rich successfully blocked the transfers, or claimed exclusive right to the opera, and on 18 December he advertised the piece with all singers "performing their Parts as formerly"—eliciting Mrs Tofts's protest. As the Coke Papers make plain, Vanbrugh was busily signing Rich's performers to lucrative contracts, and the actors realized that a major change was not far off.[59] Late in the autumn, Estcourt wrote from a sickbed to Sir John Stanley, begging that his benefit play be scheduled "before any alteration of affairs happen among us." He wrote to the Lord Chamberlain the same day, explaining his inability to attend a meeting the next day which, he guesses, "brings with it some method and Turne in our Affairs."[60] Rich struggled for a while to hang onto his performers, relying in part on intimidation. Thus in early December eight musicians (Banister, Le Sac, Lullie, La Tour, Paisible, Babel, Roger, and Dieupart) "were turn'd out of Drury Lane Play house . . . upon suspicion of being concern'd in the Project of Acting Opera's in the Haymarket."[61] They were, of course, promptly hired by Vanbrugh. Such squabbling continued through November and December and finally degenerated into public name-calling in the theatres' ads for 26 December. Kent put an end to all this jockeying when on 31 December he issued the order of union.

Whereas by reason of the Division of her Majestys Comedians into two distinct houses or Companys the Players have not been able to gaine a reasonable Subsistance for their Encouragement in either Company nor can plays always be Acted to the best Advantage. And Whereas the Charge of Maintaining a Company of Comedians with performers of Opera in the Same House is now become too great to be Supported. Therefore to remedy those inconveniences and for ye better regulation and Support of the Theatres I do hereby Order and Require

That all Operas and other Musicall presentments be perform'd for the future only at her Majestys Theatre in the Haymarket under the direction of the Manager or Managers thereof with full power and Authority to receive Admitt and Employ any performer in Musick Dancing etc. whom he or they shall judge fitt for their Service and I do hereby Strictly charge and forbid ye said Managers from and after the 10th of January next to represent any Comedies Tragedys or other Entertainments of the Stage that are not sett to Musick or to erect any other Theatre for that purpose upon pain of being silenced for breach of this my Order. I do Likewise hereby give to the Manager or Managers of the Theatres in Drury Lane & Dorset Garden etc. full power and

Authority to receive and Admitt into their Company any players or Actors of Tragedy or Comedy they shall think fitt to entertain notwithstanding any Articles or engagements they may be under in any other Play house at the same time strictly charging and requiring the said Managers not to performe any Musicall Entertainments upon their Stage or to receive into their Service any Dancers or performers in Musick other than such Instrumentall Musick as are not employ'd in the Operas and are Necessary for such Entertainments upon the like pain of being silenced for breach of this Order. And for ye greater encouragement of the Above Nam'd Theatres I do further Order and Require that no person Society or Company of Undertakers whatever do presume to erect any other Theatre or to represent Comedys Tragedys Operas or other Entertainments of ye Stage except ye Above Managers of the Theatres in Drury Lane Dorsett Garden and of the Theatre in the Hay Market as is before appointed as they shall Answer the Contrary at their perill. Given under my hand and seale this 31st of December 1707 in the Sixth Year of her Majesty's Reign.

Kent[62]

This document is interesting on a number of counts. Some scholars have assumed that the Haymarket was failing and that the authorities were once again rescuing the group which happened to have official influence. Fuller knowledge of the competitive circumstances suggests a rather different interpretation. Kent's first point is not that the theatres were losing money—they were not—but that the actors were not making enough. I take the phrase "nor can plays always be Acted to the best Advantage" to refer to destructive repertory collisions. Swiney's Haymarket Company, lacking only the few experienced actors left at Drury Lane, could certainly cast any play to advantage. But neither company benefited from opening new plays against one another, or against operas, as they had been doing the previous two seasons. And a vital point which gets overlooked by those who favor the "failing Haymarket" theory is that Rich was apparently pleading inability to support both an acting company *and* an opera company. Whether this was the simple truth, or whether Rich was hoping to keep opera, or whether he was angling for a bargain which would leave him a united acting company, we cannot determine without more evidence.

We might expect the actors to object to being sent back to Rich, but if they protested, no record of the protest has come down to us. From

Cibber's dedication of *The Lady's Last Stake* to Lord Chamberlain Kent I would deduce that Kent gave the actors assurance of decent treatment. I quote from the 1708 quarto, adding in brackets comments Cibber printed in his *Apology*:

The Stage has for many Years, till late, groan'd under the greatest Discouragements, which have been very much, if not wholly owing to the Mismanagement or Avarice of those that have aukwardly govern'd it. Great Sums have been ventur'd upon empty Projects, and Hopes of immoderate Gains; and when those Hopes have fail'd, the Loss has been tyranically deducted out of the Actors Sallery. And if your Lordship had not redeem'd 'em [—This is meant of our being suffer'd to come over to *Swiney*—] they were very near being wholly lay'd aside, or at least, the Use of their Labour was to be swallow'd up in the pretended Merit of Singing and Dancing. [What follows relates to the Difficulties in dealing with the then impracticable Menager . . .] I don't offer this as a Reflection upon Musick, . . . but it has been the Misfortune of that, as well as Poetry, to have been too long in the Hands of those, whose Taste and Fancy are utterly insensible of their Use and Power. And tho' your Lordship foresaw, and Experience tells us, that both Diversions wou'd be better encourag'd under their separate Endeavours, yet this was a Scheme, that cou'd never be beat into the impenetrable Heads of those that might have honestly paid the Labourer their Hire, and put the Profits of both into their own Pockets. Nay, even the Opera, tho' the Town has neither grudg'd it Pay nor Equipage, from either the Wilfulness or Ignorance of the same General, we see, was not able to take the Field till *December*.

. . . Yet since your Lordship has so happily begun the Establishment of the separate Diversions, we live in Hope, that the same Justice and Resolution will still persuade you to go as successfully through with it.

But while any Man is suffer'd to confound the Industry and Use of 'em, by acting publickly, in Opposition to your Lordship's equal Intentions, under a false and intricate Pretense of not being able to comply with 'em; the Town is likely to be more entertain'd with the private Dissentions, than the publick Performance of either, and we [the Actors] in a perpetual Fear and Necessity of petitioning your Lordship every Season for new Relief.[63]

Having been paid in full at the Haymarket, the actors apparently wanted a guarantee of the same treatment as the price of their return to Rich.

The Union of 1708 ended the Lincoln's Inn Fields experiment. The physical premises had been abandoned three years earlier, and the cooperative organization had entirely ended when Vanbrugh took over the license, but only with the official abolition of competition between acting companies was the spirit of the venture wholly extinguished. Looking back and judging by hindsight, we may guess that had Lincoln's Inn Fields driven Rich out of business in the first three seasons and regained the use of the Drury Lane theatre—a very real possibility—it would have operated quite successfully as long as internal bickering did not become too severe. The United Company before it and the monopoly directed by the Triumvirate after 1710 managed to do so. Lincoln's Inn Fields's problems lay a) in the internal organization of the cooperative company in its first years, and b) in destructive competition coming just when theatrical circumstances were depressed. Both companies suffered from the effects of the Collier controversy. Calhoun Winton is certainly correct in saying that the would-be reformers were not playgoers[64] —but the climate of moral opprobrium cannot have helped the theatres attract the new middle-class audience they needed.

The Union of 1708 was brought about by power politics. By no means should it be considered a parallel to that of 1682: neither company was in anything like a state of collapse, as the King's Company once had been. Competition was still genuinely vigorous in 1706–7. Indeed, in some ways the Haymarket-Drury Lane competition after October 1706 drew the battle lines more clearly than had been the case for some time. Whether the two companies could have gone on indefinitely is a matter of conjecture—and one made irrelevant by Vanbrugh's determination to gamble on the fascinations of opera. We can fairly say, however, that there were fewer signs of impending collapse in 1706–7 than there had been five or six years earlier. The 1706 reorganization was a compromise and in effect an experiment designed to see whether straight plays could again prove economically viable. The combination of Swiney's good management with the infusion of new blood he brought appears to have revitalized the Haymarket Company. By 1708 most of the original Lincoln's Inn Fields stars were dead, retired, or nearing the end,[65] but the new generation, headed by Wilks and Cibber, might well have flourished under Swiney and the 1706 arrangement.

In decreeing a new union the Lord Chamberlain plainly intended to eliminate competition for a limited audience, thus making life easier for both houses. Unfortunately, neither Kent nor Vanbrugh nor Swiney had any idea how expensive opera would prove to be, and they did not arrange for a subsidy in the separation agreement. Vanbrugh never fully understood or accepted Queen Anne's indifference. He and Marlborough, as well as other men of influence, tried without success to interest her in subsidizing opera.[66] Had Anne given the Haymarket the support George I later did, the theatrical picture between 1705 and 1714 might have been vastly different. The fact that a capable and experienced manager like Swiney could not make opera pay tells us what an uphill proposition opera was.[67] As things fell out after the union, opera quickly proved ruinously unprofitable; Rich's actors rebelled again; and chaos ensued. When the Triumvirate (which originally included Doggett) took over the acting company in 1710, they immediately adopted a conservative repertory policy, relying heavily on stock plays and adopting a double-bill format. Despite the reestablishment of a second acting company in 1714 English drama was not fully to regain its vitality, or the theatres their competitive zest, until the boom triggered by the startling success of *The Beggar's Opera* nearly two decades later.

APPENDIXES
NOTES
INDEX

APPENDIX A

The Petition of the Players, P.R.O. LC 7/3

[Cover annotations in a different hand.]

Petition of Players.
Articles of pretended
Greivances.
(1694)
(with an inclosure)

To the Right Honorable the Earle of Dorsett
Lord Chamberlaine of his Majesties Household

The Humble Petition of their Majesties
Servants & Comoedians.

Sheweth

That your petitioners whose names are here Subscribed being noe longer able to suffer & support themselves under the unjust oppressions & Violations of almost all the By lawes Customes & usage that has been established among us from ye beginning & which remained unviolated till after Dr Davenant sold his patent & shares to his Brother Alexander under whome and by whome severall Titles have been claimed by diverse persons And sometimes a Trust in him onely pretended whereby many have been defrauded with other pretenses & Combinations whereby severall persons have been Lett in who seek after their owne Interest to recover their Debts By which meanes Our Rights & the agreed Methods wee were in for soe many yeares together hath been in a manner wholly changed and all our just Rights & priviledges taken from us by the New Managers of the playhouse under the pretended claimes of such Conveyances as by the particulars here annexed appeare.

225

Our humble petition to your Lordshipp is that out of your goodnesse & Compassion you would be pleased to appoint a day of heareing our just Complaints & if wee make out what we alledge to deliver us from our Oppressions which are soe intollerable & heavy that unlesse releived wee are not able to act any longer.

And your petitioners shall ever pray etc.

Thomas Betterton	Elizabeth Barry
Cave Underhill	Ann Bracegirdle
Edward Kenniston	Suzanna Verbruggen
William Bowen	Elizabeth Bowman
Joseph Williams	Mary Betterton
Thomas Doggett	Ellen Leigh
George Bright	John Bowman
Samuell Sandford	

1   Dr Davenant sold his patent & shares as he thought to his Brother Alexander for 2300*ll*. Sir Thomas Skipwith & Mr. Christopher Rich since Mr Alexander Davenant fled have produced Deeds to prove Mr Alexander Davenants name was onely made use of That it was their money the patent & Shares was Bought with That Mr Alexander Davenant farm'd the profitts of those shares of them at 6*ll* per weeke throughout the yeare play or not play which 6*ll* per weeke the said Mr Alexander Davenant constantly paid for about 5 yeares together in all which time Sir Thomas & Mr Rich never declared the patent was in them but Lett the World beleive the Right was in Alexander Davenant which gave him Credit & authority to lay the ffoundation for all the Cheates & fforgeries he was afterwards found guilty of Couzening Mrs Barrey of 6 or 800*ll* & divers others of severall thousands.

2   When Dr Davenant came of age their was a promise made by him to the then Sharers. In Consideration of their Interest in the Cloaths Scenes Bookes & properties that when any of them should leave playing (giveing fair warning) or should be disabled by age or any accidents every whole sharer was to have 100*ll* paid him and soe more or lesse according to their severall proportions or if a sharer dyed it was to be paid to his Widdow. & it was actually paid to Mr Smith after he left the stage. It has been confirmed to the players since under the hands of Mr Killigrew & Mr Thomas Davenant Yet is now refused us by the present Managers of the playhouse.

3   Wee were persuaded to part with our Interest in the aftermoney (which is the money received[?] for the fourth & fifth Acts) which brings in 400 or 500*ll* per annum which they were to have for 16 Yeares for the payment of 1000*ll* Debt & now they have ingrossed so Considerable a part of the profitts they would force us into shares againe threatening some they will shutt up the doores if they will not Consent to it.

4   The profitt money which is raised by Mulcts imposed on Ourselves & the servants attending the Theatres which is noe part of the profitts ariseing from playing & which was always disposed of by the principle Actors as to them seemed most Convenient & which Sir William Davenant & Mr. Thomas Killigrew never laid any claime to [line dropped here?] by the present Managers.

5   The present Claimers have declared there shall be noe play given out when they feare there will be but a small audience or to act but as many dayes in the Week as they shall think fitt thereby to deprive the Actors and servants of their sallaryes and the Renters of their Rent though it has been alwayes the Custome for them to take the one with the other the bad with the good.

6   When wee parted with Our shares the Managers promised to continue to us all the Customary priviledges of shareing Actors but now every thing is taken from us, the whole Course & Method of the Dukes Theatre totally changed. All things are Ordered at the will & pleasure of the present Claimers severall turned out for noe crime & without warning & ignorant insufficient fellowes putt in their places with many other Arbitrary Acts too long to insert following the indirect wayes begunn by Mr Alexander Davenant tending to the ruine & destruction of the Company & treateing us not as we were the Kings & Queenes servants but the Claimers slaves.

7   Mrs Barry made an Agreement with Dr Davenant Mr Killigrew Mr Smith & Mr Betterton for 50*s* per weeke & the profitt of a play every yeare. Upon a second agreement with Mr Thomas Davenant it was added if the dayes charge being deducted there wanted of 70*ll* they were to make it up. What was above 70*ll* she was to have. This agreement has been performed to her many yeares but now the present Claimers refuse to make the 70*ll* good to her if the dayes Receipt fall short of it & beside would take a third part of the profitt of Mrs Barry's play from her to give to Mrs Bracegirdle.

8   When Mr Betterton quitted his share quarter & half quarter he agreed
        with Mr Killigrew & Mr Alexander Davenant for a sallary of 5*ll* per
        weeke and a present of 50 Guineys at one Yeares end which they
        termed his Vacation present. He should have had a perruck but last
        Yeare it was not made to him and now they have ingrossed the after-
        money they would bring him into share againe & would lessen him a
        quarter & halfe a quarter though he presumes he is not lessen'd in his
        acting. When Mr Thomas Davenant left the management of the Play
        house Sir Thomas Skipwith & Mr Killigrew publiquely desired Mr
        Betterton to take all the care of it which he did & for which he might
        very reasonably have expected some gratification but instead of it have
        rewarded him with all manner of ill usage & Vexations.

9   Att the Union there was a Conveyance of 5*s* per day for every day any
        play should be acted in the Kings Theatre to the Lady Davenant for
        fruit mony by Mr Killigrew who as we have heard had 50 Guineys
        (for his Consent) by Dr Davenant Mr Smith & Mr Betterton. This 5*s*
        per day is constantly entered in the Treasurers Booke, Yet Mr Rich
        takes it into his owne Custody & has not paid any of it to the persons
        who bought it of the Lady Davenant which persons now threaten to
        sue Mr Betterton for it.

10   Mr Rich refuses to pay the 20*ll* for the Organ in St Brides Church
        subscribed by the Order of Mr Killigrew & Mr Thomas Davenant.
        Hee refuses to pay Mr Atterbury Lecturer of the said Church what
        has been allowed to all his predecessors.

11   Mr Williams by Agreement with Mr Killigrew & Mr Thomas Dave-
        nant had 4*ll* a weeke sallary. The present Claimers offered him 10*ll*
        to signe a paper they offered him, which he refuseing they have
        thought fitt to take 20*s* per weeke from him without declareing to
        him the reasons for it or giveing him any warneing according to the
        Known Method of the playhouse.

12   Mrs Bracegirdle reasonably proposeth to pay the Constant Charge of
        an old play & what more shall be agreed to by her. The play will
        bring in [blank space] playing. What ever she can gett above by the
        Assistance of her freinds is all she desires for her selfe.

13   Mrs Verbruggen desires 5*s* per weeke may be added to her Sallary.

14   Mr Killigrew about halfe a yeare since did promise of himselfe to raise
        Mr Doggett equall in Sallary to any other under Mr Betterton as
        Judgeing it due to his merritt. But afterwards without any reason

from Mr Doggett he did revoake the said promise & refused to give him any more then an Addition of 10s per weeke to his sallary which Mr Doggett was willing to agree to Knowing it was not in his owne power not their inclination to doe him Justice. [blank space] Agreement is not Yet performed nor will they give him any Assurance when it shall be.

15 Mr Bright in Consideration of haveing studyed a great many of Mr Leighs parts & for what he saveth them besides in Danceing desireth an Addition of 5s per weeke to his present sallary which in Justice he ought to have had long agoe.

APPENDIX B

The Reply of the Patentees, P.R.O. LC 7/3

[The cover bears annotations in two different hands, but the date printed by Nicoll (1: 370) is no longer on the document.]

Betterton et al.
&
Skipwith Bart. et al.

To attend Lord Dorset at Sir
Robert Howards at Westminster
Munday 17 December 94 between
10 & 11 a Clock.

[10 December 1694]

Sir Thomas Skipwith Bart
Answer to Bettertons
Allegations before Lord
Dorset

[Portions of the reply were written in broad pen strokes or underlined. Because they form a precis of the argument when read consecutively, I have italicized those words and sentences.]

> The Answere to ye Petition & Articles of Pretended Greivances Presented to the right Honorable The Earle of Dorsett Lord Chamberlayn of their Majesties Houshold by Mr Thomas Betterton & others by name of their Majesties Servants & Comedians.

> The present Patentees of the Theatres saving their Right etc. say

> That his late Majestie King Charles ye Second out of his Especiall Grace & meer Motion upon Sir William Davenants Surrender of former

letters patents Granted by his Royall ffather King Charles ye ffirst of ever
Blessed Memory in ye ffourteenth Year of his Reigne did give & grant unto
Sir William Davenant his heirs & Assigns ffull power License & Authority
to build a Theatre or Playhouse with necessary Tyreing & Retireing Roomes
within ye Citties of London & Westminster or ye Subburbs thereof wherein
Tragedies Commedies plays Operas Musick Scenes & all other Entertainments of ye Stage whatsoever might be shewn & presented. And did give
& grant *unto Sir William Davenant his heirs & Assigns* & every of them ffull
power License & Authority from time to time *gather together Enterteyn
Governe priviledge & keep such & so many players & persons to Act plays as he or
they* from time to time *should think meete* which said Company should be the
Servants of his then Majesties Royall Brother James Duke of Yorke & to
consist of such Number as ye said Sir William Davenant his heirs or Assigns
should from time to time think meete. And such persons to permitt &
continue at & during ye pleasure of ye said Sir William Davenant his heirs
or Assigns without ye Impeachment or Impediment of any person or persons whatsoever. And did thereby give & grant unto ye said Sir William
Davenant his Heirs & Assigns full power to *make such allowances to the Actors
and other Persons Imployed* in Acting *as he or they should think fitt*. And that ye
Company should be Under ye *sole government* & Authority of ye said Sir
William Davenant his heirs & Assigns. *And all scandalous & mutinous persons*
should from time to time be by him & them Ejected & Disabled from
playeing in ye said Theatre. And wills & Grants that Onely *the said Company
& one other Company Erected or sett up by Thomas Killigrew Esquire & none other
should be permitted at any time afterwards within ye Citties of London & Westminster* or ye subburbs thereof to Act Comedies Tragedies etc. & Declared
all other Companys *Silenced* and Suppressed As by ye said letters patents
relation unto them being had may more at large appeare.
That his said late Majestie *King Charles ye Second* ye twenty-fifth day of
Aprill *in ye fourteenth Year of his Reigne* Granted one other Patent to ye [?]
said Thomas Killigrew Esquire for ye Erecting of another Theatre with ye same
priviledges & power of Enterteyning Governing and calling a Company as
are before mentioned in Sir William Davenants patent. And *to be ye King
& Queens Company as by* ye same Patent may appear. *Both which patents were
by Indenture Dated ye fourth of May 1692 [recte, 1682] made between Charles
Killigrew Esquire of ye one parte And Dr Davenant Thomas Betterton &
William Smith of ye other parte United.* And all ye benefitts priviledges
powers & Authoritys before mentioned are covenanted & Agreed to be as
one from thenceforth forever *Subject to ye Provisoes conditions & Agreements
therein conteyned.* And that *all plays then after to be Acted should be acted by* the
Company then Employed or after to be Employed at the Dukes Theatre &

by *such* other person & persons *as Mr Killigrew & Dr Davenant their heirs &*
Assigns should from time to time direct & appoint & not otherwise having Regard Nevertheless & to be Subject to ye same Rules Method & manner of
Government used at ye Dukes Theatre soe far forth as ye same should be
Judged by Mr Killigrew & Dr Davenant their heirs & Assigns respectively
most convenient & beneficiall & soe as they did order & Governe ye same
for ye good of all persons concerned according to ye best of their Powers
& Judgements. And by ye said Indenture *Mr Killigrew was & is to have 3*
shares in Twenty of ye cleere proffitts & to disperse & dissolve ye Kings Company of Players forthwith as by ye said Indenture amongst divers covenants
& Agreements therein conteyned may more at large appear.

And thus having in breif sett before Your Lordship ye ffoundation of ye
playhousses & where ye Government by their Majesties patents are directed
and appointed wee shall in ye next place proceede to give Your Lordship
an Account how matters stand in a Cause in Chancery now depending
before ye Right Honorable Sir John Sommers Knight Lord Keeper of ye
Great Seale of England wherein Mr Killigrew is Plaintiff And Dr Davenant
Mr Betterton & others are ye Defendants And then wee shall proceed to
Answere ye Articles which Mr Betterton & his Mutinous ["persons," written and deleted] Companions (as ye patent is pleased to term them) have
presented unto Your Lordship. The End of Mr Killigrews Bill is to have a
true account of all ye Receipts of ye Theatres from May 1682 And alsoe of
all payments and disbursements & to have his proportion thereof being 3
shares in 20 of ye cleere proffitts And alsoe an Equall Power in ye Government & Management And touching Payment to sharing Actors Ground
Rent of ye Dukes Theatre now called ye Queens Theatre Taxes Reparations,
ye 2 ffront houses there, fforfeit Mony, ffruite Mony, & 3s 4d a day, paid to
Mrs Lacy & other matters. To which Bill Dr Davenant Mr Betterton &
severall other Defendants did putt in their Answers which are very long &
have Submitted to ["have," written and deleted] an account & have referred
themselves to ye Judgement of ye Court whereupon divers witnesses were
Examined on both sides And upon hearing ye Cause the seventh of December 1691 It was referred to Sir Robert Legard one of ye Masters in Chancery
to take & state ye said Account And ["also," written and deleted] therein
to rectyfie ye state of ye Government. Sir Robert Legard after further Depositions ["is," written and deleted] taken before him made his Report And
therein reported severall things Specially to ye Court & in particular ye
Government & Management of ye Theatres & how he found it to stand on
ye Deeds & prooffes taken in ye Cause.

To which report both sides have filed Exceptions which are not yett argued.
Having stated this matter of ffact as 'tis truely Lyeing before my Lord

Keeper & by him unDetermined wee shall now proceed to Answer ye Articles by Mr Betterton Exhibited before Your Lordship.

And ffirst ["may it please your Lordship," written and deleted] as to Mr Bettertons alledging that Sir Thomas Skipwith & Mr Rich by letting ye World beleive ye Right of ye patent & Shares was in Alexander Davenant gave him Creditt & Authority to lay ye ffoundation ffor all ye Cheats & fforgeries that Alexander Davenant was found guilty of by Couzening Mrs Barry of 6 or 800*ll* & others of severall Thousands.

Answere

May it please Your Lordship Mr Alexander Davenant fled in October 1693. And it has not appeared to us that any Cheats or fforgeries have been pretended to be done by him till about ½ a Year before he fled. Whereas ["that," written and deleted] Dr Davenant (by reason that Mr Bolesworth one of his wives Trustees had not Executed ye Conveyances of ye Patent & shares as well as Mr Betterton ye other Trustee had done) did in July 1690 enter into a Bond of 3000*ll* penalty to Mr Rich that Mr Bolesworth should Execute ye same within 3 Moneths then next (though he hath not Yett done it) And tis Well known that Sir Thomas Skipwith & Mr Rich when the rent was behind Spoke of this concerne to divers persons in so much that Mr Davenant compleined of ye unkindness in soe doeing. And Mr Betterton may Remember that ye Writings though soe drawn & Ingrossed at Mr ffolkes Chamber ye same were Sealed at Mr Serjeant Pembertons Chamber (who was of Counsell for Sir Thomas Skipwith). And Mr Rich paid Mr Betterton 2000*ll* of ye Purchase Mony by a Note on Sir ffrancis Child when all ye Writings were putt into Mr Riches Custody & never were out of his Custody. And Mr Davenant never had them one Minute whereby to Cheate or Countenance a cheat Nor doth Mr Betterton or Mrs Barry or any other person that we have heard of pretend to have any Mortgage or Grant of ye said patent or those shares or any parte of them. But she hath declared that she lent Mr Davenant ["4000," written and deleted] 400*ll* in Aprill 1693 upon a share granted or Supposed to be granted by Sir William Davenant to one Cheston & 200*ll* more in May 1692 of some Rent Issueing out of ye Dukes Theatre that Mr Ashburnham gave to Mr Thomas Davenant. And that as for ye other 200*ll* that she hath ye Doctor's Bond for it as well as his Brothers. Tis true that Mr Alexander Davenant farmed ye said patent & 2 shares as he farmed ye shares of divers other persons pretended that he best Understood with ye Assistance of Mr Betterton to Mannage ye affairs of ye Theatres to ye Best Advantage & that Sir Thomas Skipwith & Mr Rich were Obleiged to sell ye same patent & Shares for 2400*ll* to Mr Alexander Davenant as they cost but Mr Davenant was not

Obleiged to repurchase ye same. The 6*ll* per Weeke was often paid at ye
office at ye Playhouse and it was well known to diverse persons: But Mr
Rich lent more Monys to Mr Alexander Davenant then he received for his
parte of the Rent insomuch that Mr Davenant when he went off Owed Mr
Rich on Bonds & a Note above 600*ll*. And to Sir Thomas Skipwith & his
late ffather to whom he is sole Executor by Bonds & other securitys above
700*ll* 10*s* which is still oweing. & Sir Thomas Skipwith & Mr Rich have
declared themselves Willing to sell ye said Patent & 2 shares to Dr Davenant or any other for ye said principall sums of 2400*ll*—600*ll* & 700*ll*
with Interest for ye same respectively at 6*ll* per Cent per Annum & their
charges & ["that," written and deleted] they ["would," written and deleted]
will discount what Mr Alexander Davenant paid upon ye ffarm aforesaid or
otherwise ever since. And Sir Thomas Skipwith ever since 1687 hath sent
Notes for persons to see plays Gratis which tis beleived Mr Betterton could
not be Ignorant off. Now May it please Your Lordship for Mr Betterton to
charge Sir Thomas Skipwith & Mr Rich in such a Scandalous manner to
have layd the ffoundation of Mr Alexander Davenants Cheats & fforgeries
& for Mr Betterton to gett divers other persons as he has done to signe ye
same when severall of them hath since Declared that they neither read nor
heard read ye Paper annexed to ye said Petition wherein those Sandalous
words are mentioned shows what Sort of a Man Mr Betterton is. And they
hope Mr Betterton & ye rest of ye Petitioners shall be Ordered by Your
Lordship to make satisfaction for ye Injury thereby done. For Sir Thomas
Skipwith & Mr Rich do not brand Mr Betterton for a Cheat or Conjorer
though he did really conceal from ye World ye Mortgaging of his Rent of
6*ll* per Weeke in the Queens Theatre for many Years ye same being but
lately discovered to Mr Rich by one from ye Mortgagee. Wee are further
forced humbly to Inform your Lordship that it has been given out in
Speeches by Dr Davenant and Mr Betterton what a great proffitt 6*ll* a Week
for 5 Years brought in to Sir Thomas Skipwith for ye consideration aforesaid. Yett they were pleased to forgett that for 2 Years last & upwards he
hath not had after ye rate of 1*ll* per Cent per Annum & Likewise to fforgett
The 600*ll* & ye 700*ll* before mentioned to be oweing by ye said Alexander
Davenant at his goeing off besides another Debt of 500*ll*. And Mr Betterton is also pleased to fforgett mentioning ye Advantageous Bargains he has
made in ye Playhous by receiving for 20 Years last past after ye rate of 20*ll*
per Cent per Annum for Monys laid out by him towards building ye Dukes
Theatre.

2   As to ye second Article concerning Dr Davenants promise when he came
of Age of giving 100*ll* to a whole sharing Actor for their Interest in ye
Cloaths Scenes Bookes & propertyes etc.

Answer

May it please Your Lordship wee know nothing of any such promise nor hath Dr Davenant made mention of any such either in ye Indenture of Union or in the Conveyances of ye patent or 2 Shares& wee have been told that ye 100*ll* given to Mr William Smith was upon an other consideration well known to Mr Betterton who can tell whether Mr Thomas Sheppy Robert Nokes James Nokes Thomas Lovell John Mosely Henry Turner & Thomas Lilleston who were formerly sharing Actors who had any such sums paid them upon ye Account aforesaid. But wee are Informed if a sharer went off or dyed Sir William Davenant putt another in his Roome & such new sharer was to give 500*ll* pounds security for his good behaviour & observing ye Orders & Rules of ye Company before he was to be admitted to such share. & when Mr Betterton went out of Share in January 1692 he did not desire any such thing nor did Mr Betterton, Mr Mountfort Mr Leigh or Mr Bowman when they setled ye priviledges of sharing Actors & came into share on 26 September 1692 make any such Demand. And if Mr Thomas Davenant Deputy Mannager appointed by word of Mouth onely hath pretended to grant any such thing he might as well with Submission to Your Lordship grant away other persons shares of Rent or proffitts. Sir William Davenant had sold of ye greatest parts of the shares in his life time before he could carry on ye Management of ye Play house. And ye Doctor hath since sold ["of," written and deleted] ye patent & some of ye shares without Subjecting ye same to any such charge or Incumbrance as may appear by ye conveyances. Nay Dr Davenant & Mr Betterton have sworn in their Answeres in Chancery that Dr Davenant could not by any Act he could doe prejudice ye grants ["of," written and deleted] made by Sir William Davenant his ffather. And Mr Killigrew for his parte sayth that he doth not know that he hath Obleiged himselfe to ye said pretention.

3   As to ye Aftermony which Mr Betterton pretends to be perswaded into & as he thinks is so great a Bargain etc.

Answer

May it please Your Lordship Itt seemeth something strange to us for Mr Betterton at this time of Day to find fault with that which he soe much Labored in Conjunction with Mr Alexander Davenant near a Year before it was done to bring about as may appear by an Affidavit in Chancery by him ye said Betterton made for ye Effecting thereof it being strongly presumed to be Mr Bettertons own project he being so zealous to have it done. Yett Not withstanding Mr Betterton & severall others have under their hands & Seals requested & desired ye Patentees and Adventurers to take ye After

Mony for 1000*ll* to pay of 1000*ll* Debt of ye Theatres which was contracted during his Management. Yet it will cost them above 1600*ll* before all will be paid. However to avoid disputes it has been Offered Mr Betterton that if he would discount his Sallarys & Gratuities by him received since ye time he parted with his proportion of share in ye After Mony & take what would have been his proportion of share ever since that time & now come into share again ye said Mr Betterton should be admitted into his proportion of ye said After Mony dureing his being an Actor sharer if he thought it worth his while lett ye After Mony be what it will which hath not yett brought in 400*ll* per Annum.

4   As to ye fforfeit of ["Mony," written and deleted] Actors being a Mulct Imposed on themselves Mr Betterton thinks that to ["be," written and deleted] no parte of ye proffitts but that it ought to be disposed by ye principall Actors as they think fitting.

Answer

May it please Your Lordship wee think with submission This is like ye rest of Mr Bettertons Actions he designing thereby to Curry ffavour with ye rest of his Companions drawn into this Mutiny. The Mulcts are not Imposed on ye Actors & Musitians to the end they should forfeite but to keep them from forfeiting for ye Dammage that ye patentees & Adventurers susteined by a fforfeit is a Greater loss to them then ye Recompence of ye Mony fforfeited for ye same. And Mr Betterton knows that by *ye Decree in ye Court of Chancery it is & hath been* brought into ye Receipt & divided as other monys are & soe he & ye other Acting sharers desired it might be on ye twenty-sixth September 1692 when after a long contention between Mr Betterton Mr Mountfort Mr Leigh & others ye Priviledges of ye sharing Actors were setled to all their contents & satisfactions And entered into ye Day Booke as may there appear.

5   As to Acting but so many Days ["in," written and deleted] a Week & takeing ye bad with ye good etc.

Answer

May it please Your Lordship it allways has been in ye Breast of ye patentees & Adventurers & their deputed Managers to Act but on such days as they think fitt. But we may Observe to Your Lordship that ye company Acted in ye last Year more days then ever was before when Mr Betterton Managed. And wee do not Question but that now Mr Betterton is left out of ye Management the Company will be permitted to Act more days in a Year then ever Mr Betterton thought fitting ffor he was greatly displeased to think ye Young People Acted ye last vacation near 30 Days without Mr

Betterton Mr Williams Mr Bright Mr Kinaston Mr Sandford or Mrs Betterton and each Man & Woman which Acted with them got enough to mainteyn them very handsomely when in former long vacations ye Young Actors have been forced to borrow Moneys from ye patentees & Adventurers for their ["asistance," written and deleted] subsistence which created a Debt upon ye Company when they began to Act again at Michaelmas. Tis true That Mr Rich being tennant of ye Kings Theatre at 3*ll* per diem on Acting days and being called on as Assignee of Sir William Davenants patent for 7*ll* a day reserved for ye Queens Theatre on Acting dayes & for all Sallarys Wages & Debts whatsoever & being Likewise Obleiged to pay 3 parts in 20 of ye Cleere proffitts to Mr Killigrew & his Assigns And alsoe ye other Adventurers Clayming under Sir William Davenants patent requiring an Account of him for their shares hath declared that in Case ye Receipts do not Answere ye constant & Incident Charges they cannot in reason desire to have ye play house doors open to pay Money out of his own pockett. Nor was it ever a Custome for ye patentees to be Obleiged to any such thing. If they were they might Quickly be ruin'd for that ye Receipts are some days under 20*ll* & yett ye full rent & sallarys are required which amount to above 30 *ll* per diem besides Incident Charges. & though Mr Betterton would have ye Patentees & Adventurers take ye bad with ye good Yett Mr Betterton hath not kept to that rule of late Years but when there hath been good Receipts then to be in share but when bad then in Sallary whereas it was the Custome with Sharing Actors to take ye bad with ye good and runn ye same risque with ye Patentees & Adventurers.

6   As to ye sixth Article of taking away sharing Actors priviledges & altering ye Course & ye method of ye Dukes Theatre etc. following ye Indirect means begun by Mr Alexander Davenant & treating ye Petitioners not as ye King & Queens Servants but Slaves & Putting people out without Warning & putting in Insufficient ffellows.

Answer

Wee humbly Inform Your Lordship that Mr Betterton And Mr Bowman soon after ye Death of Mr Mountfort & Mr Leigh to witt on ye sixteenth of January 1692 [i.e., "1692/3"] requested to be in Sallary untill ye beginning of ye then next vacation onely but they have kept in Sallary ever since although Mr Betterton hath often promised that he would be Willing at any time to come into share again. We do not know that any Customary priviledges of sharing Actors have been denyed. And as to ye Indirect means begun by Alexander Davenant tis well known Mr Alexander Davenant did nothing of Moment in ye ["Management" *altered to* "Manageing,"] of ye Theatres without Mr Betterton but from 1687 till Mr Davenant went off in 1693 all things were done as Mr Betterton would have it & he gave out what Plays he would during that time as well as ye last Year by which means very little could be Divided or thrown off to pay Debts out of ye Receipts & on ye fourteenth of July last above 189*ll* was runn in Debt as appears by ye Day Booke which we were forced to pay out of ye after Mony besides some Bills not then brought in. & wee have reason to think that Mr Alexander Davenant did begin indirect courses in 1687 by Adding without ye consent of Mr Killigrew or ye Adventurers a quarter & a ½ quarter to Mr Bettertons share & about a Year after by adding a Vacation present of 50*ll* Guineas more for his Generall care & Allowing him to brow beate and discountenance Young Actors as Mr Giloe Carlisle Mountfort & others & keeping in Impropper persons in partes & turning out putting in & advancing whom he pleased & other such like arbitrary Acts. & Wee do not know what he means by our turning out without Warning or putting in Insufficient fellows & therefore wee shall onely offer unto Your Lordships consideration whether it can be supposed that the patentees can soe far forgett their own Interest as to dismiss deserving men to Enterteyn Insufficient ffellows. Besides that with Mr Bettertons leave ye patentees doe humbly conceive that it lyes in ye patentees breast to change their servants as they think fitt according to ye power given by ye said patents & as it was heretofore practised at ye Dukes Theatre It appearing by ye proofes taken in ye said Cause in Chancery & by ye Masters Report that ye Sallarys & allowances to ye Actors servants & persons Imployed in that Theatre were altered Limmitted Diminisht or Increast as ye Governor of ye said Company & ye sharers of ye Cleere proffitts or their Managers thought fitt. And ye said Actors were taken into shares and their shares altered Increased or diminished & sometyms taken into Sallarys again as was thought fitt by ye Governor & ye said sharers Adventurers of ye Cleer proffitts for ye time being & their deputed Managers as by ye said proceedings more at large May appear. Wee humbly Inform your Lordship that wee allow sallarys to ye persons that now complayn beyond what was ever formerly paid to any Man or Woman belonging to ye Kings Theatre & Mr Betterton for his & his Wives Acting have for ye 2 last Years received out of ye Play house after ye rate of 10*ll* per Weeke besides 6*ll* per weeke for Rent Whereas Sir Thomas Skipwith & Mr Rich Who are purchasers to ye value of 3600*ll* for they have other Interest besides that which they bought of Mr Davenant did not receive full 30*ll* ye last Year.

7   As to ye seventh Article concerning Mrs Barry.

Answer

May it please Your Lordship That Mr Betterton himselfe took notice that

Mrs Barry made so great Advantage of a Play given her one day in ye Year that ye same with her Sallary was more then his 5*ll* per Weeke. And wee Observing that although ye receipts of late had been lesse then usuall yett ye Constant & Incident Charges are higher & consequently needfull to be Retrencht & Mrs Barry having declared that Mr Thomas Davenant had released her of her bargain And that she would not be Obleiged to Play unless she came to a new Agreement with us Itt was propossed that she would continue at her Usuall Sallary of 50*s* per Weeke & remitt one-third of ye proffitts of ye Days Play to Mrs Bracegirdle which we beleived would by ye Addition of Mrs Bracegirdles ffriends so Increase ye Receipts as that Mrs Barry would not be a great looser.

8   As to Mr Bettertons Quitting his share quarter & ½ quarter for 5*ll* per Weeke & ye Vacation present of 50 Guineas & a Perruke for last Year & now (ye After Mony being gone they would bring him into share which is less then he had by a quarter & a ½ which he thinks strange being not at all lessened in his Acting. And that he Expected some gratification for his Management ye last Year but in stead thereof have rewarded him with all manner of Ill usage & Vexation.

Answer

Wee humbly Inform Your Lordship that Mr Betterton never had upon Account of his Acting when he was at ye best any more then one Actors share till Dr Davenant sold his patent for from May 1682 to 1687 by prooffe in Chancery it appears that he had but one share & ½ a quarter & this ½ quarter was in parte of satisfaction for his care in ye Management. And Mr Smith had ye like when he was an Actor & Joint manager with Mr Betterton but when Mr Smith went out of ye house And Mr Thomas Davenant in 1687 came into ye Management & had 3*ll* 10*s* for his trouble then Mr Betterton had a quarter & ½ a quarter of a share Added to him by Alexander Davanant for what private Consideration is unknown to us which was continued to Mr Betterton till about ffebruary 1689. Then Mr Betterton was in Sallary in September 1691 at 5*ll* per Weeke & a Vacation present of fifty Guineas for his generall care. Then he came into share again & had but one Actors share till about September 1692. And then on 26 September 1692 when ye Agreement about ye After Mony & ye Acting sharers priviledges were setled he came into one share and a quarter but Mr Mountfort & Mr Leigh dyeing in December folloueing Mr Betterton on ye sixteenth January 1692 [i.e., "1692/3"] came into Sallary again at 5*ll* per Weeke & fifty Guineas for his generall Care by name of a vacation present but Mr Betterton well knows why he was then permitted to leave his share & quarter & go into Sallary onely for that Year Which wee shall not now discover unless he pleases. It is true Mr Betterton doth not think himselfe lessen'd in his Acting but ye Patentees & Adventurers to their sad Experience find that a Man at 60 is not able to doe That which he could at 30 or 40. He hath put himselfe into all great parts in most of ye Considerable plays Especially in ye Tragedys & Yett when he Acts a great parte we must be forced to Act an Ordinary Play one or 2 dayes after as Scapin Monsieur Ragou & such like to Ease him & soe loose what wee gott on ye day he played. Whereas there are Actors enough in ye House to Act good plays Allways & Mr Betterton himselfe could formerly have Acted a great parte 4 or 5 dayes in a Weeke when he was a Sharer & before he became so Aged. And with Submission to Your Lordships better Judgement Mr Betterton has noe Just reason to Complayn for he has had fifty Guineas for his generall care & pains in lookeing after Rehearsalls & giving out Plays ye last Year Vide Acquittance. And alsoe he has had 50*ll* for his care & trouble to gett up ye Indian Queen though he hath not yett done itt which with summs & what he & his Wife hath received for Acteing & his rent of 1*ll* per diem amounts to above 16*ll* per Weeke for every Weeke ye Company Acted ye last Year. Therefore we hope Your Lordship will Judge Mr Betterton ["to be," written and deleted] very Ungratefull in his behaviour to his Superiors That as soon as a proposition was made him in a very civill manner he Instead of giving a Civill Answer presently drew all ye Actors together to joyne in a Combination against ye Patentees & Adventurers & in stead of lessening their Demands to promise them great allowances to stand by him which comes ye more unexpected from him because ye last Year when Mr Doggett Bowen & others Mutined Mr Betterton declared they ought to be Ejected ye House & by his perswasions they were denyed to be received till they Quitted ye Combination & each Man treated onely for himselfe. Mr Betterton was told that as for ye perruck something should be considered to be given him in Leiu thereof though this of a perruck is an Innovation & may prove of great Inconvenience by reason all others will graft upon it to have ye like Allowance. That wee did desire Mr Betterton to take care of lookeing after due Rehearsalls & gieving out of plays & to consider what new Cloaths should be necessary. But wee very often attended our selvs & treated with ye Poets & as for ye Care of Inspecting ye Receipts & disbursments in seeing all ye Rents & Sallarys duely paid Examining all Tradesmens Bills taking an Account of ye Wardrobe & lookeing after ye reparations of ye Theatres Christopher Rich took ye whole Super Intendancy thereof & hath putt ye Books in a Regular & Methodical way & yett ye said Rich has not had any Allowance for his trouble & care therein. It was Mr Bettertons duty to come to Rehearsalls in such Plays where he had a parte himselfe without being gratified for it. And when he had no parte himselfe he often failed of coming & besides his diligence was not such as was reasonably Expected from him by which means he left us in Debt July last above 189*ll* besides about 60*ll* more on bills oweing. But since he was put out of Management there has been already considerable Sharings of Cleere proffitts. And Mr Betterton for ye care he tooke as principall Actor in ye nature of a Monitor in a Schole to looke after rehearsalls & giving out plays had a Gratification of 50 Guineas besides ye Compliment of his Wifes 50*s* a Week & Yett Mr Betterton is pleased to Complain off Ill Usage and Vexation.

9   As to ye 5*s* per diem ffruite Mony claymed for every day there is any Acting at ye Kings Theatre & for which Mr Betterton is threatned to be sued for.

Answer

May it please Your Lordship Sir William Davenant Immediately after ye King granted him his patent not knowing otherwise how to carry on ye charge of Acting without great Summs of Money to buy Apparell Habitts & propertys Machins & other decorations sold out to ye Honorable Mr Ashburnham late Cofferer of his Majesties Houshould ye Honorable John Hervey Esquire ye Lord Lonnelly[?] & several other persons diverse parts & shares in ye proffitts thereof all which Interested persons or ye persons Clayming under them ought to have been made partys to ye Granting of ye said 5*s* per diem & to have some consideration as well as ye Lady Davenant Dr Davenant Mr Killigrew Mr Betterton. Tis true Mr Killigrew acknowledges that he had 50*ll* which he is ready to bring into Cash & my Lady Davenant we hear had 400*ll*. Wee would faine[?] know what Dr Davenant & Mr Betterton had neither of whom wee presume would consent to such a constant Charge without a Sum of Money or some consideration paid for ye same though wee are Informed that Mr Betterton onely hath Obleiged himselfe while he is an Actor. Mr Betterton Mistakes in saying it is constantly entered in ye treasurers books It not having been entered since January last but Mr Rich hath been Warned by severall of ye persons Interrested not to pay it it being an Unjust charge on their shares & nothing thereof mentioned in ye Indenture of Union but a Clandestine bargain made afterwards. However Mr Rich is willing to doe what shall be Judged Right & Equitable for him to doe in this casee being Indempnified therein.

10   As to Mr Riches refusing to pay 20*ll* for ye Organs in St Brides & alsoe Mr Atterbury ye Lecturer what has been allowed to his predecessors.

Answer

Wee do humbly ["Inform your Lordship," written and deleted] answere that Itt is not Mr Rich alone but near 20 other persons concerned that refuse to pay ye said 20*ll* for ye Organ by Reason it is not with Submission to your Lordships Judgement Equitably placed for Mr Betterton would have it paid by ye adventuring sharers of ye Cleere proffitts onely now he is himselfe in Sallary when as ye Rent of 7*ll* per diem ought to pay it all or at Least ye one Moyety thereof which if Mr Betterton will undertake for ye persons Clayming ye 7*ll* per diem we will Undertake for ye Sharers to pay ye other Moyty. That Mr Betterton lives in one of ye ffront Houses & has done for many Years & has not Yett paid any Rent for it but wee hope he will (in some short time think fitt to pay it without putting us to ye trouble of Recovering it by Law) or troubling Your Lordship therein as alsoe Taxes ground Rent & Repairs. And he as Tennant ought to pay Mr Atterbury what is due wee conceiving it a wrong done by Mr Betterton to ye sharers when he managed to pay ye Lecturer and his parish dutys out of ye generall Receipts of ye play house when it should have gone out of his own Pockett it being ye Tennants Tax. It can be made appear that Mr Betterton was to pay 20*ll* a Year for ye House he now lives in & that a Lease thereof was drawn & Ingrossed from Mr {"Betterton," written and deleted} Ashburn- ham Mr Hervey & others to him thereof at that Rent. That no one of ye proporietors of Rent or share live in St Brides parish Except Mr Betterton & although he has 20*s* per diem rent out of ye Playhouse Yet he would pay no Taxes Repairs Ground Rent or parish dutys but bring all in to ye Charges of ye Patentees & Adventurer when no other player or proprietor pretend to any such priviledge. The parson of ye parish is paid about 3*ll* 11*s* a Year for Tythe of ye Queens Theatre but nothing is demanded by Mr Atterbury ye Lecturer but free Guift. Yett he was paid in July last 15*s* due for 3 quarters at Midsummer last past & ye Clerke of ye parish of St Brides would have had 20*s* a Year for serving Mr Betterton with Weekely Bills of Mortality which Mr Rich can have in St Giles's parish for 5*s* a Year. But why should Mr Betterton putt all his dutys on ye proprietors of ye Cleere proffitts unless every Actor and Actress should doe ye like which if they were permitted to doe it would {"be," written and deleted} in all be at least 100*ll* per Annum to ye Companys Charge.

11   As to Mr Williams Claym of 4*ll* per Weeke sallary.

Answer

Wee Humbly Inform Your Lordship that when Mr Mountfort & Mr Leigh were alive Mr Williams had never above 3*ll* per Weeke Sallary or 3 quarters of a share for Acting. That about August 1692 Mr Williams left ye house for about ½ a Year but Mr Mountfort & Mr Leigh both dyeing in Decem- ber 1692 Mr Williams was asked to act again & he being pretty sensible of

our necessity of him at that time Imposed upon us & would not come in to
Act unless he had 4*ll* per Weeke for that Year which Mr Thomas Davenant
agreed to give him for that Year as we are Informed & therefore we offered
him 3 quarters of a share & 10*ll* in Consideration of some Charges he said
he had been about Apparell more then a Comedian which he after a fort-
nights consideration refusing we sett him at 3*ll* per Weeke which we think
is as much as he can pretend to deserve for he knows that ye last Year Mr
Powell & Mr Verbruggen did Act his parts above 30 times he making
himselfe Incapable thereof by his own means for he & severall others if they
can gett their Sallarys paid them matter not whether ye patentees & Adventurers gett any thing.

12   As to Mrs. Bracegirdle proposition of having parts of ye Cleere proffitts
of an Old Play.

Answer

May it please Your Lordship we did before she askt any thing propose ye
third of ye proffitts of a Play in ye Answer to ye seventh Article concerning
Mrs Barrys mentioned & there fore wee have ye greater Reason to take her
Joyntly in Bettertons Mutiny most Unkindly & humbly hope Your Lordship will think it reasonable her pretentions be left to our Consideration
since we were ye first movers of advancing her.

13   May it please Your Lordship as to Mrs Verbruggen who is at 50*s* per
Weeke Sallary we thinke it Enough & beleive that she hath askt 5*s* a Weeke
more because Mrs. Bracegirdle had a proposition made to her as aforesaid.

14   As to Mr Doggetts demanding a Sallary Equall to any person Under Mr
Betterton & Clayming it as a promise from Mr Killigrew as due to his
Meritt.

[Answer]

Wee are forced to trouble Your Lordship with acquainting you that Mr
Doggett was taken into ye Playhouse in 1690 at 10*s* per Weeke from being
a Stroler & in ffebruary 1692/3 he entred into Articles under hand & Seale
to serve ye play hous at 40*s* per Weeke & to give 9 Acting Months notice
under hand & seale when he should have a Mind to leave ye Company. And
we having to please him upon the request of Mr Betterton & Mrs Barry
allowed him 10*s* a Weeke more. We thought he would have been conten-
tented but We find he is never satisfyed for about 3 Weeks agoe by a Note
under his hand he Demanded 3*ll* a Weeke for one Year Act or not Act.
Now with Submission to Your Lordship Wee think ffitt to hold him to his
Articles to give Warning ["to," written and deleted] if he finds himselfe
Agreived. As to what Mr Doggett accuses Mr Killigrew off he Answers

that he made no such promise or If he did give him some Incouragement It was in consideration of his success in one single parte but his naturall defect of voice & Lungs often failing him & but 2 Sufficient Arguments for Sallary [words dropped?] Mr Killigrews Judgement. Besides my Lord Mr Killigrew as Mr Betterton & ye Rest well knows cannot doe any Act that contradicts ye Deed of Union to which he referrs himselfe for Your Lordships better satisfaction.

15   As to Mr Brights studing up many parts of Mr Leigs & what he saveth ye Company by dancing desires an Addition of 5s a Weeke to his Sallary.

Answer

Wee humbly observe to your Lordship to take notice how willing Mr Betterton was to take subscriptions to his petition of greivances that he draws in Men that were not aggreived. For this Bright was told that he should have 5s per Weeke added to his Sallary or share in proportion thereunto before any proposition was made to Mr Betterton upon which ye Petition was grounded. But Mr Bright stands bound by articles under hand & Seal at 40s a Weeke Sallary.

Now my Lord having given Your Lordship ye foregoeing Answers to ye persons that think themselves aggreived Vizt to Mr Betterton, Mrs Barry, Mr Williams Mrs Bracegirdle, Mrs Verbruggen Mr Doggett & Mr Bright— Wee Humbly begg Your Lordships patience that we may Observe something concerning ye other 8 persons that signed Mr Bettertons Petition without mentioning any greivances whose names are as followeth Mr Bowman, Mr Underhill Mr Kynaston, Mr Sandford, Mr Bowen, Mrs Betterton, Mrs Leigh, & Mrs Bowman—

1   My Lord Mr Bowman might have spared his complaint & not have given this trouble to Your Lordship because about 3 Weeks before he signed ye Petition he agreed under his hand & Seale to take 3ll per Weeke for this Year or accept of 3 quarters of a share which was what he had when he last went out of share in January 1692/3 & before that time he never had above 3ll per Weeke Sallary.

2   Mr Underhill has 3ll per Weeke Sallary which with Submission to Your Lordship we thinke is more then he deservs by reason he Acts but very Seldome.

3   Mr Kinaston has 3ll per Weeke although he Acts but seldome which we did not offer to lessen although we reasonably may.

4   Mr Sandford stands at 2ll 10s per Weeke which was not offered to be lessened although by reason of his Indisposition & his voice often failing he is able to Act but Seldom.

5   Mr Bowen is under hand & Seale to serve ye Company at 40*s* per Weeke
& 9 Acting Months notice which Articles are not yett Expired. Yett he was
advanced 10*s* per Weeke ye last Year which Mr Betterton declared he
thought twas 5*s* more then he desired or deserved & Mr Bowen about a
ffortnight before he signed ye Petition declared himselfe satisfyed. But
though he is easily drawn to Mutiny yett he studys his parts very quickly
& Acts with vigour.

6   My Lord Mrs Betterton is at 50*s* per Weeke which has been constantly
paid her in Complement to Mr Betterton she not appear[ing] in any parts
to ye satisfaction of ye Audience.

7   Mrs Leigh since her Husbands death hath been raised 10*s* a Weeke being
at 30*s* a Weeke which we think full Enough being as much as ever Mrs
Cory had who was Extraordinarily well received by ye Audience.

8   Mrs Bowman was Added 5*s* per Weeke since the eighteenth October last
she being now at 30*s* per Weeke Notwithstanding she was under hand &
Seal at 25*s* per Weeke. She being a Child bearing Woman some other must
learn ["her," written and deleted] some of her parts or else those playes she
is in cannot be acted. She being asked why she signed ye Petition she
Answered onely because Mr Betterton whom she calls ffather desired her
soe to doe.

Now my Lord we desire to name to your Lordship such Actors & Actresses
who have not signed Mr Bettertons Petition which are as follow:
Vizt

Mr Powell	Mrs Aylyffe
Mr Verbruggen	Mrs Hodgson
Mr Trefusi	Mrs Knyght
Mr Lee	Mrs Rogers
Mr Horden	Mrs Perryn
Mr Harland	Mrs Lawson
Mr Cibber	Mrs Kent
Mr Harris	Mrs Lucas
Mr Pinkethman	Mrs Temple
Young Kent	

My Lord wee are very Sorry that ye generall though false Complaints of Mr Betterton & his companions have forced us to soe long an Answer which we could not possibly avoid being desirous to stand fair in Your Lordships Favour & cleared from ye false Imputations of Mr Betterton.

APPENDIX C

Personnel in the Spring of 1695

[The following tabulation is based on Appendixes A and B and *The London Stage*, part 1. The date indicates the actor's first known association with a Patent Company.]

I. The Lincoln's Inn Fields Company, drawn from three sources
  A. Signers of the Petition of the Players
        Thomas Betterton (original Duke's Company)
        Cave Underhill (original Duke's Company)
        Edward Kynaston (original King's Company)
        William Bowen (ca. 1688–89)
        Thomas Doggett (1690)
        George Bright (Duke's Company, 1678–79)
        Samuel Sandford (original Duke's Company)
        Mrs Barry (Duke's Company, ca. 1673–74)
        Mrs Bowman (ca. 1692–93)
        Mrs Betterton (original Duke's Company)
        Mrs Leigh (Duke's Company, ca. 1672)
        John Bowman (Duke's Company, ca. 1673)
  B. Members from the patentees' list of nonsigners
        Joseph Trefusis (1688–89)
        Joseph Harris (King's Company, 1669–70)
        Mrs Hodgson (1692–93)
        Mrs Perin (1690–91)
        Mrs Lawson (1691–92)
  C. Other origins
        Mrs Boutell (out of retirement)
        William Smith (out of retirement)

D. Renegades

    Joseph Williams and Mrs Verbruggen
      signed the petition but returned
      to the Patent Company.

    John Verbruggen did not sign the petition
      but joined the Patent Company.

II. The Patent Company

  A. People who did not sign the Petition of the Players

      George Powell (1686–87)
      John Verbruggen (1687–88)
      Michael Lee (1689–90)
      Hildebrand Horden (1694–95)
      Mr Harland (1694–95)
      Colley Cibber (1690)
      William Pinkethman (1692–93)
      Thomas Kent (1690–91)
      Mrs Knight (King's Company, 1676)
      Mrs Rogers (1692–93)
      Mrs Kent (1692–93)
      Mrs Lucas (1693–94)
      Mrs Temple (1693–94)

  B. Nonsigners unnamed by the patentees in their reply

      Mrs Verbruggen (ca. 1682)
      Miss Cross (1694–95)
      Jo Haynes (King's Company, 1667–68)
      John Mills (new in Rich's Company, 1695)

APPENDIX D

The Lincoln's Inn Fields Sharing Agreement

[The terms of this agreement were apparently written down as the result of a meeting with the Lord Chamberlain to settle disagreements over actor transfers, 26 October 1696. The copy text, P.R.O. LC 7/1, pp. 44–47, is followed by permission for Doggett and Verbruggen to switch companies (not transcribed here), and the date of the meeting. A fair copy of the Sharing Agreement alone exists in LC 7/3. It differs somewhat in spelling and punctuation, and in a few words ("Item" for "That is to say," "decease" for "death"), and the word "pounds" in the fifth paragraph, which I have added to my transcription in brackets. The fair copy lacks the signers' statement of "Free consent" and the list of signatories.]

Whereas Charles Earle of Dorsett and Middlesex Lord Chamberlaine of His Majesties Household etc. did in pursuance of His Majesties pleasure & Command give and grant full power Licence & authority unto Thomas Betterton, Elizabeth Barry, Anne Bracegirdle John Ver Brugen, John Boman, Cave Underhill George Bright and Elizabeth ["Lee," written and deleted] Leigh His Majesties sworne servants & Comedians in Ordinary and to the Major part of them Theire agents and Servants from time to time in any Convenient place or places to act or represent all manner of Comedies Tragedies etc. of what kind soever But so as to be under His Lordshipps Government and Regulation.

And Whereas ye said Thomas Betterton Elizabeth Barry Anne Bracegirdle John Verbrugen John Bowman Cave Underhill George Bright and Elizabeth Leigh have taken ye Tennis Court in Little Lincolns Inne Feilds and paid a greate fine and doe pay a Great rent for ye same and at an Extraordinary Charge & Expence have converted ye same into a Theatre or Playhouse where they now act Comedies Tragedies etc.

And further the said parties being necessited to provide every thing anew for the Carrying on soe Great an undertakeing as all variety of Cloaths Forreigne habitts Scenes properties etc. which must be paid out of the publique Receipts by the persons above named proportionable to the severall Shares & proportions each of them have in ye proffitts of the said playhouse

It is therefore resolved and agreed by the Consent of ye whole Company that the Shares doe never exceed the number of Tenn.

It is further Resolved and agreed that every whole sharer dyeing or quitting the Company fairely shall after ye Expiration of five yeares from the Establishment of the Company have the summe of One hundred [pounds] payd him or his Executor after his Death by the rest of the Sharers at Two Equall payments within the space of Three months after his Death or Quitting the Company as Theire interest and due for theire Shares in Cloaths Scenes properties etc. That is to say the summe of Twenty pounds to a whole sharer for the first yeare, Twenty pounds more for ye second yeare and soe on to One hundred pounds at ye five Yeares End And soe to all other parts of shares in proportion to a Whole share.

But in Consideration of the great Expences ye first three yeares being more then reasonable can be supposed for the like Terme to come It is agreed that any whole sharer dyeing at or after the Expiration of Three yeares shall have the summe of One hundred pounds payd His Executor as well & fully as if the whole Terme of Five yeares was Expired so in proportion to every under Sharer That is to say this payment to be made upon no other account but the Death of the party.

If any sharer be made incapable of His Business in the Company by sickness or any other accident every whole sharer so disabled shall have forty shillings per week allowed him every Week the Company shall Act And every person under the degree of a whole sharer shall have an allowance in proportion to his part of a Share he then enjoyed when he was so disabled.

If any Sharer shall hereafter be received into any proportion of Share he shall be obliged to signe the said Articles and be Conformable to all Orders and agreements made by the Company before his admission.

If any sharer be adJudged incapable of acting he shall not be obliged to acquitt his share and take the Salary provided in that Case above mentioned before a Twelve Month be Expired in which ["place," written and deleted] space of a Twelve month if he recover so as to attend his Business as formerly he shall then enjoy his share as formerly.

If any hyred Servant whose Salary Exceeds Twenty Shillings the Week be made incapable of his Business by sickness or any other accident on the Stage he shall have such a Weekly allowance proportionable to his Salary as the Majority of the Sharers shall Settle upon him.

If any Actor in Share or Sallary shall Quitt this Company and afterwards shall by Acting or otherwise assist any other Company he shall be incapable of receiveing any Benefitt of these Articles. And alsoe every Actor

Quitting the said Company shall be obliged to give sufficient Security for his performing the Conditions of this Article before he shall receive his proportion of Cloaths etc.

It is further agreed by the Consent of ye whole Company that as the number of Sharers are not to Exceed Tenn so no person shall have any proportion of above one share in consideration of Acting.

To these above mention'd Articles
to Testifye theire full and
Free consent the partyes
Conscerned have Severally
sett Theire hands

Thomas Betterton	Elizabeth Barry
John Verbruggen	Anne Bracegirdle
John Bowman	Elizabeth Leigh
Cave Underhill	
George Bright	

APPENDIX E

Verbruggen's Petition

[This undated petition was written on a single sheet and probably delivered in person, since it is unaddressed. It is now bound into P. R. O. LC 7/3 near the end of part 1.]

To the Right Honorable the Earle of Jersey Lord
Chamberlain of her Majesties Household

The Humble Petition of John Verbruggen.

Sheweth

    That Mr William Smith One of the cheife Actors & Sharers of the Company in Lincolns Inn Feilds dying about Michaelmas 1696 & the Company being in great distress for one to performe his parts your petitioner upon their extraordinary Sollicitations & fair promises Withdrew himselfe (by the Lord Chamberlains Leave) from the Company in Covent Garden, where he was a principall Actor, & ingaged himselfe as a sharing Actor & Manager in this Company in the stead of the said William Smith.

    That by Articles of Agreement dated twenty-seventh October 1696 made between Mr Betterton Mrs Barry Mrs Bracegirdle Mr Bowman Mr Underhill Mr Bright & Mrs Leigh then sharing Actors of the said Company on the one parte & your petitioner on the other parte It was agreed that your petitioner should be admitted to have as well one Share in Ten to be divided of the Common Stock of Scenes Clothes properties etc. As also of all the moneys profits & perquisites in any manner arising from the said playhouse as

252

fully & proportionably & in such manner as any other sharer to Commence from the first of January then next.

That your petitioner on his parte did thereby covenant to conforme himselfe to the Rules of the Company & that he should proportionably with the other sharers pay all Debts relating to the said playhouse.

That Mr Betterton having then one share & an halfe quitted halfe a quarter of his share to your petitioner & it was also agreed That your petitioner should have 20s a week paid him out of the Generall Receipts as assistant Manager to Mr Betterton So that your petitioner for acting & manageing might have an equivalent with him.

That your petitioner was accordingly admitted into the said share & salary & was then informed that the Debts did not exceed 200ll. [Marginal note in another hand, cancelled: "leave to look in ye books."]

That sometime after your petitioner complained to them how small a share of profits came to him, not sufficient for a bare subsistance & desired to have an account of Receipts in Generall & subscription moneys & how the same were disposed of & desired a list of the debts but could never to this time obtain the same.

And as for Mr Bowman Bright Underhill & Mrs Leigh they are aggreived in the same manner & observe that Mr Betterton Mrs Barry & Mrs Bracegirdle have made Gains to themselves by benefit plays & other wise.

That about Michaelmas last they told your petitioner that the debts of the Company were about 800ll and after an attendance on your Lordship Itt was agreed on That no sharer should have any benefit play but that all the Clear profits should be applyed to discharge the Debts, till all should be paid saving that some parte of the profits in the meantime should be shared for a bare subsistance only.

That this last winter the Receipts have been extraordinary great especially ever since the Italian Woman hath sung & yet they pretend the Debts are not all paid although they have stopt your petitioners management money of 20s per week & for 7 monthes last past have not paid him for his dividend full 30ll although the persons at sallary have been abated many days pay. So that your petitioner hath reason to believe that more moneys have been stopt then really the debts amounted to & yet they pretend that many debts are still owing, but your petitioner could never obtain a just account of them. And now Mr Betterton who appeared before Sir John Stanley with your petitioner & with him protested against all benefit plays hath ordered Bills to be printed for Othello to be acted on ffryday next with singing by the Italian Woman for his own benefit & tis said she is to sing twice more in plays for Mrs Barry & Mrs Bracegirdle & then to leave of. So that those three design

still as they have done to reap all the benefit to themselves to the wrong &
Damage of your petitioner & the rest of the Company & leave your petitioner
lyable to the Debts they pretend due.

That ever since Mr Betterton and your petitioner were before Sir John
Stanley He hath constantly declared against any sharers having any benefit
plays & hath signifyed as much by notice under his hand (purporting that he
expected his proportionable share of all profits arising by sharers benefits after
charges deducted) directed to Mr Betterton & the rest of the sharers.

Your petitioner now humbly prays your Lordship to give Order

First That a List of such debts as have been paid since Michaelmas
last & of such debts as are still owing, if any & of such Debts as were owing
& to whom when your petitioner came first into the Company in 1696 may
be forthwith delivered to your petitioner. [Marginal note in another hand:
"leave to examine ye books."]

Secondly That all the Books & papers of accounts may be produced
together with all the subscriptions & an Accountant on your petitioners be-
halfe permitted to peruse & examine the same whereby your petitioner may
be truly informed of all matters & what his share & proportion according to
his Contract amounts to ever since his coming into the Company & that right
may be done him therein without a suite at Law. [Marginal note in another
hand: "a liberty to examine subscriptions."]

Thirdly That in case your Lordship thinks fit That your petitioner
shall play his part in Othello on ffryday next That then the Receipts of that
day & afterwards all others of like kind (after payment of usuall charge) may
be divided amongst all the sharers according & in proportion to their shares
& which is pursuant to your petitioners Originall Contract & that Mr Smith
the Treasurer be ordered to pay the same accordingly.

And your petitioner shall ever pray etc.

NOTES

Chapter 1:
The Organization and Management
of the Patent Companies, 1660–1668

1 For a detailed account, see John Freehafer, "The Formation of the London Patent Companies in 1660," *Theatre Notebook* 20 (1965): 6–30.

2 See *The Dramatic Records of Sir Henry Herbert*, ed. Joseph Quincy Adams (New Haven: Yale University Press, 1917), pp. 87–88.

3 For details of the patent grant see Hotson, chaps. 5 and 6. See also *Survey of London*, vol. 35 (London: Athlone Press, 1970), chap. 1.

4 See John Freehafer, "Brome, Suckling, and Davenant's Theatre Project of 1639," *Texas Studies in Literature and Language* 10 (1968): 367–88.

5 *The Dramatic Records of Sir Henry Herbert*, pp. 113–15.

6 Ibid., pp. 119–23.

7 The whereabouts of Davenant's patent, if extant, is unknown. My copy text is a transcription in P.R.O. C66/3009 (cited without date in *Survey of London*, 35:112). In 1720 *The State of the Case, Between The Lord Chamberlain . . . and Sir Richard Steele, [etc.]* printed a "True Copy" of the patent which includes a further clause promising no certainty of profits. Percy Fitzgerald accepted this version without identifying it (*A New History of the English Stage*, 2 vols. [London: Tinsley Brothers, 1882], 1:73–77). Since the Killigrew patent, P.R.O. C66/3013, contains no such clause, I am reluctant to accept it as genuine.

8 Hotson, p. 200.

9 The fullest study is Arthur F. White's "The Office of Revels and Dramatic Censorship during the Restoration Period," *Western Reserve University Bulletin*, n.s. 34 (1931): 5–45. The reader should also consult Edward A. Langhans's *Restoration Promptbooks*, forthcoming.

10 See *The Cheats*, ed. Milton C. Nahm (Oxford: Blackwell, 1935).

11 Bodleian MS Rawl. Poet 195, fols. 49–78. See Judith Milhous and Robert D. Hume, "Two Plays by Elizabeth Polwhele: *The Faithfull Virgins* and *The Frolicks*," *Papers of the Bibliographical Society of America* 71 (1977): 1–9.

12 See *The Poems and Plays of William Cartwright*, ed. G. Blakemore Evans (Madison: University of Wisconsin Press, 1951), p. 85.

13 P.R.O. LC 5/137, pp. 332–33, and Freehafer's interpretation, "Formation of the London Patent Companies," pp. 20–21.
14 See Hotson, pp. 177–78.
15 See Freehafer, "Formation of the London Patent Companies," pp. 25–26, and P.R.O. LC 5/137, p. 343.
16 A copy is preserved in *The Dramatic Records of Sir Henry Herbert*, pp. 96–100.
17 See Hotson, chap. 4.
18 On sales of shares, see Hotson, pp. 219 ff.
19 See Gerald Eades Bentley, *The Jacobean and Caroline Stage*, 7 vols. (Oxford: Clarendon Press, 1941–68), I: 43–47.
20 See Hotson, p. 244.
21 See George Chalmers, *An Apology for the Believers in the Shakspeare-Papers* (London: Thomas Egerton, 1797), pp. 529–30, for a transcription of an arbitrators' report in the P.R.O., now unlocatable.
22 See Hotson, pp. 243–44, and H. J. Oliver, "The Building of the Theatre Royal in Bridges St.: Some Details of Finance," *Notes & Queries* 217 (1972): 464–66.
23 Hotson, p. 249.
24 See Hotson, pp. 255–56, and *Survey of London*, 35: 31–32.
25 The hypothetical calculations which follow are my own, but they are based on information in *The London Stage*, pt. 1, pp xlix–lvi, lxx–lxxi.
26 Cited by Hotson, p. 222.
27 For performance totals later in the century compare Edward A. Langhans, "New Restoration Theatre Accounts, 1682–1692," *Theatre Notebook* 17 (1963): 118–34, and Hotson, p. 308.
28 P.R.O. C7/486/74, transcribed in *The Works of John Dryden*, vol. 10, ed. Maximillian E. Novak and George R. Guffey (Berkeley: University of California Press, 1970), pp. 539–47.
29 *Roscius Anglicanus*, p. 41.
30 Pepys, 20 November 1660. Quotations are from *The Diary of Samuel Pepys*, ed. Robert Latham and William Matthews, 11 vols. in progress (London: Bell, 1970–).
31 Note Killigrew's boasts to Pepys, 2 August 1664, 12 February and 9 September 1667.
32 *Apology* 1:91.
33 See Freehafer, "Formation of the London Patent Companies," pp. 26–27.
34 P.R.O. LC 5/137, p. 343.
35 See Gerald Eades Bentley, *The Profession of Dramatist in Shakespeare's Time* (Princeton: Princeton University Press, 1971), chap. 10.
36 Bentley, *The Jacobean and Caroline Stage*, 1: 330–31.
37 The fullest consideration is by Gunnar Sorelius, "The Rights of the Restoration Theatrical Companies in the Older Drama," *Studia Neophilologica* 37 (1965): 174–89.
38 *The Dramatic Records of Sir Henry Herbert*, p. 90.
39 *Biographical Dictionary*, 2: 135.
40 P.R.O. LC 5/139, p. 375. P.R.O. LC 5/12, p. 212, lists plays reserved for Killigrew's company.
41 Samuel Butler, *Satires and Miscellaneous Poetry and Prose*, ed. René Lamar (Cambridge: At the University Press, 1928), pp. 142–43.
42 P.R.O. LC 5/138, p. 15.

43 Pepys, 27 January 1664; Evelyn, 5 February 1664.
44 Letter by Katherine Philips, cited in *The London Stage*, pt. 1, p. 74.
45 See William Van Lennep, "Henry Harris, Actor, Friend of Pepys," *Studies in English Theatre History In Memory of Gabrielle Enthoven* (London: Society for Theatre Research, 1952), pp. 9–23.
46 Pepys, 28 September and 4 October 1664.
47 *Roscius Anglicanus*, p. 26.
48 Pepys, 25 March 1668.
49 Ibid., 7 January 1669.
50 For details see James M. Osborn, *John Dryden: Some Biographical Facts and Problems*, 2d ed. (Gainesville: University of Florida Press, 1965), pp. 200–207. Charles E. Ward, in *The Life of John Dryden* (Chapel Hill: University of North Carolina Press, 1961), p. 57, dates the King's Company offer to Dryden "sometime in May" 1668, but he cites no evidence for this statement.
51 Dent points out that even the Italian public had no access to opera until the Teatro San Cassiano opened in Venice in 1637, and Cardinal Mazarin did not succeed in mounting an Italian opera in Paris until 1647. *Foundations of English Opera* (1928; reprint ed., New York: Da Capo, 1965), pp. 44–48.

Chapter 2:
Betterton's Management
Experience, 1668–1694

1 See Hotson, pp. 226–27; and Arthur H. Nethercot, *Sir William D'avenant* (1938; reprint ed., New York: Russell and Russell, 1967), pp. 408–12.
2 7 April 1668.
3 Printed by Hotson, p. 228. The staff of the P.R.O. could not locate this document for me (cited by Hotson as C24/1144/11) when I tried to consult it in the summer of 1976.
4 For further details, see Hotson, pp. 229–30, and my article, "The Duke's Company's Profits, 1675–1677," *Theatre Notebook* 32 (1978): 76–88.
5 *Roscius Anglicanus*, p. 35. *Biographical Dictionary*, 2: 269–70.
6 Both documents are in P.R.O. LC 7/3. See Appendix B and Nicoll, 2: 276.
7 For details, see my article, "Thomas Betterton's Playwriting," *Bulletin of the New York Public Library* 77 (1974): 375–92.
8 See Edward A. Langhans, "A Conjectural Reconstruction of the Dorset Garden Theatre," *Theatre Survey* 13 (November 1972): 74–93.
9 On Harris see Oscar L. Brownstein, "The Duke's Company in 1667 [recte, 1677]," *Theatre Notebook* 28 (1974): 18–23. For Betterton's testimony, see Hotson, pp. 233–34.
10 P.R.O. C6/250/28. Printed in full by Hotson, pp. 356–76. Quotation from p. 369.
11 P.R.O. C6/316/21.
12 On this elaborate production, and the involvement of the Court with the theatre, see Eleanore Boswell, *The Restoration Court Stage* (1932; reprint ed., New York: Barnes and Noble, 1966).
13 The Nell Gwyn letter is cited by Nicoll, 1: 319,n. Dorset served as Lord Chamberlain from 1689 until 19 April 1697.
14 See Cibber, *Apology*, 1: 194 and n.

15 See Nicoll, 1: 319–20, for a convenient list.
16 *Mr. Goodman the Player* (Pittsburgh: University of Pittsburgh Press, 1964).
17 See Curt A. Zimansky and Robert D. Hume, "Henry Shipman's *Henry the Third of France*: Some Problems of Date, Performance, and Publication," *Philological Quarterly* 55 (1976): 436–44.
18 *Covent Garden Drollery*, ed. G. Thorn-Drury (London: Dobell, 1928), pp. 2–3.
19 Hotson, p. 258.
20 See "A Prologue Spoken at the Opening of the New House," *The Prologues and Epilogues of John Dryden*, ed. William Bradford Gardner (1951; reprint ed., Mamaroneck, N.Y.: Appel, 1971), pp. 60–61.
21 P.R.O. LC 7/1, p. 4.
22 P.R.O. LC 5/141, p. 307.
23 P.R.O. LC 7/1, p. 5.
24 P.R.O. LC 5/190, fol. 134v.
25 See Hotson, p. 259, who cites a 1696 lawsuit between Kynaston and an heir of Wintershall.
26 P.R.O. documents of 9 September 1676 and 22 February 1677 (LC 5/141, pp. 455, 539).
27 P.R.O. LC 5/142, p. 98 (30 July).
28 For details, see Hotson, pp. 261–62.
29 Petition of the King's Company, printed by Osborn, *John Dryden*, pp. 200–207.
30 See P.R.O. LC 5/143, p. 69, and Nicoll, 1: 326–27.
31 Details are known from a Chancery suit. See Hotson, pp. 264–65, and Wilson, *Mr. Goodman*, pp. 68–69.
32 John Harold Wilson, "Theatre Notes from the Newdigate Newsletters," *Theatre Notebook* 15 (1961): 79–84.
33 *Mr. Goodman*, p. 71, and P.R.O. C7/133/82.
34 P.R.O. LC 5/140, fol. 456. A month later the return of the scenery was demanded (LC 5/140, fol. 471).
35 *Roscius Anglicanus*, p. 35.
36 See Hotson, p. 263.
37 *Mr. Goodman*, p. 53.
38 P.R.O. C6/316/21. William Smith's answer, quoted by Hotson, is essentially identical, but in the last few lines Betterton takes up issues Smith does not touch.
39 Printed in Charles Gildon, *The Life of Mr. Thomas Betterton* (1710; reprint ed., New York: Augustus M. Kelley, 1970), pp. 8–9.
40 For the former, see Add. MS 20,726. For the latter, P.R.O. C10/297/57 (n.d.; ca. 1700?). The two do not differ in any important particulars, though Add. MS 20,726 mistakenly gives the date as 14 May, instead of 4 May 1682. P.R.O. C6/316/21 confirms the correct date.
41 P.R.O. C6/316/21.
42 See Hotson, p. 271 for the usurpation suit. My information about the Drury Lane lease is from Hotson, p. 273, and C10/360/16. The separately financed scene-house was also leased to the United Company in 1683 for nineteen years, after the King's Company actors who built it had failed to pay the ground rent. See *Survey of London*, 35: 31–32. The fate of its much-disputed, much-depleted stock is not known, though Mohun's suit (discussed below) implies that it was taken over by the United Company.

43 *Roscius Anglicanus*, pp. 39–40.
44 P.R.O. LC 5/191, fols. 102v–3, 105.
45 *The London Stage*, pt. 1, pp. lvi, xliii.
46 For details see Hotson, pp. 288–89, and Langhans, "New Restoration Theatre Accounts."
47 Preface to *The Treacherous Brothers* (1690).
48 See Hotson, pp. 228–29 for what little is known.
49 See Diana de Marly, "The Architect of Dorset Garden Theatre," *Theatre Notebook* 29 (1975): 119–24, who challenges the traditional vague attribution to Wren.
50 Add. MS 36,916, fol. 233, cited in *The London Stage*, pt. 1, p. 190.
51 See P.R.O. LC 5/14, p. 73 for an order to Sir Christopher Wren to inspect the building "for his Majesty's safety," since "information hath beene given that there is a defect in a Wall."
52 For some account of ordinary staging practices, see Montague Summers, *The Restoration Theatre* (1934; reprint ed., New York: Humanities Press, 1964), chap. 6. The best account of the subject remains Edward A. Langhans's dissertation, "Staging Practices in the Restoration Theatres 1660–1682" (Yale, 1955).
53 For these categories, see Hume, chap. 5.
54 Descriptions are from *Roscius Anglicanus*, pp. 33, 34–36, 40–42.
55 *The Works of John Dryden*, vol. 15, ed. Earl Miner and George R. Guffey (Berkeley: University of California Press, 1976), p. 28, reprints the sketch from Scott's edition of the *Works*. See also the relevant note, p. 372.
56 *Roscius Anglicanus*, pp. 35–36.
57 Cited in *The London Stage*, pt. 1, p. 334. If we allow generous box office receipts of £50 × 200 days = £10,000, less conservative house charges of £25 per day (£5,000) and profit for twenty shareholders of £60 a year (£1200) as in 1676, the total expenses come to £6,200, which leaves only £3,800 to stage all shows.
58 In the first published edition of "The Play House, a Satyr," licensed 8 January 1689, Robert Gould included the line, "*The Emp'rour of the Moon*, 'twill never tire."
59 *A Brief Historical Relation of State Affairs*, 6 vols. (Oxford: Oxford University Press, 1857), 2: 435.

Chapter 3:
The Actors' Rebellion
of 1694–1695

1 See Hotson, pp. 296–97, for summaries of the charters involved.
2 See Langhans, "New Restoration Theatre Accounts."
3 Hotson, p. 286. For examples of anti–Thomas Davenant sentiments, see Charles Killigrew in P.R.O. C6/316/21, and Rich's statement in the Reply of the Patentees that Thomas was appointed "by word of mouth onely" (art. 2).
4 See the Reply of the Patentees, arts. 6 and 8. According to the accounts published by Langhans, Thomas Davenant received £2 10s. Killigrew thought his salary was 40s. (P.R.O. C6/316/21).
5 P.R.O. C6/316/21.
6 See John Harold Wilson, "Players' Lists in the Lord Chamberlain's *Registers*," *Theatre Notebook* 18 (1963): 25–30. Smith's will is found in PCC 1696, fol. 149, PROB 11 433.

7 His obituary, in *The Flying Post*, 28 December 1695, is printed by Montague Summers in his edition of *Roscius Anglicanus*, p. 168.

8 Hotson, p. 286.

9 Wilson, "Players' Lists"; Hotson, p. 290; warrants in P.R.O. LC 5/151, p. 369, and LC 5/148, p. 145.

10 See *The Complete Works of Thomas Shadwell*, 5 vols., ed. Montague Summers (1927; reprint ed., New York: Blom, 1968), 5: 403, for a transcription of Shadwell's letter of protest. See *The London Stage*, pt. 1, p. 419, on *The Old Batchelour*. In 1694 Thomas Davenant was still known to hold a fraction of a share in the company, but he was dead by the time Rich made his report in answer to Sir Edward Smith, September 1705 (P.R.O. C8/599/77).

11 P.R.O. LC 5/151, p. 369.

12 The only other candidate ever proposed is Elkanah Settle. See Frank C. Brown, *Elkanah Settle: His Life and Works* (Chicago: University of Chicago Press, 1910), pp. 95–97. But Brown is more concerned with proving Settle the adapter than with his qualifications as a machinist.

13 *Biographical Dictionary*, 2: 84.

14 See Hotson, p. 293.

15 *Apology*, 1: 188. Powell, who was violently jealous of Betterton and had been chafing against his authority since at least 1690, was eager. But Mrs Bracegirdle, who had grown up as a ward of the Bettertons and who played rather different sorts of roles than Mrs Barry, prudently refused. The patentees regarded her desertion as "most Unkindly," since they "were ye first movers of advancing her" (Reply of the Patentees, art. 12).

16 See P.R.O. LC 5/149, fol. 16 for details. The actors known to have treated with him are Leigh, Nokes, Mountfort, and Mrs Corey.

17 P.R.O. C5/284/40. Hotson specifies December (p. 293), but I cannot find testimony to the month.

18 *Apology*, 1: 190, 192.

19 See P.R.O. LC 5/151, p. 397 for Dorset's scheduling of the hearing, dated 7 December 1694.

20 For these documents, see Hotson, pp. 296–97. In 1704 the patentees imply that their patent claims were not believed until they had shown evidence of Alexander Davenant's sales to the actors (P.R.O. C5/284/40).

21 Reply of the Patentees, art. 1 and added comment 8. Mrs Bowman was, briefly, a ward of Betterton in 1692–93, before her marriage. See the *Biographical Dictionary*, 2: 201.

22 P.R.O. C6/438/34 gives us this information.

23 According to *The London Stage*, Mountfort died 9 December 1692, Gillow in May 1687 (Company Roster 1686–87). Summers gives a death date of 11 July 1691 in his note on Carlisle, but without a source (*Roscius Anglicanus*, p. 236). The *Biographical Dictionary*, 3: 73, gives 12 July.

24 See Hotson, p. 290, and art. 6 of the Reply of the Patentees. Art. 3 tries to make light of the amount of aftermoney, saying that it has "not yett" amounted to £400 per annum. If it were even £350 a year, the debt would not take long to repay.

25 *Apology*, 1: 192.

26 P.R.O. SP 44/74/2 (and 44/73/20, which is worded differently but records the same information).

27 *Apology*, 1: 192–93.
28 P.R.O. LC 7/3, documents of 19 and 22 March 1695.
29 *Roscius Anglicanus*, p. 43.
30 Cibber, *Apology*, 1: 194; Robert W. Lowe, *Thomas Betterton* (1891; reprint ed., New York: AMS, 1972), pp. 143–44.
31 See Hotson, p. 306; see also *A Comparison between the Two Stages*, p. 12.
32 *Apology*, 1: 200.
33 Documents in P.R.O. LC 7/3.
34 *Apology*, 1: 193.
35 See chap. 5 below. The patentees did not, of course, own either Drury Lane or Dorset Garden—they merely held rental agreements on them.
36 P.R.O. LC 7/1 and 7/3. For a full transcription, see Appendix D. The Lord Chamberlain's papers give us no explanation of this "greate fine." Might it have been fees paid for legal documents drawn up?
37 See Donald C. Mullin, *The Development of the Playhouse* (Berkeley: University of California Press, 1970), pp. 68–69.
38 Mrs Barry was under the impression that she had bought some United Company stock from Alexander Davenant, but that she had not made any money from it, nor did the stock give her authority in the company. (Sec. 1 of the Petition of the Players and of the Reply of the Patentees.)
39 Cibber, *Apology*, 1: 194. See also *A Comparison between the Two Stages*, p. 9.
40 P.R.O. C8/599/74. This corroboration is particularly useful because the suit is nearly contemporary, unlike Cibber's book.
41 The actors prudently specify that retirement benefits will not be given to anyone who is moving to another theatre, or who fails to give adequate guarantees of not doing so. A glance at Doggett's checkered history shows why this provision was needed.
42 E.g., John Harold Wilson, *A Preface to Restoration Drama* (Boston: Houghton Mifflin, 1965), chap. 4.
43 See especially Emmett L. Avery, "The Restoration Audience," *Philological Quarterly* 45 (1966): 54–61, and Harold Love, "The Myth of the Restoration Audience," *Komos* 1 (1967): 49–56.
44 John Loftis, *Comedy and Society from Congreve to Fielding* (Stanford: Stanford University Press, 1959), p. 15.
45 See Hume, chap. 9.
46 Harry William Pedicord points out that after 1750, when enough evidence is available to permit conclusions, "only 17 people in every 1,000 [in London] attended" the patent theatres. *The Theatrical Public in the Time of Garrick* (1954; reprint ed., Carbondale: Southern Illinois University Press, 1966), p. 43. While we cannot extrapolate back directly to the 1695 situation, a percentage this small in the middle of the next century is an indication of the tiny number of potential customers to be sorted out from the general London population at a time when the audience base was changing.
47 *Bishop Burnet's History of His Own Time*, 6 vols., 2d enl. ed. (Oxford: Oxford University Press, 1833), 5: 18–19.
48 *CSPDom*, 1689–90, p. 3: 16 February 1689. Cf. an earlier proclamation, *CSPDom*, 1663–64, p. 240, which deals only with unlicensed seditious works.
49 See D. S. Thomas, "Prosecutions of *Sodom: or, the Quintessence of Debauchery*, and *Poems on Several Occasions by the E of R*, 1689–1690 and 1693," *The Library*, 5th

ser., 24 (1969): 51–55, and David Foxon, *Libertine Literature in England, 1660–1745* (New Hyde Park, N.Y.: University Books, 1965).

50 See *The London Stage*, pt. 1, p. 403 (17 December 1691). Earlier in the year, in a somewhat similar vein, official orders had cut short the summer fair: "Bartholomew faire by order of the Lord Mayor and Aldermen is to bee kept but for 3 days this yeare because its a season of great debauchery" (8 August 1691).

51 *The Gay Couple in Restoration Comedy* (Cambridge: Harvard University Press, 1948), p. 135.

52 See Hume, chaps. 9, 10.

53 *The London Stage*, pt. 1, pp. lxix–lxx.

54 P.R.O. C10/297/57, transcribed by Hotson, p. 300. That sheet of parchment had evidently become detached and was no longer with the suit in the summer of 1976.

55 *Apology*, 1: 195.

Chapter 4:
The Success of the Rebels,
1695–1698

1 See Shirley Strum Kenny, "Theatrical Warfare," cited in the Preface.

2 *A Comparison*, p. 7. Sixteen is not an exaggeration: see Appendix C. "The Theatre at the Bear Garden" probably refers to the baiting ring at Hockley-in-the-Hole.

3 Letter from Robert Jennens to Thomas Coke, 19 November 1696, cited in *The London Stage*, pt. 1, p. 470. The "new play" was Vanbrugh's *The Relapse*, and its triumph may indeed have saved the company.

4 Hotson implies that Philip Griffin, who had acted with the King's and United companies until 1692, became manager at Drury Lane in 1695 and held the post for some years. "An additional expense was incurred when Skipwith and Rich appointed Captain Griffin as manager of their tail-end of a company—a post which he held until his journey to Ireland in 1699" (p. 300). But I can find no evidence to support this assertion. Griffin appears in *The London Stage* roster for Rich's Company in the spring of 1695, but there is no record of him with the company in 1695–96, 1696–97, or 1697–98 until 2 June 1698, when he is specially advertised as "formerly a famous Actor, and lately Captain of a Company of Foot in His Majesty's Service, through the Wars in Ireland." According to Clark, he went to Dublin in the fall of 1699. (See William Smith Clark, *The Early Irish Stage* [1955; reprint ed., Westport, Conn.: Greenwood, 1973], p. 114.)

5 *Apology*, 1. 232.

6 See his dedication to Rich of *The Cornish Comedy* (1696).

7 *A Comparison*, p. 106.

8 The Articles of Agreement are in P.R.O. LC 7/3.

9 Few of Doggett's roles are known for this period, so we cannot really determine the effect of his desertion upon the company. His Sailor Ben in *Love for Love* was considered irreplaceable, and in later years he returned to the London theatre to do guest appearances in that play.

10 *A Comparison*, p. 17. The cast list in the 1696 edition gives Doggett as Young Hob.

11 P.R.O. LC 5/152, p. 40.

12 P.R.O. LC 5/192, fol. 109.

13 P.R.O. LC 7/1.

14 The contract is in P.R.O. LC 7/3. See also the *Biographical Dictionary* entry on Cibber, and chap. 5 below for his play *Xerxes* (which Rich was happy to have refused, since it failed at Lincoln's Inn Fields).

15 Such orders were issued 16 April and 25 July 1695, and 26 October 1696 (P.R.O. LC 7/1), and reiterated by Sunderland when he took the post, 27 May 1697 (LC 5/152, p. 15).

16 *Animadversions on Mr Congreve's late Answer to Mr Collier* (1698), pp. 34–35, cited in *The London Stage*, pt. 1, p. 486.

17 See Dilke's "Epistle Dedicatory."

18 One of the few later Lincoln's Inn Fields "warfare" pieces is the epilogue to *The Italian Husband* (November 1697), but it was written by Drury Lane's Jo Haynes, who would have been hearing the metaphor there.

19 *Roscius Anglicanus*, p. 45.

20 See *Don Quixote*, pt. 3; *The Roman Bride's Revenge; The Cornish Comedy; Woman's Wit;* and *A Plot and No Plot* for examples of Patent Company plays with smutty epilogues. See also Nicoll, 1: 266.

21 See Curtis A. Price's excellent dissertation, "Musical Practices in Restoration Plays, with a Catalogue of Instrumental Music in the Plays 1665–1713" (Harvard, 1974), for a very helpful account of music and musicians on the Restoration stage.

22 *Roscius Anglicanus*, p. 46; *Biographical Dictionary*, 2: 85.

23 The castle of Namur surrendered on 1 September 1695 after a summer-long siege (Stephen B. Baxter, *William III* [London: Longmans, 1965], p. 329). Motteux did the libretto, Eccles the music for the masque that was printed that fall. No public performance is recorded; but so small a piece would have been part of a multiple bill and, before daily newspaper ads, our chances of knowing about it are slim.

24 Prologue to *The Anatomist*.

25 Sybil Rosenfeld, *A Short History of Scene Design in Great Britain* (Oxford: Blackwell, 1973), pp. 55 ff.

26 For example, the swans that dance and fly in act 1 are probably left over from *The Fairy-Queen*.

27 See the prologues to *The Innocent Mistress* (late June), *The Deceiver Deceived* (November), and less specifically *The Unnatural Mother* (ca. September) for humor at the expense of *The World in the Moon*.

28 The publication of *Heroic Love* was advertised in the 17–21 February *London Gazette*.

29 Preface to the anonymous *The Fatal Discovery*.

30 Quoted in *The London Stage*, pt. 1, p. 490. Peter the Great spent 11 January through ca. 28 April in and around London (*CSPDom*, 1698).

31 See Dryden's letter to Mrs Steward, quoted in *The London Stage*, pt. 1, p. 509.

32 *Apology*, 1: 217–18. The play was *The Provok'd Wife*.

33 See the Introduction by Lucyle Hook to the Augustan Reprint Society edition (1967).

34 *A Comparison*, pp. 7–9.

35 See Eugene Hulse Sloane, *Robert Gould*, pp. 35–37.

36 Cited in *The London Stage*, pt. 1, p. 476.

37 *Roscius Anglicanus*, p. 44; *Apology*, 1: 197.
38 P.R.O. C8/599/77. The figure probably represents the entire 1694–95 season. At least it cannot be an accurate count for the last three and a half months, being far too high: at a generous estimate that period might have included fifty-eight acting days.
39 *Apology*, 1: 202.
40 Other reprints this year are *The Country-Wife, King Arthur, Macbeth,* and *The Souldiers Fortune*.
41 *Apology*, 1: 205–6.
42 See Maximillian E. Novak, "The Closing of Lincoln's Inn Fields Theatre in 1695," *Restoration and Eighteenth Century Theatre Research* 14 (May 1975): 51–52.
43 *Roscius Anglicanus*, p. 44.
44 Ibid.
45 Ibid. Anne Bracegirdle thereby lost an amusing mad scene in which the character she played thinks she is Cupid.
46 *A Comparison*, p. 20.
47 P.R.O. C8/599/77.
48 See P.R.O. LC 7/1 and 7/3 (printed by Nicoll, 1: 341, n. 1) for the Lord Chamberlain's reprimand to the managers of the company at "ye Theatres of Drury Lane & Dorsett Gardens" for acting both new and revived plays without the permission of the Master of the Revels.
49 Posthumously produced, the play had been rejected by the United Company and was quite dated. Gildon reports in his dedication that a "Faction" caused its failure, which is not surprising in view of the treatment of sex in the play. He also says that Verbruggen *read* his part—though he hastens to add that the reading was so well done that "he lost nothing in the Force of Elocution, nor Gracefulness of Action." We have no information as to why the shortchanging occurred.
50 Cibber refers to Powell's "bouncing *Borgia*" (*Apology*, 1: 228). The Little Girl epilogue to *Bonduca* (October 1695) reminds the audience, "You heard me t'other Day in Young Queen *Betty*."
51 *The Indian Queen* had been a point of contention between the patentees and rebels (see the Reply of the Patentees, art. 7). I doubt the junior company could have mounted the production in the spring of 1695, as *The London Stage* suggests.
52 Dilke specifies that he got his author's benefit.
53 Charles Gildon, *The Lives and Characters of the English Dramatick Poets* (London: Leigh and Turner [1699]), p. 111.
54 Gildon, *Lives and Characters*, p. 115.
55 *A Comparison*, p. 20.
56 The following scenes and machines from *Albion and Albanius* reappeared in *Brutus*: Augusta attended by Cities and Thamesis by Rivers, along with Hermes's Raven Chariot (from 1. 1 of Dryden's play); the Poetical Hell of 2. 1; Juno's Peacock, Dover, the Cave of Proteus, and Apollo's Throne from 3. 1. The stage directions are copied almost verbatim from those Betterton provided Dryden. Some costumes were probably also reused—a Watermen's Dance occurred in *Albion and Albanius*, 1. 1. The only major scene from another opera, the "Palace of the Corinthian Order," came from *Psyche*, act 3. These pieces ranged from ten to twenty years old and, even if refurbished, may have looked dated. Powell can scarcely have been unaware that he was lifting from Betterton.

57 P.R.O. C8/599/77.

58 *Roscius Anglicanus*, p. 44.

59 P.R.O. C8/599/77. Among plays reprinted this year, the following are more or less definitely associated with the Patent Company: *The City Heiress, Don Sebastian, Marriage A-la-Mode, Sauny the Scot,* and *Secret-Love*. See *The London Stage*, pt. 1, pp. 484–85.

60 *Apology*, 1: 200. Following quotation from 1: 218.

61 In P.R.O. C8/599/74 Sir Edward Smith et al. mistakenly assert that the £7 rent on Dorset Garden accrued only when that theatre was used; they also state that in the last ten years the rent has not been paid even for those few days.

62 For a more balanced view, see the *Biographical Dictionary*, 2: 85 ff. The authors speculate that Valentine was written for Joseph Williams, perhaps extrapolating from Cibber's account of Williams's return to Drury Lane (*Apology*, 1: 201). Montague Summers, also without citing his evidence, says Williams was originally cast as Scandal (*The Complete Works of William Congreve*, 4 vols. [Soho: Nonesuch Press, 1923], 1: 25).

63 See *The London Stage* headnote to the 1697–98 season.

64 See the preface to Walker's *Victorious Love*.

65 See David Ogg, *England in the Reigns of James II and William III* (Oxford: Clarendon Press, 1955), pp. 424 and 435.

66 See Calhoun Winton, "The London Stage Embattled: 1695–1700," on the subject of the reforms being sought (*Tennessee Studies in Literature* 19 [1974]: 9–19).

Chapter 5:
Cutthroat Competition,
1698–1702

1 Booth joined Lincoln's Inn Fields in 1700, according to the *Biographical Dictionary*, 2: 212. Taken literally, the "ten years" would have been 1695–1705, after which Betterton ceased to lead the company.

2 *A Comparison*, pp. 104–5.

3 *Apology*, 1: 315,n.; Nicoll, 1: 340.

4 Kenny, "Theatrical Warfare," p. 133.

5 *Apology*, 1: 238–39, 255–56.

6 He joined the United Company about 1689, probably with experience in Dublin. Both Betterton and Rich had reservations about him (see the Reply of the Patentees, Added Comment No. 5), and he was not a sharing actor at Lincoln's Inn Fields. See the *Biographical Dictionary*, 2: 251–57.

7 Printed in *Love and Business* (1701). *The Complete Works of George Farquhar*, ed. Charles Stonehill, 2 vols. (1930; reprint ed., New York: Gordian, 1967), 2: 295–96.

8 Kenny ("Theatrical Warfare") cites the Pix and Farquhar verses, but she dismisses the incident too lightly.

9 On Mme Subligny's visit, see Robert D. Hume, "A Revival of *The Way of the World* in December 1701 or January 1702," *Theatre Notebook* 26 (1971): 30–36.

10 The following information comes from a series of answers given by Skipwith, Rich, and Baggs from March 1702 to July 1704 in P.R.O. C5/284/40.

11 The few performances listed at Dorset Garden in *The London Stage* during this

time are either nontheatrical (13 May 1700) or subscription concerts (March–May 1701).

12 For the union sublease, see Hotson, p. 273. The other relevant Killigrew suits are P.R.O. C6/438/55 (April 1700) and C10/297/57 (n.d.; ca. 1700).

13 P.R.O. C10/261/51, Killigrew et al. vs. Skipwith and Rich, bill of complaint.

14 P.R.O. C10/261/51, Answer, 4 February "1702/3." This answer also verifies the lease to Betterton. The patentees claim not to have known about the lease problems before Killigrew's complaint, but Rich evidently bullied someone into showing him the Betterton-Watson lease in October 1702.

15 See the *Survey of London*, 35: 31, 117,n.

16 See the prologue to *The Island Princess*, and the contract for an opera in LC 7/3, taken by Sybil Rosenfeld and others as referring to *The Virgin Prophetess* (transcribed by Nicoll, 1: 382).

17 Similar comments occur in prologues to the following Drury Lane productions: *The Humour of the Age* (1701), *The Unhappy Penitent* (1701), *The Funeral* (1701), *The Inconstant* (1702), *The False Friend* (1702), and others.

18 P.R.O. LC 5/152, p. 15 (4 June 1697), and p. 162 (18 February 1699); and LC 7/3 (24 January 1696), printed by Nicoll, 1: 341,n. For a later order, see Nicoll, 2: 282 and the *Daily Courant* of 24 January 1704.

19 Alfred Jackson, "The Stage and the Authorities, 1700–1714 (As Revealed in the Newspapers)," *Review of English Studies* 14 (1938): 53–62, citation from p. 56, n. 3.

20 See Garnet V. Portus, *Caritas Anglicana* (London: Mowbray, 1912), pp. 48–49 and 93. This study of the laws and the attempts of the Societies for the Reformation of Manners to enforce them deserves to be better known.

21 See, for example, P.R.O. KB 27/2147, Rex Roll No. 9, and KB 33/24/8 for complaints against the Lincoln's Inn Fields actors for profanity in a performance of *Love for Love* on 25 or 26 December 1700. From the quotations given we may deduce that Doggett (as Sailor Ben), in particular was adding ad lib profanity.

22 Joseph Wood Krutch, *Comedy and Conscience after the Restoration*, rev. ed. (New York: Columbia University Press, 1949), chaps. 5–7.

23 John Holt, *Modern CASES Argued and Adjudged in the Court of King's Bench at Westminster, In the Reign of Her late Majesty Q. ANNE*, comp. Thomas Farresley (London: J. Nutt, 1716), p. 17: "Term Pasch. 1 Annae in B.R. Information against the Play-House for Acting profane and lewd Plays, and they being bound by Recognizance to try it made up the Record wrong, *viz. Lincoln's-Fields* for *Lincoln's-Inn-Fields*, thinking to be acquitted upon that Variance; but *Holt* ordered it to be found Specially, and Mr. *Attorney* moved to have their Recognizance estreated."

24 See Krutch, pp. 173–76.

25 Alfred Jackson, "London Playhouses, 1700–1705," *Review of English Studies* 8 (1932): 291–302, esp. p. 293. See also a satirical letter in *A Pacquet from Wills* (1701), quoted by Sybil Rosenfeld, *The Theatre of the London Fairs in the 18th Century* (Cambridge: At the University Press, 1960), p. 2.

26 *Post Man*, 10–13 July 1703.

27 Ogg, *England in the Reigns of James II and William III*, pp. 470–85, esp. pp. 472, 483.

28 See Willard Thorp, "A Key to Rowe's *Tamerlane*," *Journal of English and Germanic Philology* 39 (1940): 124–27.

29 *A Comparison*, p. 22. In his edition, Wells notes that Bracegirdle—the celebrated virgin—is not in the dramatis personae, and suggests that she appeared in the final tableau, as she may have done. But he seems not to have been aware that she was a very competent singer, and is most likely to have played Venus in the dialogue with Cupid in act 3.

30 For the reversal of dates of these productions, see Judith Milhous and Robert D. Hume, "Dating Play Premières from Publication Data, 1660–1700," *Harvard Library Bulletin* 22 (1974): 374–405, esp. pp. 400–402.

31 See Robert Newton Cunningham, *Peter Anthony Motteux, 1663–1718* (Oxford: Blackwell, 1933), for biographical details.

32 See Arthur Colby Sprague, *Beaumont and Fletcher on the Restoration Stage* (1926; reprint ed., New York: Blom, 1965), pp. 85–86. Sprague quotes from *The State of the Case . . . Restated* (1720). Although the assertion was made after Motteux's death, many of this pamphleteer's observations are accurate, which increases the likelihood that this one is too.

33 *A Comparison*, p. 25.

34 *A Comparison* does not mention older adaptations like *The Tempest, King Lear, Timon*, and perhaps *Coriolanus*, all of which had recently been in the active repertory.

35 The 1700 quarto was published under Fletcher's name; Vanbrugh did not take credit for it then or include it in any collection of his works during his lifetime. See *The Complete Works of Sir John Vanbrugh*, ed. Bonamy Dobrée and Geoffrey Webb, 4 vols. (1927–28; reprint ed., New York: AMS, 1967), 2: 88.

36 Cited in *The London Stage*, pt. 1, p. 496.

37 Lord Cholmondeley gave Balon a present of 100 guineas above his large salary from Lincoln's Inn Fields. See *The London Stage*, pt. 1, p. 510 (8 April 1699).

38 *Works*, 4: 4 (letter of 25 December 1699).

39 Sybil Rosenfeld identified this dancer as L'Abbé in "The Restoration Stage in Newspapers and Journals, 1660–1700," *Modern Language Review* 30 (1935): 445–59, esp. p. 450,n.

40 *Life of Betterton*, p. 155.

41 *Apology*, 1: 316.

42 Preface to *Ximena* (1719).

43 Cited in *The London Stage*, pt. 1, p. 515.

44 Ibid., pp. 518, 520.

45 In vol. 1 of his *Genuine Works in Prose and Verse* (London: Tonson, 1732), Granville published this prologue with a footnote explaining that Gormon was "A famous Prize-Fighter." As late as 1703 he was advertised as fighting at Hockley-in-the-Hole (*Post Man*, 21–24 August).

46 For some of the anticipatory fuss, see Alfred Jackson, "Play Notices from the Burney Newspapers 1700–1703," *PMLA* 48 (1933): 815–49, esp. p. 820; and Jackson, "London Playhouses," p. 295.

47 Rosenfeld, *A Short History of Scene Design in Great Britain*, pp. 57–58.

48 Hotson, p. 279,n.

49 See *The London Stage*, pt. 2, pp. 51, 56, 106.

50 Prologues and epilogues to the second part of *Massaniello* and *Love and a Bottle*

chortle over Miss Cross's "elopement" to France. She had been one of Drury Lane's principal speakers of smutty verse in previous years. The epilogue to *The False Friend* is a late example of such a piece, though it is not nearly so explicit.

51 *Apology*, 1: 316.

52 See M. A. Shaaber, "A Letter from Mrs. Barry," *Library Chronicle* 16 (1950): 46–49.

53 *The Letters of John Dryden*, ed. Charles E. Ward (1942; reprint ed., New York: AMS, 1965), No. 59.

54 Lotteries had been licensed under James II, according to Henry Morley, *Memoirs of Bartholomew Fair*, rev. ed. (London: Chatto and Windus, 1880), p. 226. But by 1700, the Court of Common Council for London was trying to regulate them. See Jackson, "The Stage and the Authorities," p. 55.

55 *Roscius Anglicanus*, p. 45.

56 Anon., *The Laureat: or, The Right Side of Colley Cibber, Esq.* (London: J. Roberts, 1740), p. 102.

57 See the *Tatler*, no. 42, 16 July 1709.

58 The prologue is to the anonymous *Feign'd Friendship*. Stonehill deduces a run of nine performances for *Love and a Bottle*, but his grounds are insufficient. See *Works*, 1: xv, 5. The days between premiere and publication were not necessarily devoted to performances of this play, and we have only an approximate premiere date in any case.

59 Eric Rothstein, *Restoration Tragedy* (Madison: University of Wisconsin Press, 1967), p. 171.

60 Vanbrugh, *Works*, 4: 4.

61 *Roscius Anglicanus*, p. 45.

62 See *A Comparison*, pp. 23–25; *Roscius Anglicanus*, p. 45.

63 *The London Stage*, pt. 1, p. 523.

64 Ibid., p. 520, deduces this from a preface (missing in the copy I have seen) which mentions Farquhar's play.

65 See *A Comparison*, pp. 26–27.

66 Preface to *Ximena* (1719).

67 *The Dramatic Works of William Burnaby*, ed. F. E. Budd (London: Scholartis Press, 1931), pp. 407–8.

68 P.R.O. C8/599/77. Curtis A. Price points out that half the lost plays he has identified from published music or from marginalia in music manuscripts belong to this season ("Eight 'Lost' Restoration Plays 'Found' in Musical Sources," *Music & Letters* 58 [1977]: 294–303).

69 *Roscius Anglicanus*, p. 45.

70 *A Comparison*, p. 96.

71 Hazelton Spencer, *Shakespeare Improved* (1927; reprint ed., New York: Ungar, 1963), p. 124.

72 Preface to *Ximena*.

73 See Krutch, p. 170.

74 *The London Stage*, pt. 2, p. 15.

75 *Roscius Anglicanus*, pp. 45–46.

76 See Vanbrugh, *Works*, 2: 154; *A Comparison*, pp. 95–96.

77 See *A Comparison* for an extended hostile analysis of this play.

78 *HMC Egmont* (1909), 2: 208.

79 See Stonehill's introduction to his edition of Farquhar's *Works* for details of the

personal element in this exchange between Oldmixon and Farquhar (1: xviii–xix). For the prologue, added to *The Constant Couple* for the performance of 13 July 1700, see 1: 89–90.

80 Cited by Jackson, "London Playhouses," p. 296.

Chapter 6:
The Years of Uncertainty,
1702–1705

1 *Apology*, 1: 301, 315 ff., among other places. Both Cibber and Downes talk as if Congreve were a shareholder in Lincoln's Inn Fields, but his name is not on any official documents connected with the theatre.

2 For example, Richard Hindry Barker, *Mr Cibber of Drury Lane* (New York: Columbia Univ. Press, 1939), pp. 61–62. Scholars concerned with the Haymarket or opera summarize these years in one paragraph. See Donald C. Mullin, "The Queen's Theatre, Haymarket," *Theatre Survey* 8 (1967): 84–105, and Daniel Nalbach, *The King's Theatre 1704–1867* (London: Society for Theatre Research, 1972). Avery treats the first years of the century almost not at all in his introduction to pt. 2 of *The London Stage*.

3 Following the practice of Vanbrugh, Congreve, Downes, Cibber, and other people concerned with theatre in London at the turn of the seventeenth century, I have chosen to call the theatre Vanbrugh built "the Haymarket." Designation by monarch seems anachronistic at a time when theatres were casually identified by location. Legally the monarch held control of the other theatre too, as witness the silencing of Rich, 6 June 1709: even after the productions were restricted to opera, no one called it the opera house officially. The "Little Theatre in the Haymarket" does not impinge on this study, since it opened in 1720 and housed no permanent company in its first decade.

4 Nicoll, 1: 384–85. Since the full text of Verbruggen's Petition is otherwise unavailable, I have included a transcription of it in Appendix E.

5 P.R.O. C8/599/74 is Smith's bill. His fellow complainants were William Shiers, Thomas Savery, and Robert Gower, Apothecary.

6 Hotson, p. 302.

7 Not given in P.R.O. C6/316/21 or C10/297/57, but cf. notes made for Killigrew in British Library Add. MS 20,726.

8 In P.R.O. C8/595/71 Killigrew admits that he and the patentees did not agree on the subject of management, and dates their dispute from the year 1695.

9 On the Dorset Garden investors' returns, see Hotson, p. 232.

10 See P.R.O. C8/599/77.

11 P.R.O. C8/604/5 (15 February 1705/6). The same list of dates was given in reply to Sir Charles O'Hara, Henry Harris, and other Dorset Garden shareholders in P.R.O. C5/284/40.

12 P.R.O. C8/620/35. Rich also bribed court officials, according to Cibber (*Apology*, 1: 328).

13 See Hotson, p. 397.

14 He is wrong about the time of Smith's death, and we have reason to question his account of the New Theatre's need for him—points discussed in chap. 4.

15 Our knowledge of subscriptions prior to 1708 is very hazy. For a discussion, see the introduction to pt. 2 of *The London Stage*, pp. lix–lx.

16 For details see my article, "The Date and Import of 'Verbruggen's Petition' in Public Record Office LC 7/3," *Archiv*, in press.
17 The complaint is in P.R.O. LC 7/3.
18 P.R.O. LC 7/3 (undated). It probably occurred soon after Anne became Queen, 8 March 1702, since many prosecutions on the subject were still on the docket.
19 P.R.O. LC 7/3.
20 The *Biographical Dictionary*, 2: 87, dates Brown's "Amusements" "ca. 1695," although the *NCBEL* says that series was published in 1700 and lists a French source for parts of it.
21 P.R.O. C8/599/77 (15–20 September 1705). No one from the New Theatre contingent speaks to this issue in the answers preserved.
22 *A Comparison*, p. 25 (final italics added).
23 William Taverner used this play as the basis for *The Female Advocates*, performed at Drury Lane in 1713. Whether he was responsible for the first version we have no evidence.
24 *The Lunatick* (London: B. Bragg, 1705). Publication was advertised in the *Post Man*, 8–10 March 1705.
25 *Apology*, 1: 232.
26 Epilogue to *The Princess of Parma*.
27 *Apology*, 1: 252–53.
28 See Clark, *The Early Irish Stage*, though his dates for personnel are not always reliable.
29 *Apology*, 1: 252.
30 We know that the theatres hired the following adjunct performers, though our lists are almost certainly incomplete. Fractions represent shared performers.

		Singers	Dancers	Musicians
1702–3	LIF	5	7½	?
	DL	9	7½	7
1703–4	LIF	10	5 (no women?)	3
	DL	11	15	3
1704–5	LIF	4½	9	?
	DL	8½	10	4

31 Doggett: LIF, 1702–3, 1703–4; DL, 1704–5; LIF, 1705–6. Bowen: DL, 1702–3; Dublin, 1703–4; LIF, 1704–5, 1705–6. Powell: LIF, 1702–3, 1703–4 (part season); DL, part of 1704, 1704–5 until the opening of the Haymarket. Powell was thrown out of the Haymarket and Drury Lane was forbidden to hire him in November 1705 (P.R.O. LC 5/154, p. 124; summarized by Nicoll, 2: 287; excerpts printed by Nalbach, *The King's Theatre*, p. 9).
32 See Emmett L. Avery, "Some New Prologues and Epilogues, 1704–1708," *Studies in English Literature* 5 (1965): 455–67, esp. 458–59.
33 P.R.O. LC 5/152, pp. 202, 220.
34 *Roscius Anglicanus*, pp. 46–47.
35 For details of the spurious publication of *Squire Trelooby*, see John C. Hodges, "The Authorship of *Squire Trelooby*," *Review of English Studies* 4 (1928): 404–13; and Graham D. Harley, "*Squire Trelooby* and *The Cornish Squire*: A Reconsideration," *Philological Quarterly* 49 (1970): 520–29. Neither takes up the question of the authenticity of the cast, but if (as Hodges argues) the first version was published to capitalize on performance, the cast was probably accurate.
36 *Roscius Anglicanus*, p. 52.

37 *The London Stage*, pt. 2, p. 27. Cf. Jackson, "Play Notices from the Burney Newspapers," p. 834.

38 *Apology*, 2: 67.

39 See my article, "New Light on Vanbrugh's Haymarket Theatre Project," *Theatre Survey* 17 (1976): 143–61.

40 See Edward A. Langhans, "Players and Playhouses, 1695–1710, and Their Effect on English Comedy," *Theatre Annual* 29 (1973): 28–39.

41 See Curtis A. Price, "The Critical Decade for English Music Drama, 1700–1710," *Harvard Library Bulletin* 26 (1978): 38–76.

42 See my article, "The Date and Import of the Financial Plan for a United Theatre Company in P.R.O. LC 7/3," *Maske und Kothurn* 21 (1975): 81–88.

43 See Robert J. Allen, "The Kit-Cat Club and the Theatre," *Review of English Studies* 7 (1931): 56–61, and Kathleen M. Lynch, *Jacob Tonson, Kit-Cat Publisher* (Knoxville: University of Tennessee Press, 1971), pp. 56–66.

44 See J. A. Downie, "Defoe's Review, the Theatre, and Anti-High-Church Propaganda," *Restoration and Eighteenth Century Theatre Research* 15 (May 1976): 24–32.

45 John Loftis, *The Politics of Drama in Augustan England* (Oxford: Clarendon Press, 1963), p. 35.

46 See James R. Sutherland, "The Circulation of Newspapers and Literary Periodicals, 1700–30," *The Library*, n.s. 15 (1934): 110–24.

47 "Lincoln's Inn Fields, 1704–1705," *Theatre Notebook* 5 (1950): 13–15.

48 The *Daily Courant*, 4 and 5 October 1703, announces the Patent Company's return.

49 Clark, *Early Irish Stage*, p. 205.

50 See Curtis A. Price's dissertation, cited in chap. 4, n. 21 above.

51 See Avery's introduction to pt. 2 of *The London Stage*, pp. cxxxi–cxxxii, for a discussion of the meaning of this word in the period.

52 *The London Stage*, pt. 2, p. xciii.

53 The *Post Man*, 10–13 July 1703.

54 P.R.O. LC 5/153, pp. 433, 434, summarized by Nicoll, 2: 282.

55 *Mr Collier's Dissuasive from the Play-House* (1703; rpt. in *Collier Tracts, 1703–1708*, ed. Arthur Freeman [New York: Garland, 1973], pp. 14–15).

56 *The London Stage*, pt. 2, p. 50. See further, Arthur H. Scouten, "The S.P.C.K. and the Stage," *Theatre Notebook* 11 (1957): 58–62.

57 The last major printed assaults which Winton cites, those by Arthur Bedford of Bristol (1706) and John Disney of London (1708), had no directly traceable results ("The London Stage Embattled," pp. 15–17).

58 See *The Dramatic Works of William Burnaby*, pp. 348 and 447–48.

59 See *Love's Contrivance* and *The Faithful Bride of Granada*.

60 *The London Stage*, pt. 2, p. 35, erroneously places it in May, but see the *Daily Courant*, 13 March.

61 *Roscius Anglicanus*, p. 46. In 1715 it was advertised as not having been acted for ten years.

62 See the preface to *Ximena*. The play did become popular during the Triumvirate management of Drury Lane.

63 *The London Stage* date (November) is wrong by about a month. A reference in the prologue places it before the start of the Michaelmas term, 23 or 24 October.

64 See Emmett L. Avery, "New Prologues and Epilogues," pp. 458–60. This pro-

logue was printed with an answering epilogue from Drury Lane, but the play which it introduced is not known. "Its Heroes from its Ensigns fled" refers to the most recent transfers of Doggett and Powell.

65 Letter 42 in *The Post-Boy Robb'd of his Mail* [ed. Charles Gildon], 2d ed. (London: B. Mills for John Sprint, 1706).

Chapter 7:

The Haymarket Years and the

Union of 1708

1 Price, "The Critical Decade," p. 47. For further details of Vanbrugh's agreement with his subscribers and other information bearing on the establishment of this theatre, see my "New Light on Vanbrugh's Haymarket Theatre Project."

2 Portland MS PW2.571 (Nottingham University Library).

3 See Vanbrugh, *Works*, 4: xi, xxiii, xxiv, and 1: xxviii.

4 Both Vanbrugh's undated proposal and Haym's protest of 1 March 1705/6 in the Baroness's name are included in P.R.O. LC 7/3. They are summarized by Nicoll, 2: 288–89.

5 John Genest, *Some Account of the English Stage*, 10 vols. (1832; reprint ed., New York: Burt Franklin, n.d.), 2: 333; Cibber, *Apology*, 1: 326.

6 Rich's protest is in P.R.O. LC 7/3. For the letter to Keally, see *William Congreve: Letters & Documents*, ed. John C. Hodges (New York: Harcourt, Brace, and World, 1964), No. 22.

7 For details, see my article, "An Annotated Census of Thomas Betterton's Roles, 1659–1710," *Theatre Notebook* 29 (1975): 33–43, 85–94.

8 Fiske, *English Theatre Music in the Eighteenth Century* (London: Oxford University Press, 1973), p. 33. Fiske errs in saying there were twenty-four performances the first season.

9 For example, see Congreve's enthusiastic report on *The Judgment of Paris*, 21 March 1701, in *The London Stage*, pt. 2, p. 9.

10 Preface by Thomas Clayton to *Arsinoe, Queen of Cyprus* (London: Tonson, 1705).

11 P.R.O. LC 7/3, attached to a letter of 9 December 1705. The distinction is not entirely clear in the transcription printed in *Congreve: Letters & Documents*, No. 71.

12 Rosenberg, "A New Move [*recte*, Motive] for the Censorship of Owen Swiney's 'The Quacks,'" *Notes & Queries* 203 (1958): 393–96.

13 *Letters & Documents*, No. 20. We have no evidence as to when Congreve began work on his unproduced *Semele*, but by the time Eccles had completed the music (January 1707), the Haymarket was restricted to nonoperatic performances. Congreve had long since left the management. Indeed, he and Eccles were negotiating with Rich to put on *Semele*. For a fine analysis of the music, see Stoddard Lincoln, "The First Musical Setting of Congreve's *Semele*," *Music and Letters* 44 (1963): 103–17. Lincoln's dating is incorrect; the first issue of the *Muses Mercury* was published after 21 January 1707 and before 28 January, as references in it to the Shakespeare subscription series indicate.

14 Vanbrugh, *Works*, 1: xxi–xxii.

15 *Annals of Opera 1597–1940*, 2d ed. (Genève: Societas Bibliographica, 1955), 1: 113–14. The key piece of evidence is the rare dual-language edition (London, 1705).

16 *Apology*, 1: 325.

17 Nalbach, p. 7. *The Triumph of Love* was performed at the Haymarket in November 1712.

18 Fiske, pp. 33–35. Curtis A. Price doubts that a wholly "new set of Singers" was imported but suggests that some were borrowed from Drury Lane ("The Critical Decade," pp. 46–47, 53). He names the Baroness. However, neither she nor Haym is listed on the Drury Lane roster for 1704–5, so I see no reason to doubt that her contract with Vanbrugh was straightforward and unencumbered by obligations to Rich.

19 *The Complete Works of William Congreve*, 4 vols., ed. Montague Summers (Soho: Nonesuch, 1923), 4: 80–81.

20 *Apology*, 1: 321–22.

21 *The Post-Boy Robb'd of his Mail*, pp. 342–47.

22 Transcribed by Percy Fitzgerald (who cites no source) in *A New History of the English Stage*, 1: 259–60. Fitzgerald misdates the petition by two and a half years. Suzanna Mountfort the younger was among the signers; since she joined Drury Lane on 14 June 1705 we may probably date the petition within the following two weeks. Curtis A. Price cites a broadside form of the petition in the Burney newspaper collection; he dates it ca. September 1706 ("The Critical Decade," p. 55,n.). Still another version exists in New York Public Library Drexel MS 1986.

23 The following people who signed the petition to Kent remained at Drury Lane in 1706–7: Estcourt, Williams, Pinkethman, Norris, Bickerstaff, Mrs Cross, Cherrier, Ramondon, Mrs Moore, Mrs Lindsey, and Mrs Mountfort. Those who moved to the Haymarket were Wilks, Cross, Kent, Cibber, Mills, Mrs Oldfield, Fairbank, Keen, Mrs Powell, and Mrs Mills. The rest are not listed as active in London that year, though some, like Mrs Knight, returned to the stage later.

24 P.R.O. LC 7/3. Summarized by Nicoll, 2: 289–90.

25 *Roscius Anglicanus*, p. 48.

26 Ibid., p. 49.

27 Granville, *Genuine Works in Verse and Prose*, 2 vols. (London, 1732), 1: [8], preface to *The British Enchanters*.

28 For a full account of *Camilla*, see Lowell Edwin Lindgren's Ph.D. thesis, "A Bibliographic Scrutiny of Dramatic Works Set by Giovanni and His Brother Antonio Maria Bononcini" (Harvard, 1972).

29 Fiske, pp. 41–44; Hume, p. 479.

30 *Roscius Anglicanus*, pp. 49–50.

31 *Letters & Documents*, No. 23.

32 The agreement in P.R.O. LC 7/2, fol. 1, does not mention the alternative sum of £700 a year given in Cibber's account (*Apology*, 1: 330–37). For other discussions of this union, see Barker, *Mr Cibber*, pp. 63–66, and Price, "The Critical Decade," pp. 54–60.

33 Nineteenth-century transcription in New York Public Library MS Drexel 1986, fols. 10–10v.

34 John Harold Wilson, "Theatre Notes from the Newdigate Newsletters," pp. 79–84. Curtis A. Price prints a full transcription of a draft order on these terms from the Coke Papers in "The Critical Decade," pp. 56–57.

35 *Congreve: Letters & Documents*, No. 26.

36 BL Add. MS 38,607, Document 57 (Winston transcription of a Coke original, present location unknown). The document is unsigned and undated.
37 *Apology*, 1: 335.
38 In the 1904 edition of *Grove's Dictionary* (s.v. Swiney), Julian Marshall quotes a letter of 5 October 1706 from Swiney to Cibber, then in his possession, to the effect that Swiney had just taken a lease on the Haymarket at £5 a day, "although Rich might have had the house for £3 or £3: 10s. a day." At what date Rich was negotiating to lease the Haymarket is unclear. Perhaps this refers to the April talks. Cibber's first advertised appearance in the 1706–7 season was 17 November.
39 BL Add. MS 38,607, Document 50 (Winston transcription), a letter of 9 December 1706. The performance advertised for 10 December 1706 was duly canceled. However, the work was performed the following 22 March "With all the Original Scenes, Machines, and Decorations" but with no mention of singing and dancing.
40 Barker, *Mr Cibber*, p. 66.
41 Avery, "New Prologues and Epilogues," p. 462.
42 Cited in *The London Stage*, pt. 2, p. 139.
43 Shirley Strum Kenny, "A Broadside Prologue by Farquhar," *Studies in Bibliography* 25 (1972): 179–85.
44 Letter of 14 May, transcribed by Albert Rosenberg, "New Light on Vanbrugh," *Philological Quarterly* 45 (1966): 603–13.
45 *Apology*, 1: 336. In a letter to George Granville, Lord Lansdowne, 16 December 1712, Barton Booth said that at the Haymarket he had "far'd not much better than before" so far as money was concerned (Add. MS 38,607, Document 8). However, Booth was lobbying to become a manager then, and it was to his advantage to slight previous managers.
46 Harvard Coke Papers, Document 47.
47 P.R.O. LC 7/3, letter of 27 January 1706/7.
48 Harvard Coke Papers, Document 37.
49 See Curtis A. Price, "The Critical Decade," pp. 60–61.
50 The last day Verbruggen is known to have played in London was 19 August 1707. Clark, *The Early Irish Stage*, pp. 123–24, concludes from an Irish promptbook and from the London benefit for his orphan that Verbruggen died in Dublin before he had appeared onstage there. But a petition for reinstatement after the 1708 Union by Verbruggen, Pack, Mrs Porter, and Mrs Bradshaw suggests that Verbruggen returned to England (Harvard Coke Papers, Document 56). We have no reference to him before the benefit for his orphan, 26 April 1708, though the other three petitioners were back onstage by the first week in February.
51 P.R.O. LC 7/3, letter of 22 October 1707.
52 "The Queen's Theatre, Haymarket."
53 *Apology*, 2: 2, 5.
54 Vanbrugh, *Works*, 4: 20–22.
55 See Hotson, pp. 386–97, for depositions in the Skipwith-Brett dispute over ownership of the part-shares in the patent.
56 *Works*, 4: 16 (24 February 1708).
57 A. M. Broadley, "Annals of the Haymarket" ("King's Theatre" volume—scrapbook), p. 35 (Westminster Public Library).

58 Harvard Coke Papers, Document 54.

59 Ibid., Document 12.

60 Add. MS 38,607 (Winston transcriptions), Documents 38, 39.

61 Harvard Coke Papers, Document 54. As we learn from Vanbrugh's "List of Ye Musick Proposd" (Coke, Document 18), Rich's suspicions were well founded.

62 Scribal copy in BL Add. MS 20,726. I have not been able to find the original in the P.R.O. referred to by Lowe in his notes to Cibber's *Apology*, 2: 49.

63 Cf. *Apology*, 2: 46–48.

64 Calhoun Winton, "Sentimentalism and Theater Reform in the Early Eighteenth Century," in *Quick Springs of Sense*, ed. Larry S. Champion (Athens: University of Georgia Press, 1974), pp. 97–112.

65 Mrs Bracegirdle had retired, and Mrs Barry did so the next year. Verbruggen died in the spring. Betterton played only on special occasions after 1707, and Underhill appeared even less often. Doggett was in and out of London doing guest spots. George Powell was increasingly handicapped by drink.

66 Vanbrugh, *Works*, 4: 16, 21.

67 "Colman's Opera Register" reported for 14 January 1713: "Mr Swiny Brakes & runs away & leaves ye singers unpaid ye Scenes & Habits also unpaid for," BL Add. MS 11,258.

INDEX

L'Abbé, M (dancer), 134, 139, 161, 167, 195

Actresses: specified in patent grants, 6, 21; in men's clothes, 22; perform without men, 22, 31, 182, 200; direct shareholders in the Lincoln's Inn Fields Company, 72

Adams, Joseph Quincy, 255

Addison, Joseph: *Cato*, 188; *Rosamond* (with Clayton), 213

Allen, Robert J., 271

Animadversions on Mr Congreve's late Answer to Mr Collier, 263n

Anne, Queen of England, 75, 126–28, 131, 181, 183–84, 190–91, 216, 221, 270

Argalus and Parthenia (Glapthorne), 22

Arnold, Mr (actor), 117

Ashburnham, Mr (shareholder), 233, 241, 242

Aston, Anthony (actor), 110

Atterbury, Mr (lecturer at St. Brides), 228, 241–42

Audience: changing tastes of, 51, 75–78; "Ladies" in, 76; change in curtain time to accommodate, 77, 149; soldiers in, 172; servants admitted gratis to the upper gallery, 149

Avery, Emmett L., 145–46, 166, 172–73, 178, 261, 269, 270, 274

Ayliff, Mrs (singer), 87, 100, 133, 245

Babel, Charles (musician), 217

Baggs, Zachary (treasurer), 155, 158, 265

Bailey, Samuel (actor), 117

Baker, Katherine (actress), 204

Baker, Thomas: *The Humour of the Age*, 137, 139, 145, 266; *Tunbridge Walks*, 172, 182–83; *Hampstead Heath* (*An Act at Oxford*, revised), 205

Balon, Jean (dancer), 112, 120, 134, 135, 138–40, 267

Banister, John (musician), 136, 217

Banister, John, Jr (musician), 136

Banks, John: *The Destruction of Troy*, 44; *Cyrus the Great*, 102; *Vertue Betray'd*, 103; *The Albion Queens* (*The Island Queens*, revised), 180; mentioned, 98

Barker, Richard Hindry, 269, 273–74

Baroness, the (Joanna Maria Lindelheim, singer), 192, 272, 273

Barry, Elizabeth (actress), 36, 59, 61, 67, 68, 83, 90, 98, 99, 101, 104, 107, 117, 139, 144, 160–61, 163, 166, 185, 226–27, 233, 238, 239, 243–44, 247, 249, 251–53, 260–61, 268, 275

Bartholomew Fair, 41, 96, 135, 136

Bathurst, Villiers (commentator), 142

Baxter, Stephen B., 263

Bayly, Richard (counsel for the Duke's Company), 152

Bedford, Arthur, 271

Bedford, William Russell, Earl (later Duke) of, 124

Bedingfield, Edward (commentator), 47

Beeston, William (manager), 4, 8, 17

Behn, Aphra: *The Emperor of the Moon*, 46, 48, 174–75, 259; *Abdelazer*, 54, 100; *The Younger Brother*, 102; *The Rover*, 204; *The City Heiress*, 264; mentioned, 42, 98

Bentley, Gerald Eades, 256

Betterton, Mary (actress), 28, 30, 58, 65, 226, 236, 240, 244–45, 247, 260

Betterton, Thomas (actor, manager): Davenant's apprentice and disciple, x, 24–25, 58; business morals of, x, 159–61; experience as manager, 3, 26–48 passim; early experience with new plays, compared to 1695–1708, 19; with Mary, raises Anne Bracegirdle, 28, *The Roman Virgin* (adapted from Webster), 28; provides scripts, 28–29; *The Amorous Widow*, 29; *The Woman Made a Justice*, 29; coaches future queens in *Calisto*, 30; part in the

277